COGNITION, EDUCATION, and MULTIMEDIA:
Exploring Ideas in High Technology

Edited by
Don Nix
IBM, Thomas J. Watson Research Center
Rand Spiro
University of Illinois at Urbana—Champaign

LEA LAWRENCE ERLBAUM ASSOCIATES, PUBLISHERS
1990 Hillsdale, New Jersey   Hove and London

Lawrence Erlbaum Associates, Inc., Publishers
365 Broadway
Hillsdale, New Jersey 07642

Library of Congress Cataloging-in-Publication Data

Cognition, education, and multimedia : exploring ideas in high
technology / edited by Don Nix, Rand Spiro.
    p.   cm.
    ISBN 0-8058-0036-0
    1. Computer-assisted instruction. 2. Cognition. 3. Experiential
learning. I. Nix, Don. II. Spiro, Rand J.
LB1028.5.C5258   1990
371.3'34—dc20   89-39923
                                                          CIP

Printed in the United States of America
10 9 8 7 6 5 4 3

Contents

3

**Computers and Videodisc Technology for Bilingual
ASL/English Instruction of Deaf Children**
Vicki L. Hanson and Carol A. Padden

49

4

Literacy as Search: Explorations Via Computer
John T. Guthrie and Mariam Jean Dreher

65

5

**Anchored Instruction: Why We Need It
and How Technology Can Help**
*John D. Bransford, Robert D. Sherwood, Ted S. Hasselbring,
Charles K. Kinzer, and Susan M. Williams*

115

6
Should Computers Know What You Can Do With Them?
Don Nix   143

7
Cognitive Flexibility and Hypertext: Theory and Technology for the Nonlinear and Multidimensional Traversal of Complex Subject Matter
Rand J. Spiro and Jihn-Chang Jehng   163

Introduction

Don Nix
IBM, Thomas J. Watson Research Center

It is important that people who think about cognition, learning, and education, and who do not operate solely within the boundaries of classroom exigencies and traditional computer approaches to classroom education, explore the value of computers in education. Such explorations may provide outlines of feasibility, if and where they exist, for ways to use computers in education. These guidelines, if forthcoming, would augment, amplify, clarify, nullify, and/or replace guidelines both from traditional approaches and newer approaches.

Computers present a set of choices to the educational system. In this book, the *educational system* usually refers to K–12. Computers have become a topic of concern, debate, argument, dogmatism, and inquiry among a varied assortment of people who are interested in the fate and effects and purposes of the educational system.

One reasonable point of view is that computers, although perhaps in many ways different than other implements of classroom activities (such as books, workbooks, kits, teachers, peers, clean-up time), will be contained within the existing system and will, in time, be another such implement without contributing any special qualities. That is, this point of view is that computers will be contained by the existing system, and will not result in fundamental changes to it.

There are many reasons computers may have no significant effect on the way education occurs. Schools tend to be conservative systems over a period of time. Other "technologies" have emerged that have been expected by proponents and opponents as well to make fundamental changes to schools. Examples include radio, television, teaching machines, and open classrooms. These technologies have not, in general, been significant agents of change. Teachers, and by extension the mentality of school education, it has been stated, view reality as if it were motionless (Friere, 1962). The reality of the school is relatively fixed, in terms of content materials, role relationships, and political status within the larger society.

Another reason why computers may not impact school education in a fundamental way is based on economics. Schools have relatively little money for materials. Computers that have potential for new approaches to education, learning, and thinking, very often tend to be expensive because they require speed, large memory, sophisticated graphics, sound, video, and touch. In contrast, computers that are typically purchased for use in schools tend to be bottom of the line, whatever the current state of the art is in software and hardware. To see the power available in a current computer, one can walk into a business establishment. To see the lowest common denominator, one can go to a school.

However, even if schools were rich, and open to radical change, there is still a serious limitation to the brave new world of computerized educational reform. How many philosophers, psychologists, academicians, teachers, educators, researchers, and developers, actually know what a fundamentally different and effective instructional medium should be like? Who knows how to explicate such a medium so that in principle it could be run on a computer?

And who knows him or herself how to actually program this new medium in unique ways, without having to interact with a set of computer people who although specialists with computers, are not equipped to comprehend a computer application from a human, educative point of view? The steps required to get from a good idea in education, to an implementation of it, and then successive and timely modifications of it, are circuitous. Thinking about an application as complex as one involved in learning, and thinking about how to make a computer run such an application, are simply different ways of thinking, with incompatible ruling classes.

Computers present enormous difficulties for the innovative exploration of ideas, for people with computer expertise. For people who are not computer experts, or who do not want to be, computers are often intractible, or at least a major sidetrack to the consideration of the issues that brought one to the computer in the first place. Perhaps a text editor or spread sheet or hypertext system exists that, as advertised, is easy for the computer novice to learn. Putting together a drill and practice program to teach a well-defined and limited skill may be possible. However, iteratively creating an educational medium which is defined in the process of implementing it, concerning a learning goal that itself is in the process of emerging, is qualitatively and quantitatively more difficult.

This book focuses mainly on this issue of how people who may have ideas about education that are well-founded and worth exploration, may actually get a computer to explore these ideas with a limited amount of distortion. We are not necessarily assuming that schools will be rich enough or that the necessary computers will be inexpensive enough to enable practical application of good ideas. We are not necessarily assuming that schools will be congenial to radical, or any, change. On the other hand, if the question is to be answered about whether or not computers have the potential of offering something useful to the educational process, then people who are involved in the noncomputer disciplines need to be involved. If computers are to become an attractive medium to the school establishment, then such people need to be able to explore their ideas in actual classroom and related settings. If computers turn out to be a mistake, considering effort, cost, and possible function, we should be in the position of knowing this based on a thorough, exploratory period of trying out ideas.

The chapters in this book are related in several ways. First, they are related through the use of an experimental language, HANDY, as the medium for exploring the ideas represented. HANDY was created (chapter 6 by Nix for some detail on HANDY) to be a computer language and environment for providing control of a strategic set of capabilities new computer technologies provide. Important examples include multitasking objects, animated graphics, videodisc, videotape, audiotape, voice synthesis, digitized voice, touch, the ability to create new commands, and to link to standard programs written in languages such as C, BASIC, Pascal, FORTRAN, and others. It is unusual for this type of facility to be integrated in one system. It is particularly unusual for this facility to be integrated in a system that is accessible to users who are not professional computer programmers. The idea in creating HANDY was to make this "high-tech" orientation available for iterative, exploratory use by people who, because of a particular expertise and interest in the fields of cognition and education, intend to experiment with computers in education.

The chapters in this book are also related through the concept of *experiential learning*. This term refers to qualities of a learning environment that are intended to relate the learning to one's life outside a normal classroom or related academic situation. This can include such qualities as fun, self-motivation, intrinsic interest of content to be learned. In normal life, as is well known, children learn through participation in activities and thoughts triggered by their lives as humans. There is often a feeling of ownership concerning what they know. In the abnormal world of a school setting, such self-directed learning is unusual for the majority of children.

Experiential learning can also include the avoidance of a rigorous distinction of content along department lines. That is, social studies is not something you have to stop doing in order to do math. In fact, social studies is not necessarily a body of knowledge at all. The distinction between social studies and math is invented, and presented to children as *natural*. This dichotimization is not necessary. Reality may be fragmentary, but not exclusively along the lines of a pamphlet of course offerings.

One prominent way computers can be used to produce an albeit computerized version of an approach to experiential learning is through the use of multimedia technology. Another way is to base the content to be learned on life-like settings. The chapters in this volume show examples, in varying degrees, of these approaches.

A third important interrelationship among the chapters in this book is that each one is based on a theoretical point of view that is not derived from traditional computer-based instruction, or from the world of computers at all. Areas represented include various linguistic and psychological aspects of the study of cognition. In some cases, chapters include empirical studies. In other cases, chapters focus on sketching approaches that are empirically evaluated. In all cases, the reasoning behind the computer implementation is the central contribution. This is why each chapter was included. The chapters have been sequenced roughly in terms of type of content that is the point of interest, whether the content is relatively specific, or involves a range of skills.

Gildea, Miller, and Wurtenberg (chapter 1) present research on the learning of words. The approach to creating a system that enables children to learn meanings of new words uses an approach they refer to as *contextual enrichment*. The words are learned in a context of interest and meaning (using scenes from *Raiders of the Lost Ark*) and definitional enrichment, presented by videodisc integrated with the computer procedures for interaction. Results of the effectiveness of this approach are presented.

Chomsky (chapter 2) describes a project that makes books accessible to young children. She created a computer system that simulates aspects of the experience of reading, being read to, and having help with finding out what words and phrases mean. The child uses a "book on disc" system, with computerized support, to interactively enter the world of *Peter Rabbit*. The rationale of the process is to use the technology, books on disc, as a means of leading children to being familiar with, interested in, and reading books.

Hanson and Padden (chapter 3) have developed an exploratory system for use by deaf children who are proficient in American Sign Language (ASL), but who are not proficient in certain aspects of printed English. Thus, a bilingual computer-mediated system exists, with which the student can learn more about written English, in a self-directed mode. The English consists of computer-generated displays. The American Sign Language is conveyed in a videodisc with one of the authors signing a series of stories, as well as ASL-signed feedback messages. The system explores issues about using a bilingual approach to teach aspects of written English to the particular population.

Guthrie and Dreher (chapter 4) present some of their work in representing complex types of literacy tasks, with multiple components, and how subjects perform in locating information of various kinds in this type of domain. These tasks involve experientially familiar tasks such as dealing with airplane schedules. A cognitive process model of search is outlined, and provides the design and evaluation framework for four empirical studies they report. The computer was used to capture several aspects of the subjects' performance (e.g., time to solution, selections made to traverse the problem domain, and notepad information). This information was used to evaluate the underlying theory.

Bransford, Sherwood, Hasselbring, Kinzer, and Williams (chapter 5) present the notion of *anchored instruction,* and contrast it to older approaches to instruction. Anchored instruction is an orientation that is integrative in terms of facts, processes, disciplines. Traditional approaches tend to alienate facts from facts, and facts from cognitive processes for dealing with facts and creating new facts and hypotheses. Preliminary studies are described, and a series of planned anchored instruction educational implementations is outlined. There is also a discussion of doing your own video productions in addition to using existing materials.

The chapter by Nix (chapter 6) is focused on *self-expressive* learning. The chapter describes a series of projects in which children created their own materials, to be used to teach or entertain others. Projects include a soap opera, game show, rock video, political campaign adds, and civil rights essays, all consisting of multimedia productions planned, written, produced, and transformed into interactive computer-based events. The existence of a range of activities involved in these creations is the point of a theoretical perspective that computers can function as a decentered but enabling medium for creativity and self-exploration.

Spiro and Jehng (chapter 7) discuss the Cognitive Flexibility Theory of learning, knowledge representation, and knowledge transfer. They present an instructional approach based on this theory—a "cognitive flexibility hypertext" instructional approach for "landscape crisscrossing" in the acquisition and transfer of advanced knowledge. Key features of this instructional approach are illustrated by a functioning prototype system for teaching the complex thematic structure of the film *Citizen Kane,* a movie with a rich mulilevel network of meanings. The generality of this approach is discussed with examples of prototypes in other content domains.

In summary, the chapters in this book are working hypotheses of ways in which computers may fit into and/or transform the way education is done in classrooms. Their importance lies principally in the ideas about learning and cognition that infuse the technological manifestations. If computers end up making significant new contributions to the field of education, the explorations such as these, among others, will be responsible.

1

Contextual Enrichment by Videodisc

Patricia M. Gildea
Rutgers University

George A. Miller
Princeton University

Cheryl L. Wurtenberg
Rutgers University

Most psychologists who have studied learning from context have been word chauvinists. Clearly, contextual learning should be a broad topic, yet most attempts to study it empirically have been concerned with how words are learned from the contexts in which they are used. Moreover, this preoccupation with word learning has generally been accompanied by a further preoccupation with the sentences in which the words are used—the focus has been on linguistic learning in linguistic contexts.

The work reported here is also concerned with learning words, but it takes a somewhat broader view of the context for that learning. We have taken pains that the sentence contexts from which the words are to be learned should tell a story of some interest to the learner, and we have supplemented that narrative linguistic context with as rich a visual context as we could present. This contextual enrichment was made possible by the use of interactive videodisc.

We did not resort to interactive videodisc out of some perverse affection for modern technology. Rather, we felt driven to it by the difficulties we encountered with simpler methods of instruction. Before launching into the experimental report, a short history of how we were led to study contextual enrichment by videodisc seems appropriate.

A CONTEXT FOR CONTEXTUAL STUDIES

Students of child language generally agree that the most surprising thing about language development is how quickly very young children learn grammar. Syntax seems so complex that its mastery at an early age has rightfully grabbed center stage. Nevertheless, children's ability to follow grammatical rules is only slightly more wonderful than their ability to learn new words.

Syntactic learning and lexical learning follow very different courses. A grammar is a set of highly general, highly productive rules that children are able to master rather quickly. A vocabulary involves thousands of highly specific facts that simply have to be memorized, a process that can go on for years and years. Whereas grammatical competence is usually achieved before a child starts to school, vocabulary growth continues into adulthood. Indeed, for an intellectually active person it probably never ends.

Attempts have been made to estimate the magnitude of the vocabulary learning task in English (Nagy & Herman, 1987). Although different numerical estimates have been published, everyone who has considered the question has been impressed by the amount of information that has to be learned and the rapid rate at which the learning progresses—rates of acquisition on the order of 10 words per day are sustained throughout childhood. The kinds of experience that support such rapid and sustained learning, and the conceptual developments that accompany it, have been topics for investigation by generations of developmental psycholinguists.

This chapter focuses on how school children learn words, thus skipping the initial phases that many psychologists regard as the most interesting. But the later stages have an interest of their own.

Preschool children learn new words by ear, by hearing them spoken by familiar people in familiar situations, and thereby inferring from their knowledge of the context what concepts the unfamiliar words are being used to express. The early learning process is so efficient that some theorists have argued that children are innately prepared for it, although the details of that genetic endowment are not easily described. Once children have learned to read, however, the learning processes must be very different—beginning in about the fourth grade the average school child begins to encounter words in written forms that they have never heard used in conversational interaction—but somehow the process of vocabulary growth continues at the same rate, or even accelerates.

Although many workers around the world have observed this remarkable learning process and many research papers have been written about it, a thorough review of all that research is not necessary. Fortunately, an excellent survey has recently appeared under the editorship of McKeown and Curtis (1987). This chapter can be limited to our own work, and what we think we have learned from it.

STUDIES WITH DICTIONARIES

We began several years ago with a general curiosity about how lexical knowledge should be characterized (Miller, 1985/1986). That question led us to examine critically that remarkable artifact of our culture, the printed, alphabetical, handheld dictionary. Although the organization of information in a dictionary is very different from the organization of lexical knowledge in the long-term memory of a human being, we still began with the assumption that a dictionary gives a reasonably good description of the information that a person must master in the course of learning the vocabulary of English. That is to say, we began with the commonsense belief that if you do not know what a word means, you can always look it up in a dictionary.

That commonsense assumption is shared generally by parents and teachers, and probably underlies the practice of teaching what are called *dictionary skills* in the early grades. Because school children are going to encounter in their reading many words that they have never heard spoken, they should be able to use dictionaries to look up those unfamiliar words and so learn their meanings. And because understanding what you find when you open a dictionary requires that you understand such things as spelling, alphabetizing, parts of speech, and multiple meanings, considerable time must be spent explaining these matters.

An exercise that is widely used in such teaching is to give students a list of words that they should learn and to tell them to look up those words in a dictionary and write sentences using these. Deese (1967) noticed the curious results that can follow from this assignment. The example that Deese reported was based on the experience of a seventh-grade teacher who asked her class to look up the word "chaste" and use it in a sentence. The sentences that he quoted were:

The milk was chaste.
The plates were chaste after much use.
The amoeba is a chaste animal.

What the students had in mind becomes clear only when you look at the definition that they found in the dictionary:

chaste *adj*.1: innocent of unlawful sexual intercourse. 2: celibate. 3: pure in thought and act, modest. 4. severely simple in design or execution, austere.

We have replicated Deese's observation many times over (Miller & Gildea, 1985). With the cooperation of schools in and around Princeton we have collected about 2,500 sentences that fifth- and sixth-grade children wrote after looking up words in a school dictionary. The children were familiar with some of the words; others were unfamiliar.

When the word they looked up was familiar, the children usually managed to write an acceptable sentence containing it. When the word was unfamiliar, however, a surprising fraction of their sentences indicated clearly that they did not know what the word meant or how to use it.

We were particularly interested in what we call *substitution errors*, which were the most frequent indications of misunderstanding and which seem to give us a special insight into what the children were doing. Indeed, we now believe that, although the write-a-sentence task probably has little pedagogic value, the trick of making children use a word in a sentence before they are really ready to do so is an excellent technique for getting information about the early stages of the word-learning process.

Some examples of substitution errors should make the point. The child who wrote "The milk was chaste" illustrates a substitution error. We assume that the child searched the definition for some familiar word, landed on "pure," composed a sentence containing the word "pure"—in this instance, "The milk was pure." The child then substituted the target word, "chaste," for the defining word, "pure." The result of that simple substitution was "The milk was chaste."

Sometimes other kinds of mistakes occur, but the simple substitution strategy for dealing with the definition of unfamiliar words is often apparent even when other errors occur. (The other popular strategy, available when the dictionary entry includes a sentence illustrating usage, is to model the response after the illustrative example—but we discuss that later.)

Our hypothesis about how simple substitution errors occur can be made explicit by writing it out as a sequence of steps:

1. find the target word in the dictionary;
2. read the definition;
3. select some short, familiar segment of the definition;
4. compose a sentence using the selected segment; and
5. substitute the target word for the selected segment in the sentence.

The important thing to notice about this strategy is that sometimes, by pure chance, it can result in a perfectly good sentence. In such cases it is blind luck, not lexical understanding, that produces the acceptable result. In other words, the number of sentences that were written by following this procedure must be even greater than the frequency of simple substitution errors would indicate.

Simple substitution errors can be quite amusing. The child who read in the dictionary that "accrue" means "come as a growth" composed the sentence, "We had a branch come as a growth on our plant," then made the simple substitution to produce "We had a branch accrue on our plant." And the child who read that "transitory" means "lasting a short time" composed the sentence, "I bought a battery that lasted a short time" and then made the simple substitution to produce "I bought a battery that was transitory." One always has a favorite, of course. Ours was written by a little girl who looked up "erode" and discovered that it means "eat out, eat away," then produced "Our family erodes a lot."

The upshot of these observations was that we decided the write-a-sentence task is a good research procedure, but not a good educational procedure. The dictionary, for all its virtues as a reference book, is not a good instructional tool. Other ways of helping young readers learn the meanings of unfamiliar words should be considered.

But if not definitions, then what?

STUDIES WITH SENTENCE CONTEXTS

The natural answer is that sentence contexts should be used. One reason that sentence contexts seem so attractive is that we know young children can learn from them. After all, that is how they learned all the words they knew before they started learning to read.

At the time we turned to research with sentence contexts we were not fully aware of the difficulties that we would meet. But that was probably all to the good. In our innocence we went ahead and rediscovered for ourselves some of the difficulties that other workers were quarreling about.

We decided to compare the effectiveness of three kinds of lexical information, but still using the write-a-sentence task that we had become fond of. In a counterbalanced study, one kind of information was the definition taken from a school dictionary; a second was the illustrative sentence taken from the same dictionary; and the third was a sentence drawn more or less haphazardly from *The New York Times*.

For example, in the case of the unfamiliar verb "usurp," the definition said "seize and hold (power, position, or authority) by force or without right." The dictionary's illustrative sentence was "The king's brother tried to usurp the throne." And the sentence from *The New York Times* was "In recent years the court has tried to usurp the powers of elected branches of government by rewriting the constitution."

On first inspection, the sentence contexts seemed to yield more acceptable sentences from the students than the definitions did: only 36% acceptable with definitions, compared with 52% or 55% acceptable with sentence contexts. We were not so innocent as to take that result at face value. We had previously noted that the students have a strong tendency to model their own sentences after the illustrative sentences that they see. The apparent superiority of sentence contexts over dictionary definitions may have been nothing more than the advantage of theft over honest toil. We have tried to think what a proper control group for this comparison would be, but with little success. It may be that the children's imitative tendencies should not be controlled, but instead should be exploited.

As before, the interesting results of the study do not become apparent until you examine the actual sentences that the children wrote. Look first at some of the sentences written when they saw only the definition:

> She doesn't have an easy usurp.
>
> He has the usurp to put you in jail.
>
> He had a usurp on the pencil.
>
> He usurped my arm, hurting it.
>
> He had usurped his opponent's hair.

These are merely more examples of the simple substitution errors that we have already seen. But note that the students have not understood the significance of the parentheses in the definition. "He has the usurp to put you in jail," for example, must be based on a substitution for "power," which was not part of the definition of "usurp" at all.

More interesting are the sentences written when sentence contexts were provided:

> The blue chair was usurped from the room.
>
> Don't try to usurp that tape from the store.
>
> The teacher could wait to usurp the class.
>
> The children fought about who was going to usurp the toy.
>
> The thief tried to usurp the money from the safe.

Note here that the example sentence contains a metaphor: "throne" is used metaphorically to signify "power, position, or authority." The children thought of a throne as a piece of furniture, and assumed that "usurp" must mean, approximately, "take or steal." So they wrote sentences using "take" and made a simple substitution. That is to say, we see exactly the same kind of problem solving going on here that we saw when definitions were provided—it merely involved an additional step, guessing what the defining word should be.

The same generalization holds for the sentences based on *The New York Times* sentence:

I usurped my story.
The woman usurped the test to the girl's level.
I usurped the people's minds.
The umpire usurped the 0–3 count on the batter.
The girl has usurped by buying new clothes.

In this case the children seem to have decided that "usurp" means "rewrite" or, more generally, "change." So they composed sentences using those guesses, then made a simple substitution of "usurp" for "change."

Because the sentence contexts were not really as big an improvement over the definitions as we had hoped, we tried giving the children three contexts instead of one, on the assumption that the greater variety of uses would enable them to induce the word's meaning more accurately. Without going into the details we can simply report that three contexts were no better than one. We believe that what happened was that the children focused on one of the three illustrative sentences and ignored the other two, guessed a meaning on the basis of that single sentence, then used the simple substitution strategy that we are now so familiar with.

But if sentence contexts do not improve on definitions, what else can be done?

STUDIES WITH ENRICHED CONTEXTS[1]

As we thought about it, we realized that when preschool children were learning new words by hearing them used in context, they had a great deal more than a sentence context to go on. They usually knew the people who were talking, had a good idea what those people were trying to accomplish, could see the objects and the general situation in which the sentences were spoken. All in all, children learn their first words with very rich environmental support.

We decided, therefore, to enrich the contextual support in our studies. We decided to embed the words to be learned in a narrative, rather than in isolated sentences. And we decided to provide visual context as well as linguistic.

Many ways of using visual information to convey word meanings can be imagined. We decided on interactive videodisc as a convenient, programmable way to provide a visual context for word learning. Our initial question was how best to exploit videodisc technology for the pedagogic purpose we

---

[1] The possibility of using interactive videodisc for vocabulary instruction was first suggested to us by Michael S. Gazzaniga.

had in mind. Here we describe our initial attempts to develop a satisfactory answer.

Preliminary goals for the videodisc project were to:

- explore new ways to combine dictionary information with contextual information;
- assess what those contexts might be, both linguistic and visual; and
- develop a method for determining which contexts are best for learning different kinds of words.

The general plan for meeting those goals was to ask learners to read a text that describes an episode from a movie that they have just seen. Included in the text are certain words, specially marked, that the reader is expected to learn. When one of those words is encountered, various kinds of information about its meaning are available on request.

This general plan was spelled out in the form of an instructional session that had five parts:

1. giving a pretest to assess how many of the target words are known;
2. showing an episode from a movie[2] in order to provide a general context for the learning experience;
3. sequentially displaying paragraphs containing target words that are highlighted and paired with specific scenes from the movie;[3]
4. offering a "help session" in which the user can suspend watching the movie in order to learn more about the target words; and
5. giving a posttest to assess comprehension of the paragraphs, particularly the target words.

The experimental variables of major interest—namely, the different kinds of "help" that were offered—were manipulated in Part 4 of the instructional session.

Before describing the experiments and their results in detail, we discuss the technology used to create and run them.

---

[2] The film used in these studies was *Raiders of the Lost Ark;* it is available on videodiscs that are recorded at constant angular velocity, which makes it possible to control the display by computer commands.

[3] The text was adapted from the novel, *Raiders of the Lost Ark* by Campbell Black, which is based on the movie and follows it closely.

The HANDY Authoring Language

The equipment used for controlling the videodisc player was an IBM PC XT equipped with a Sony color monitor and the MicroKey System of Video Associates Labs that enabled the computer to control the Pioneer 2000 videodisc player.

The software was HANDY, developed by Dr. Don Nix and his associates at the IBM T.J. Watson Research Center in Yorktown Heights, New York.[4] HANDY is an experimental language for writing interactive scripts that can provide windowing and animation of objects; can control the videodisc, videotape, audiocassette tape, voice synthesizer, mouse, and touch panel devices; can implement flexible control structures based on timing, random numbers, variables, mathematical expressions, approximate answer processing, string processing, user written subroutines, user written commands, and other contingencies; and can run multiple scripts concurrently. We are indebted to Dr. Nix not only for permission to use HANDY, but for considerable assistance in designing the first version of our demonstration system.

Programming Details

The current version has several features that evolved after experience in creating its predecessors. First, files are loaded and destroyed when needed, without having complicated directories or a separate loading program that takes time and slows down the execution of the program. Second, a fraction of the number of files is required; this was possible by organizing each type of illustrative material—sentences or definitions—into a single large file. The main program shifted a "window" on the large files to show the appropriate contexts at the appropriate moment.

A third feature involves control of the videodisc player while multitasking (running several programs at once). This is accomplished by setting a place holder, stopping one program, and using a data matrix to orchestrate the options. The data matrix is a very useful feature of HANDY. Our matrix is essentially a table that contains all information about the supplementary materials: where each scene from the videodisc begins and ends, which text goes with which scene, the coordinates of each target word, the location of each definition and illustrative sentence in the larger files, and which files contain pictorial information.

Our programs for both of the following experiments are of three kinds. A main program searches directories, loads programs, starts programs, defines options, and records the users' choices. A second program controls the videodisc

---

[4] HANDY was made available to us by a special agreement with IBM.

player by starting the movie at appropriate times and coordinating the texts with the appropriate scenes by using data retrieved from the large matrix.

A third set of programs present the pictorial context options. These programs vary widely depending on the concept to be illustrated. In one case the program simply locates a single frame or picture, shows the target word in a window, and waits until the student is ready to continue. Another type of program displays a single frame and blocks out irrelevant information in the picture by calling in a red mask with a rectangular window surrounding the pertinent area of the picture; a caption is also displayed that describes the illustrated word. For example, in a scene containing a pedestal, the word PEDESTAL is displayed at the top of the screen, the descriptive sentence "The idol is on the PEDESTAL" is displayed underneath, a red background appears to zoom in, masking out all but the pedestal, and this configuration remains on the screen until the student is ready to continue. In still other cases a short scene from the movie is played. Some of these clips are played in slow motion, some are played with sound, some use the zoom-in window effect, and one even plays the scene backward. Because these procedures for showing pictures are so diverse, a separate file was created for each target word. Standardization was eventually achieved, however, by including matrices in the programs: one matrix contains all the verbal information to be displayed with the picture, and another defines the program for the videodisc player (whether to play or freeze, which frame or frames to present, whether to zoom in, and the coordinates to outline the relevant portion of a frame).

The program also records the students' activity during the instructional phase. This record is a matrix-type file that includes whether background information is requested about each target word; the kind of information selected—definition, sentence, or picture; and the order of selection. A separate program is used to administer the posttest. It records which answer is selected for each question and whether the answer is correct.

EXPERIMENT 1: COMPARING PREFERENCES FOR CONTEXTS

In Experiment 1 the learners had considerable freedom of choice: The experiment was designed to give information relevant to the following four questions:

1. Do children know when to look for help?
2. Will contexts provide by interactive video actually aid learning?
3. Will children differentially sample contextual information?
4. Do children know which kinds of information are most helpful?

The first question concerns the children's ability to monitor their own knowledge states. Would fifth graders be able to use an interactive system that presupposes a fairly complicated metamemory skill: knowing that you do not know something. Some psychologists believe that children 10 or 11 years old do not know when to look for additional information (Elvian, 1938; Looby, 1939; Schatz & Baldwin, 1986).

The second question concerns whether children will learn anything from the interaction. Although we are not attempting to develop or recommend a technology or a teaching strategy, we did hope that while we were learning from the children they might also be learning from us. From what we had read of the literature on enhanced learning using interactive videodiscs, we were fairly optimistic that children's word knowledge would improve as a result of their participation in our experiment (Bosco, 1986; Elder et al., 1985; Glenn, Kozen, & Pollak, 1984; Ramsberger, Harns, Knerr, & Hopwood, 1985).

The third and fourth questions concern the learning contexts themselves. What do children want to know about words, given that access to various kinds of information is equal. The instructional program offered three kinds of explanations about words, in addition to the narrative context in which they are embedded. Children could choose to see dictionary definitions, illustrative sentences, or illustrative scenes from the film. We were curious to see which kinds of information children might prefer, if any. Our naive intuition was that children would enjoy the pictures and the novelty of interactive videodisc, and so would sample visual information quite frequently.

The final question raises the issue of whether children know which kinds of information are most helpful for learning new vocabulary. Our previous research (Miller & Gildea, 1985) had indicated that educators may be misled concerning the optimal strategies for learning new words. Have children been taught to request the information that is most helpful?

Experimental Details. Eighteen fifth and sixth graders were recruited from the Princeton area schools. Children were paid $5 for their time and travel expenses.

In brief, for the experimental group an experimental session had three sections: (a) the movie phase—presentation of a 10-minute clip from *Raiders of the Lost Ark;* (b) the instructional phase, consisting, in Experiment 1, of a repeat showing of the movie, which would stop periodically, allowing the children to read the narrative and to ask for help about the targeted words; and (c) a vocabulary test phase. For the control group, the vocabulary test phase preceded the instructional phase. During the instructional phase, the children were required to read aloud all written materials—narrative paragraphs, definitions, illustrative sentences—in order to indicate to the experimenter that they indeed had read them.

Figure 1.1 shows an example narrative paragraph, along with an illustrative sentence and a definition, as they would appear on the screen. The definition was always presented in the position indicated in Fig. 1.1. Definitions[5] were shortened to include only the one sense of the word that was appropriate to the narrative context.

Illustrative sentences appeared in the middle position of the screen, as indicated in Fig. 1.1. As in the case of the definitions, the sentences always used the word to express the same meaning that is expressed in the narrative (rather than suggesting some new interpretation of the word). In addition to that semantic constraint, the sentences were designed to complement a scene from the movie. We refer to these scenes as the *picture contexts*. A picture context could be either a single frame or a series of frames, such as an action sequence.

The written narrative consisted of 36 paragraphs similar in length and complexity to the example shown in Fig. 1.1. Each paragraph contained either one or two words to be learned. In all, there were 58 target words.

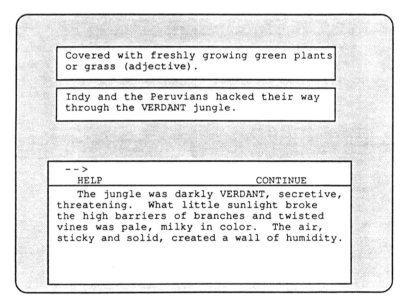

FIG. 1.1. Rough sketch of screen, showing the definition at the top, the illustrative sentence in the middle, and the narrative paragraph at the bottom, for the target word VERDANT. A mouse could be used to request HELP, or to move the arrow to select CONTINUE in order to continue with the narrative.

---

[5] From the *Longman Dictionary of Contemporary English,* which is intended for students learning English as a second language and which uses a limited vocabulary of familiar words to phase its definitions.

Words were selected to be unfamiliar to fifth- and sixth-grade students: The target words were on average introduced in 10th-grade level texts, according to the EDL Core Vocabulary List (Taylor, Frackenpohl, & White, 1969). Following the narrative, a multiple-choice vocabulary test was administered by the computer. The choices were designed to test appropriate inferences concerning use, as opposed to synonyms. For example, the word "colossal" described a boulder in the movie and narrative. The test question for "colossal" asked: Which might be colossal? The correct choice (out of four) was "elephant."

Performance for the entire session was recorded by the computer. This included recording all contexts that were sampled for each target word. The number of definitions, sentences, and pictures sampled were calculated for each subject. The order of each choice was recorded, as well as all test choices.

The entire session was designed to last an hour, but given variations in sampling and reading speed, the session sometimes lasted as long as 90 minutes. Even then, many of the children wanted to continue—in sharp contrast to children's typical reactions to a dictionary.

The subjects were divided haphazardly into two groups. An experimental group ($n=12$) interacted with the computer and took the vocabulary test at the end. A control group ($n=6$) took the vocabulary test at the beginning, then proceeded to interact with the system as the experimental group had.

It is necessary to have a way to separate familiar and unfamiliar target items, because one would not expect a learning effect for familiar words. The responses of the control group were used to determine which words were familiar and which were novel for the subjects in our sample. We classified a word as familiar when the control group answered it on the test with 75% accuracy or greater (chance is 25%). Familiar words include "alien," "humidity," "plunge," "peril," "awe," and "colossal." We classified a word as unfamiliar if the control group responded with less than 50% accuracy. Words that were unfamiliar include "verdant," "sinuous," "truculence," "arrest," and "fluid."

Note that some words might be familiar, but not in the sense that was used in the narrative. For instance, "arrest" was used in the less frequent sense of catching one's attention.

Results. In order to assess the effect of our program on vocabulary learning, test performance was compared for the experimental and control groups. Figure 1.2 shows the mean percentage correct by group.

The experimental group scored higher than the control. Familiar words, as determined by the control group, were not affected (see upper line on graph). Unfamiliar items show a large gain, from 30% (near chance) to almost 70% correct. The differences between groups are reliable considering all words ($t = 2.93$, $p < .01$), or for unfamiliar words alone ($t = 6.04$, $p < .01$).

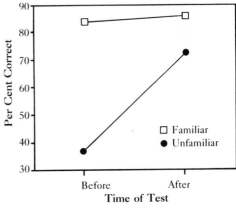

FIG. 1.2. Percent correct responses on a multiple-choice vocabulary tests administered before and after the learning session in Experiment 1. Little improvement could be seen for familiar words, but considerable learning occurred for unfamiliar words.

Scores on Objective Test (Chance=25%)

Table 1.1 shows the children's preferences for the three learning contexts, as indicated by the frequency with which each type was sampled. Data for the experimental and control groups are shown separately, but the preference patterns are similar. The percentages reflect sampling out of the total possible pool of definitions, sentences, or pictures. Overall, the experimental group sampled 29% of all possible contexts; the control group sampled 22%. For the experimental group, 54% of the definitions were selected; 21% of the pictures; and 12% of the sentences. Similarly, 49% of the definitions, 11% of the pictures, and 7% of the sentences were sampled by the control group. Regardless of when testing occurred, definitions were highly sampled and preferred; pictures were sampled much less often; and sentences were significantly the least sampled or preferred. This preference ordering is, of course, exactly the opposite of what we believed would be optimal from a pedagogical point of view.

This order of preference—definitions sampled most, illustrative sentences sampled least—was also reflected in the order of sampling. Definitions were usually sampled first, pictures second, and sentences third (if at all). Analyses

TABLE 1.1
Experiment 1: Preferences for Help, in Percentages

	Category of Help			
Group(N)	Definition	Sentence	Picture	Overall
Pretest(12)	54	12	21	29
Posttest(6)	49	7	11	22

of the combinations of contexts sampled suggest the following strategy: Sample a definition to make sure the word is known. If the word is unfamiliar or the definition is confusing, sample a picture. If the picture and definition do not provide a clear summary or synonym, sample a sentence. Sentences are chosen as the option of last resort. That is to say, sentences are never chosen first; they are frequently chosen last; and they are chosen mainly for the unfamiliar words.

The results of main concern are the effects of different context types on learning. Although the first experiment does not address this question directly, we divided the data from the experimental group into correct and incorrect answers by contexts sampled. This analysis is shown in Table 1.2.

The question is, which contexts did subjects sample when their answers were correct compared with when they were incorrect? The proportions for correct answers are reported in the top row of Table 1.2, and the proportions for incorrect answers are shown below. The most striking result is the column labeled "Nothing." This column represents the cases when no information was sampled at all and the children continued with the movie. When posttest answers were correct, no information was sampled about 18% of the time. When incorrect, no information was sampled 3% of the time or, to put it the other way round, some kind of help was requested 97% of the time. In other words, children seem to know when they need help. Moreover, they know what kind of help they want. The preference pattern already described persists: look at lots of definitions, some pictures, and a few sentences. When incorrect, it appears that more definitions are sampled, whereas sampling the other contexts remains constant. (Parenthetically, for words to which the response on the posttest would be incorrect, it looks as though the data that are missing from the "nothing" cell have shifted to the "definition" cell, but that is only speculation.)

At first we were disappointed about the implications of our data. These children, who seemed unusually bright in other respects, did not seem to know that illustrative sentences can be quite helpful, and they did not sample them enough for us to even begin to analyze their helpfulness. However, one final analysis convinced us that these children were behaving in a very

TABLE 1.2
Experiment 1: What Help Was Sampled for Correct and Incorrect
Answers on the Posttest, in Percentages

Posttest Answer (N)	Category of Help			
	Definition	Sentence	Picture	Nothing
Correct (177)	51	10	21	18
Incorrect (55)	64	13	20	3

intelligent manner. Table 1.3 shows the help that was chosen as a function of familiarity of the target words.

Again the data for familiar and unfamiliar words (as determined by the control group) are compared, but this time as a function of the kind of help sampled. We can see that the preference pattern persists, but now at a much higher rate: when the words were unfamiliar, 44% of the pictures and 21% of total sentences were chosen, as opposed to 12% and 4% respectively when they were familiar. Apparently the children were showing us what they have been taught: namely to look to definitions for help in learning the meanings of unfamiliar words.

EXPERIMENT 2: COMPARING CONTEXTS FOR LEARNING

The main goal of Experiment 2 was to make a more direct comparison of the effectiveness of dictionary definitions with the effectiveness of illustrative sentences and pictures or scenes. Because the freedom of choice allowed in Experiment 1 did not provide enough evidence to make a reasonable estimate about the relative effectiveness of all three kinds of help, our next step was to constrain the contexts that children could sample.

Experimental Details. The experimental materials and procedures were virtually the same as in Experiment 1, except that this time the movie was not shown again while the children were reading about it. The children watched the same episode from the movie and then were asked to read the story "out loud," and were told that they could request background information about the target words if they felt they needed to. The number of target words was reduced to one per paragraph, so there were only 36 words to be learned in Experiment 2. Words that were classified as familiar in Experiment 1 were eliminated.

Sixty children were randomly assigned to one of six groups (10 per group). All groups saw the episode from the movie and read the narrative description

TABLE 1.3
Experiment 1: What Help Was Sampled as a Function of Familiarity,
in Percentages

	Category of Help		
Familiarity	Definition	Sentence	Picture
High	85	4	12
Low	93	21	44

of it; the groups differed in the kinds of information they received when they asked for help.

Rationale. Experiment 2 was designed to provide information relevant to the following specific questions:

1. How do the three different contextual aids for learning compare?
2. Are the effects of helpful contexts additive?
3. How do different measures of learning compare?

The first question was investigated by assigning different kinds of contextual help to different groups of subjects. Group 1, the control group, read the narrative but were not able to request any background information. The remaining five groups had additional contexts available when they requested further information. Group 2 received only definitions. Group 3 received only sentences. Group 4 received definitions and sentences. Group 5 received pictures and sentences. Group 6 received all three contexts.

The second question concerns how contexts are combined. Is a definition a fairly effective context, a definition plus a sentence better, and a definition plus a sentence plus a picture the best of all? That is to say, do the contexts add together in some neat, predictable way? Our previous research with multiple sentence contexts led us to expect that the effects would not be cumulative. However, it is possible that definitions plus sentences can be better than the definition alone for some kinds of vocabulary tasks. The difference between previous studies and the present one is, again, the addition of an integrated narrative with visual contexts. Virtually all of the existing literature relevant to our questions concerns unrelated target words in the absence of a connected text.

Figure 1.3 illustrates a way to think about and compare the context groups. Group 1, who received the text alone, provides the data against which the performance of all the other groups can be compared. They represent a typical learning-from-context situation, with information about target words presented as part of the background knowledge about the movie and implicitly in the written narrative. At the next level of the figure are groups that additionally received one kind of context: either a definition or a sentence. At the third level are the groups who received two context types. At the final level is the group of subjects who received all three. Another way to read the figure is to compare groups along the horizontal or vertical axes. Comparing Conditions 1, 3, and 5 with Conditions 2, 4, and 6 shows the effect of adding a definition. Comparing Conditions 1 and 2 with Conditions 3 and 4 shows the effect of adding a sentence. Comparing Conditions 3 and 4 with Conditions 5

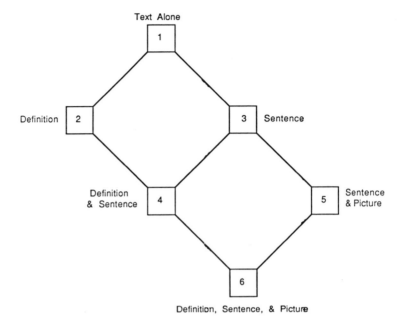

FIG. 1.3. Lattice showing relations among the six learning conditions that were evaluated in Experiment 2. (No subjects were run with pictures alone.)

and 6 shows the effect of adding a picture context. We use the additive graph when considering test performance.

The third question concerns the assessment of learning. The literature on learning from context is far from clear. Certainly one reason for equivocal results among studies relates to how learning and memory are assessed. Consequently, we measured learning and retention in three different ways: a production task (make up a sentence using the target word with all information in full view), a multiple choice test immediately following the instructional section (the same as Experiment 1); and a new delayed multiple choice test (return a week later and take a surprise test).

Our subjects were asked to return 1 week after the original learning experience, at which time, to their great disappointment, they were given the dreaded recognition and recall test. That test asked the children three different kinds of questions: either select the word's definition, or select a sentence that uses the word correctly, or describe an appropriate scene or context of use for the word. Distractor items on the multiple-choice items for sentences and definitions were sentences and definitions for other target words. Items were counterbalanced across subjects so that each subject actually saw only one type of question per target word, and each item was presented equally often for every type of help and every question type.

In addition to the objective tests given before and after the reading experience, we required the children to construct a sentence, just as we had done in our earlier research with the dictionary. Creating a sentence for a word that you have not heard before is hard work, and not a favorite pastime of fifth and sixth graders. However, children are accustomed to this request and usually respond with appropriate sentences that often sound a bit creative. We expected the kinds of sentences that we have encountered and documented previously. Our question was how various contexts, such as pictures, might affect production differentially.

Results on the Immediate Test. In Fig. 1.4, performance on the immediate posttest is compared across the six context groups: The percentage correct is shown as a function of the learning condition.

Performance ranges from 58% to 73%, where chance is 25%. Thus, all groups performed well. Even those who read the story and tried to use the target word without additional information were well above chance on the test. Comparing groups by using the "additive" graph reveals that, in general, performance for definition groups (2, 4, 6) does not differ significantly from

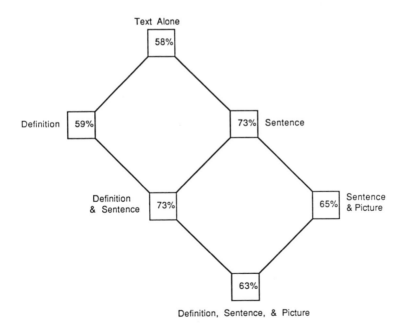

FIG. 1.4.   Percent correct on vocabulary test given immediately following the learning session, as a function of the learning condition in Experiment 2.

comparison groups (1, 3, 5), with 0–2% differences among comparison groups. Also, performance for picture groups (5, 6) does not differ significantly from the appropriate comparison groups (3, 4). However, groups (3, 4) perform significantly better than comparison groups (1, 2) who do not receive sentences.

Results on the Delayed Test. Our next question was: Do these results hold over time? Figure 1.5 presents the percentage correct on the test of retention that was taken after a 1-week interval, for each of the six groups.

Scores for the Text Alone group were comparable to their scores on the immediate test, although the two tests were quite different. Comparing the other groups with the Text Alone group, one was significantly better: the Sentence Alone group, $F (5,41)=3.85$, $p<.05$. The groups who received definitions when they asked for help are comparable to one another, as are the Picture groups. Furthermore, unlike the test a week earlier, the sentence groups are not comparable: Adding further information to the illustrative sentence such as definitions and pictures appears to hinder performance.

Can we say more about what kinds of information each group is recalling?

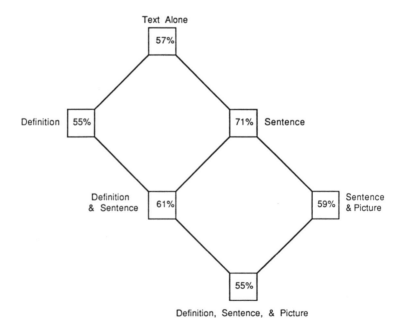

FIG. 1.5. Percent correct on vocabulary test given 1 week following the learning session, as a function of the learning condition in Experiment 2.

Another way to analyze the delayed test is to break down performance by question type: recognize the correct definition versus recognize the correct sentence versus describe a situation of use. Table 1.4 shows percentage correct on the delay test as a function of question type and the kind of help provided.

The comparison group, who saw the text alone, was correct 56% of the time for definition questions, 74% for sentence questions, and 38% for describing situations of use. We compared performance of the other groups with these scores. The group who was permitted to see definitions out-performed the comparison group on questions that asked for the recognition of *definitions*, but not on the other measures. In fact, their ability to judge correct sentences was significantly lower than the Text Alone group, and was the lowest score of all groups. It appears that, although seeing the correct definition enables a student to select the correct one a week later, definitions do not generalize to helping the student recognize or produce appropriate sentences.

The Picture groups' performances were comparable to the Text Alone group, with the exception that the Sentence and Picture group (5) recognized more definitions. It appears that in general the pictures do not add information that is helpful for remembering new words. It may be that pictures distract from information that is more helpful: illustrative sentences.

The two remaining Sentence groups, Sentence Alone (3) and Definition and Sentence (4), outperformed the comparison group on two of the three measures. The Definition and Sentence group performance was slightly below that of the Sentence Alone group. In fact, the Sentence Alone subjects, who had not been given a definition, were able to recognize definitions significantly more often than the comparison group and just as often as subjects who had been given definitions. In addition, they were the only group who were significantly better than the comparison group in describing scenes and using the new words themselves. The superior performance of

TABLE 1.4
Experiment 2: Percent Correct on Test 1 Week Later, as a Function
of Question Type and Learning Context

	Question Type		
Learning Context	Definition	Sentence	Description
1. Text Alone (Control)	56	74	38
2. Text, Definition	70*	60*	36
3. Text, Sentence	71*	77	50*
4. Text, Def, Sent	64	73	46
5. Text, Sent, Picture	68*	65	37
6. Text, Def, Sent, Pict	58	70	33

*Differ significantly from Text Alone, $p<.05$

the Sentence group a week later cannot be due merely to recognizing information they have seen before.

Results on Sentence Production Task. The final results concern the sentences that the children produced on-line. With all the contextual information
about target words in full view, children composed a sentence using the target
words. Our analysis examined differences between groups in terms of the
number of sentences that used the target words correctly and types of errors
when they occurred.

Three raters independently judged whether the children's sentences were
acceptable or unacceptable. For unacceptable sentences, judges indicated
reason(s) for their ratings. Materials were rated without knowledge of context
condition. A sentence was counted as unacceptable if one or more judges
rated it to be. Agreement among the judges was quite high: all three agreed
on 92% of the sentences.

The following sentences are representative of those judged to be unacceptable.

I have a VERDANT in the back of our yard.

He had a VERDANT sweater.

The girl was TENEBROUS because it was raining.

My trees are INDIGENOUS throughout the year.

Birds INDIGENOUS in the forest.

The dog INDIGENOUS in his doghouse.

Many of the unacceptable sentences qualify as simple substitution errors.

In general, however, most of the sentences that the children produced
were acceptable. In all, there were 2,160 sentences, or 360 sentences per
group.[6] Figure 1.6 gives the proportions of acceptable sentences as a function
of learning context.

The results of the sentence production task indicated that all learning
contexts significantly improved the students' ability to produce new sentences, compared to reading the text alone. For the comparison group (Text
Alone), who received no special information about the target words, 70% of
sentences produced were judged to be acceptable, but this proportion does
not reflect incorrect explanations and guesses about the target words. In
addition to composing a sentence, the children in this group were required
to tell the experimenter what they thought the word might mean. When all
of the sentences that accompanied misguided explanations are excluded,
only 43% remain. Because we have no comparable explanations from the

---

[6] 2,160 sentences=36 words x 10 subjects/group x 6 groups.

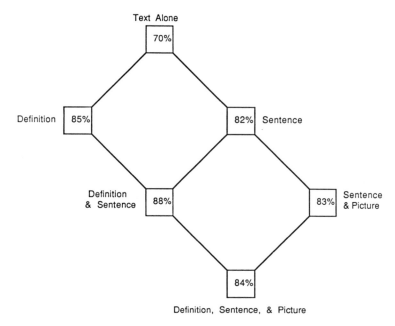

Text Alone
70%

Definition 85%   82% Sentence

Definition
& Sentence 88%   83% Sentence
& Picture

84%

Definition, Sentence, & Picture

FIG. 1.6. Percent of the sentences using the target words that were judged acceptable, as a function of the learning condition in Experiment 2.

other groups, however, we can only guess how many wrong explanations may be lurking behind many of their acceptable ones. Our previous work has shown that partial understanding is often all that is required for acceptable performance.

For the other groups, the number of errors[7] is approximately the same for all learning conditions. Additional comparisons with our previous studies using school dictionaries show that production errors were much less frequent. Thus, presenting words in an enriched context adds information that must be missing from the dictionary.

Analysis of the kinds of errors, however, did suggest some interesting differences among the groups. For the Definition Alone group (2), over 40% of the errors were attributed to using the target word as the wrong part of speech. For the Sentence Alone group (3), only about 5% of errors were grammatical errors; the most frequent errors resulted from substitution errors.

When only the most difficult words (nine items) were considered, we can

---

[7] "Errors" is not quite the right way to think about these data. The children's responses provide valuable information about what is missing from the instructional materials.

see contributions of the sentences and definitions more clearly. These turned out to be the following: "verdant," "veneration," "traverse," "truculence," "parody," "fluid," "extrinsic," "impetus," and "stand." (Difficult words were identified as those for which subjects produced 40% or more unacceptable sentences.) Again the Text Alone group (1) made significantly more errors than all other groups. The Sentence group (3) and Definition group (2) were again comparable. The Definition and Sentence group (4) now made fewer errors than either the Sentence or Definition groups. We speculate that the definitions in our sample provided more synonyms that included suitable substitutions than the children could generate on their own in the sentence condition. Sentences, on the other hand, provide better grammatical cues than definitions by using words appropriately as opposed to giving the part of speech in a code.

Results With Pictures. Up to this point, we have had little to say about the video portion of our contexts. Several recent studies have provided guidelines or lists of situations in which a picture could clarify a word's interpretation (Brody, 1984; Wisely & Streeter, 1985). Pictures can (a) establish similarities and dissimilarities, (b) provide varied examples, (c) provide a specific referent, (d) provide a simpler example, (e) provide a usual or general domain, (f) provide new information not included in the text, and (g) generate emotion. Can we find such cases in our own data?

We examined the production data for words that seemed to clarify the target words as described here.

We compared the average number of unacceptable sentences written for the nine most difficult words under three conditions: (a) by the comparison group (1), who saw text alone, (b) by the three groups (2,3,4) who received sentences or definitions, but no pictures, when they asked for help, and (c) by the two groups (5,6) who were permitted to see pictures. The comparison group produced an average of about 68% unacceptable sentences. The children who had verbal help but did not see any pictures wrote 49% unacceptable sentences. The children who saw pictures significantly outperformed the

TABLE 1.5
Experiment 2: Mean Percentage of Unacceptable Sentences
Composed with Most Difficult Words

Learning Context	Mean	St. Dev.
Text Alone (Control)	68.0	10.3
No Pictures Shown	49.1*	7.8
Pictures Included	28.5*	12.1

*Differ significantly from Text Alone, $p<.001$

others: Only about 29% of their sentences using these difficult words were rated as unacceptable.

These data may seem surprising in light of the multiple-choice tests discussed previously. There may be several explanations for the general unhelpfulness of pictures for learning novel words. One reason for this may be due to our limited sample of pictures, because our choice was constrained to what we could find on side one of the *Raiders* videodisc. Another reason may be that pictures are novel and salient, distracting attention away from the sentence contexts.

SUMMARY AND CONCLUSION

What we think we have learned from these exercises and analyses can be briefly summarized.

1. Children do know when to initiate look-up—but not what information to ask for.
2. The narrative context (Text Alone group) was sufficient for a high proportion of correct answers.
3. Helpful contexts for learning are not additive.
4. The children given illustrative sentences when they requested help outperformed all others on multiple-choice tests. Definitions add very little, and actually detract from performance over time.
5. Pictures significantly improve sentence production for many words.

Experiment 1 supports the first point: Children appear to know when to ask for additional information about unfamiliar vocabulary. They seem to prefer information in the form of a brief definition, but the definition does not always provide the most help and often leads to interesting misconceptions.

The third point restates an old adage: more is not necessarily better. Experiment 2, where contexts were prespecified, shows clearly that contextual aids do not yield additive effects.

The fourth point concerns the apparent helpfulness of sentence contexts. One might be surprised at the superior performance of the Sentence groups. The information that was sampled least in Experiment 1 appeared to be most helpful in Experiment 2. Why might that be? Of course, we know from our studies with dictionaries that definitions are not always clear and do not always contain enough information for error-free performance. Indeed, they were not written with that purpose in mind. The sentence result seems to be sensible, given that children must learn a great deal of their vocabulary from contexts of use.

What might seem surprising is that the children who saw sentences combined with additional information did not do any better than the children who saw only sentences. One possibility is that, given that definitions and pictures are preferred, they obscure other information. Once they see the definition, children may not think that they need to attend to anything else. The data for tests a week later seems to support this interpretation. Groups adding definitions and pictures to sentences do not remember as much.

Another possibility is that children who saw only sentences were performing a different task. We were able to videotape many of the children; the differences in general behavior among the context groups are striking. Those in the sentence group were extremely active. The sentences, combined with the text and the movie, seemed to provide them with a challenging game of discovery: "What does this word mean now that I have seen it used a few times?" In contrast, the children who were given definitions did not appear to be engaging in a discovery process. They said such things as, "Oh, I see, I get it," and then they went on to the next paragraph. Those who saw sentences appeared to spend more time thinking about the meaning of the word than did those who saw definitions.

Video recordings of 12 children whose reading speeds were comparable were studied in order to compare the amount of time that elapsed between reading the material on the screen and starting to compose their own sentence. Six children given only a definition took an average of 26 seconds (SD=9) between reading the text and producing a sentence. Six children who received only sentences took an average of 46 seconds (SD=16) during the same interval. It appears that an illustrative sentence alone requires or encourages subjects to spend more time, 20 seconds on the average, thinking about target words. It is our impression that children in the sentence group were generating definitions for themselves, which might explain how they were able to identify the definitions when they saw them for the first time a week later.

This account is speculative, of course, and needs to be tested. One critical question remains: if time were held constant, would the sentence advantage still hold? Also, perhaps the sentence condition is challenging and effective only for highly motivated learners, who probably are already in possession of a rich vocabulary. We did observe a great deal of variation among subjects within the various learning groups. Particularly, the effectiveness of sentences and the distraction of other information, such as definitions and pictures, differs widely. Because our subjects were not in any sense a random sample, we are not prepared to suggest that the sentence method is always the best way to teach vocabulary. Rather, in the process of developing a method to study vocabulary acquisition in enriched contexts we have stumbled across a phenomenon that looks interesting and deserves further testing.

For this reason, we decided to re-run some of the experiments previously discussed. A group of college-age subjects from Rutgers University was selected in order to compare the learning strategies and the effectiveness of illustrative sentences found in previous studies with children.

One question concerns our sampling data: Will adults prefer to sample definitions as background contexts, as our fifth and sixth graders do? Or, do they realize that sentences are helpful contexts for learning about unfamiliar words? Eighteen subjects participated as part of their psychology course requirements. Their sampling strategies turned out to be virtually identical to those found in previous studies. When adult students were unfamiliar with a target word, they sampled 59% of the available definitions, 14% of the available illustrative sentences, and 13% of the available pictures. The order of sampling was also consistent with our previous observations: sample definitions first, and sample other information if the definition seems unclear.

Another question pertains to our sentence effect: Will adults also demonstrate that illustrative sentences alone are the most helpful? It may be that adults are able to integrate more information, or focus less on parts of definitions that may be misleading.

Forty-five subjects were recruited from the same population mentioned earlier at Rutgers University.[8] Subjects were randomly assigned to one of five experimental conditions: definitions, sentences, definitions and sentences, the narrative alone, and the posttests alone. The narrative alone group participated as did the other experimental groups, except that they were given no additional information about target words. The posttests alone group serves as the control group in that they were given the tests in lieu of participation in the experiment. Their performance is used as a baseline for determining which target words are generally familiar to our population. The procedure was identical to our previous studies with children: subjects (a) watched a segment of a movie, (b) read a related story with target words to learn about, (c) were given some combination of background information about the target words, (d) were required to use targets in a sentence of their own design, and (e) were given posttests to assess learning.

The results support our previous findings. An analysis of variance revealed a significant effect of learning condition.[9] A Duncan Multiple Range test revealed three different levels of performance. The Sentence Group outperformed all others with 74% on the immediate posttest. The next three

---

[8] Students were selected from a special program for "high-risk" freshmen. Participation in the program is voluntary; however, entering students who have lower than average grades and achievement scores are targeted and encouraged to attend certain specially designed courses and smaller subsections of larger classes. We chose these students as they seem representative of the kinds of learners that we hope would benefit most from interactive video programs.

[9] Learning was assessed by eliminating familiar words. This was determined by selecting those words that were above chance performance, according to the control group.

groups did not differ significantly from one another: definition group (58%), definition and sentence group (58%), and narrative alone (49%). The control group performance was at chance (25%).

We conclude that there is a strong belief that dictionary definitions are perceived to be the most helpful and informative starting point for learning new words. Furthermore, this strategy is not merely one followed by elementary school children but one that college-age learners adhere to. We were also able to replicate and extend our findings from previous studies that show that the optimal context for explaining our target words is not the standard dictionary definition. Rather, it is an illustrative sentence that fits with a rich, narrative context. Combining such sentences with definitions does not appear to provide better contexts for learning. It appears that dictionary definitions occlude the kind of thinking that context sentences encourage.

Although our findings are still tentative, they seem sufficiently promising to merit consideration. We found in both experiments that a narrative context was sufficient for a high proportion of correct answers. In Experiment 1, overall, children sampled only about 25% of the available additional information and yet were able to answer a test with surprisingly high accuracy (even when the words were unfamiliar). In Experiment 2, when children were given a new word in an enriched context they could learn quite a bit about what it meant; they could remember a great deal of this a week later; and they could produce acceptable sentences with remarkable frequency. Looking at the results another way, the children were able to learn about 10 new words in an hour.

Moreover, the proportion of acceptable sentences produced in Experiment 2 was much higher than in our earlier dictionary experiments. Although the children who volunteered for Experiment 2 may have been academically superior to those tested in our earlier studies, we are still inclined to attribute some of the differences to the enriched context provided by the narrative and by lexical information that is easily consulted.

Meanwhile, we will continue to search for innovative ways to enrich traditional learning contexts. And we will surely continue to be amazed at how much children can teach us by misunderstanding what we thought we told them.

ACKNOWLEDGMENTS

This research has been supported by the Spencer Foundation, the James S. McDonnell Foundation, Bell Communications Research, International Business Machines, and the Army Research Institute. The views and conclusions contained in this chapter are those of the authors and should not be interpreted as representing official policies, either expressed or implied, of any of those sponsors. We are personally indebted to Robert Amsler, Robert Bernard, Stephen J. Hanson, Katherine L. Miller, and Pamela Wakefield for advice and assistance at various stages in the work.

REFERENCES

Bosco, J. (1986). An analysis of evaluations of interactive video. *Educational Technology, 26,* 7–17.

Brody, P. J. (1984). Research on pictures in instructional texts. *Educational Communication and Technology Journal, 29,* 93–100.

Brody, P. J. (1984). In search of instructional utility: A function-based approach to pictorial research. *Instructional Science, 13,* 47–61.

Deese, J. (1967). Meaning and change of meaning. *American Psychologist, 22,* 641–651.

Elder, B., Harris, C., Sticha, P., Stein, D., Kneer, C., & Tkacz, S. (1985). *Development of interactive videodisc training for army land navigation skills* (HumRRO Final Report FR-PRD-85-17). Alexandria, VA.: Human Resources Research Organization.

Elvian, J. (1938). Word perception and word meaning in the intermediate grades. *Education, 59,* 51–56.

Glenn, A., Kozen, N., & Pollak, R. Teaching economics: Research findings from a microcomputer/videodisc project. *Educational Technology, 24*(3), 30–32.

Looby, R. (1939). Understandings children derive from their readings. *Elementary English Review, 16,* 56–62.

McKeown, M. G., & Curtis, M. E. (Eds.). (1987). *The nature of vocabulary acquisition.* Hillsdale, NJ: Lawrence Erlbaum Associates.

Miller, G. A. (1985/1986). Dictionaries in the mind. *Language and Cognitive Processes, 1,* 171–186.

Miller, G. A., & Gildea, P. M. (1985). How to misread a dictionary. *AILA Bulletin,* 13–26.

Nagy, W. E., & Herman, P. A. (1987). Breadth and depth of vocabulary knowledge: Implications for acquisition and instruction. In M. G. McKeown & M. E. Curtis (Eds.), *The nature of vocabulary acquisition* (pp. 19–36). Hillsdale, NJ: Lawrence Erlbaum Associates.

Ramsberger, P. Harris, C., Knerr, C., & Hopwood, D. (1985). *Development of parallel learning strategies curricula using videodisc and standard off-line formats* (HumRRO Final Report FR-PRD-85-16). Alexandria, VA: Human Resources Research Organization.

Schatz, E., & Baldwin, R. (1986). Context clues are unreliable predictors of word meanings. *Reading Research Quarterly, 21,*439–453.

Taylor, S. E., Frackenpohl, H., & White, C. E. (1969). *A revised core vocabulary.* New York: McGraw-Hill.

Wisely, F., & Streeter, C. (1985). Toward defining the function of visuals used to support a verbal narration. *Educational Technology 25,* 24–26.

2

Books on Videodisc: Computers, Video, and Reading Aloud to Children

Carol Chomsky
Harvard Graduate School of Education

An ongoing interest of mine is providing children with access to books. The intention is to nurture a love of reading in children so they are motivated to read on their own.

What I have in mind is the kind of "access" to books that includes the desire to read as well as the availability of books. Simply having books available is not enough. Literacy develops, after all, when we read because we want to, not because we have to. Children need to discover that books are wonderful and delightful. They need to develop an easy familiarity with books, to feel anticipation when sitting down to read, to be able to find a book of interest, and to get off to a comfortable start with a new book. These are all aspects of a child's developing relationship to books and reading that can contribute in an important way to independence in reading. They are part of being in touch with books in a meaningful way.

This chapter describes an effort to expand children's access to books, through the use of new technologies. It is an account of using microcomputers and interactive videodiscs to provide this access and put children in direct touch with books.

The purpose is to encourage children to read on their own. The role of technology here, as I see it, is to motivate this independent reading. The function of the computer is to lead a child to a book, to provide the link. In this instrumental role, technology can provide a real service.

For example, a session at the computer may offer familiarity with a book. It may serve to introduce a book and facilitate getting started with it. The interactive videodisc/computer combination can offer activities such as browsing through the text and illustrations, hearing the book read aloud while following along in the text, finding out about the characters and plot, or even being introduced to difficult vocabulary that will be encountered. Such a session can be useful and interesting not only as an introduction prior to reading the book, but also, it turns out, as a follow-up after the book has been read and enjoyed.

It is intriguing to think about ways of using technology to encourage reading. This is a generation of screen-oriented youths, accustomed to television and having things come to life on the screen. It is a commonplace that television requires less of a contribution from the viewer than does reading from the reader. Using one's own internal resources and imagination to bring a story to life, as required in reading, is a much more active process, involving the reader in very different ways. It is harder. It takes more effort and more of an investment.

Why not use the familiar screen to encourage reading? Present the text of the book on the screen for viewing, while hearing it read aloud. Start with viewing, but let the goal be, as previously indicated, to lead away from viewing to reading on one's own. I have found that the combination of a videodisc and a computer offers very interesting possibilities toward this end. The work described here has this "journey," from screen to book, as its goal.

The interactive videodisc is particularly well-suited to this task. Children see the book on the screen—text, illustrations, and all. They can page through the book on the screen, hearing it read aloud while they follow along in the text. They can listen to selected portions, or even the whole book if they so choose. They can stop and ask for the meaning of words they do not know, or have idiomatic usage explained. Or they can flip through the pages, looking at all the pictures, for example, if this is helpful in deciding whether they want to read a book.

Although the program presents the book on the screen, and turns the pages, the function of the computer is far from that of a "glass book" or an "electronic page-turner." Rather it makes its own kind of contribution toward connecting children to books. The book is on the screen as an introduction, in the context of serving as a bridge to reading the book later, after the computer session is over. The computer functions as an attention-getter, while also giving real help with the actual reading. Rather than replace the reading, it facilitates it and leads up to it.

I stress this point, and keep coming back to it, because it can be so easily misunderstood. Action on the screen, and time spent at the computer, very often compete with the more reflective activity of reading and investing in literacy. Here the attempt is to overcome the competition, and exploit the screen and the computer for what they can *contribute* to literacy. Over the past few years I have been exploring ways to implement these ideas. The exploration has been rewarding, in particular because I have been working with a highly flexible system for using videodiscs under computer control. I have been able to program the system myself in IBM's programming language HANDY, a language designed for educators who are not programmers. Because I do not have to work through a programmer, but can try out ideas independently at any time, I have been able to experiment freely.

It is easy with HANDY to turn an idea into a working program. As a result, I can try out an idea with children fairly readily, and abandon it with little regret if it does not go over well. The investment was minimal. And if an activity is successful, I find out early on and can develop it, trying variations easily as I go along.

From several years of exploration with videodiscs, computers, and children, I have arrived at a number of interesting ways of presenting a book as a read-aloud. I have also developed a variety of activities for working and playing with the story and text. This is work in progress, still undergoing development and revision. This chapter describes the present state of this "books-on-videodisc" project.

LISTENING TO A BOOK READ ALOUD

Rationale

The combination of a videodisc and a computer offers new and interesting possibilities for reading aloud to children. The project described here uses computer-driven videodisc to provide an introduction to a book. The book is presented on the screen, page by page, while a voice reads the text aloud. A student may listen to a few pages, or to the entire book. Help is provided with keeping the place and with unfamiliar vocabulary.

What is the purpose of such a presentation? As one colleague asked, when I told him I was using videodiscs to read aloud to children, "Now why would you want to do a thing like that?"

Well, for many reasons. To provide an introduction to a book. To make it easier to read the book on one's own. To give practice in "listening while reading," a technique of following along in a text while hearing it read aloud, which has been shown to help with reading fluency. To review a book one has read and liked. Also for pure enjoyment, of the sort one derives from going to a poetry reading, or to the reading of a play.

Reading aloud to children can have all sorts of benefits: getting beginning readers started on books they can handle, motivating reluctant readers, helping problem readers manage with a book they would like to read, easing the task for a child of finding a book that will be interesting and involving, helping children develop judgment in choosing a book they will like.

Listening to books read aloud is an important part of children's early experience with stories and literature. Looking at the pictures, watching and turning the pages as someone reads to them, all help to familiarize young children with the pleasures a book can offer. Sometimes called the "lap method," this early exposure to books is widely recognized as an important background for reading. It is a valuable initiation into the experience and feeling of reading, preparing the way for a natural transition to reading on one's own.

The advantages of being read to continue as children start learning to read. By following along in the text as someone reads to them, children participate in the reading in a way that offers benefits on many levels of reading simultaneously. Indeed, repeated listening to a favorite story or book while following along on the page often results in children's "memorizing" the text, so that they can "read" the book aloud themselves long before their actual reading skill permits such a feat. This is a common observation of parents who find themselves called on to read and reread a favorite storybook to children whose desire to hear it can well outlast a parent's willingness to read it yet again. The day finally comes when the child picks up the book and "reads" it aloud, through a mixture of memorization and clues from the print. This kind of thorough familiarity with a book can make an important contribution as children progress to real reading.

Being read to continues to play an important and recognized role long after children have learned to read. It can solidify their knowledge of a book they are able to read on their own, and provide access to books they can't yet manage by themselves. For older students who read well, it can provide a good dramatic presentation of a well-liked book or story, bringing the language to life. Much as seeing a play, or attending the reading of a play, is a different experience from reading it on one's own, hearing a book read aloud offers a very different kind of satisfaction. Having the text available to follow provides help for students who need it, and an anchor for students who do not have problems but may simply find watching while they listen useful and enjoyable. Following the text can be particularly effective, for example, for listeners of any age at a poetry reading while poets read from their own work.

For young students, whether it be few listenings or many listenings to a particular story or book or poem, the experience is enjoyable and valuable. Ordinarily the reading is done in a "live" situation, by a parent, teacher, relative, or older friend. Here we are experimenting with letting the videodisc serve as a substitute.

Here is how we do it. We take a videodisc with a book pictured on it, page by page, accompanied by a voice reading aloud. We put the child in control of the pace of the reading, of when to turn the pages, of whether to read sequentially or skip about in the book. We provide a variety of means of "keeping the place" as the voice moves along, down each page. It is easy for the child to follow along in the text while listening to the voice.

With an appropriate dramatic reading of the book, good filming of the text and illustrations, and imaginative use of musical effects, a book can come to life before a child's eyes.

A session with a book on videodisc can serve as an introduction to a book prior to reading it on one's own. Or it can be a chance to listen to a book one has read independently and enjoyed. Or it can be used for repeated listenings to a favorite book or story, much as a child enlists the participation of a willing adult to read and reread the book of choice on any given day.

We have been working so far with young children, both preschool and elementary school age. But this scheme can be useful for students of any age, including adults. The book or text need only be appropriate for the interests, maturity, and reading level of the viewer/reader. The idea can readily be adapted for use with older students in secondary school, in adult literacy programs, or for speakers of other languages in English as a Second Language (ESL) programs.

Description

In this "books-on-disc" undertaking, we use videodiscs, under computer control, to simulate reading aloud to a listener/viewer. The program is implemented on an IBM Infowindow system, and written in the IBM authoring language HANDY. The system includes a videodisc, which shows each page of a book in succession, with accompanying voice reading it. There is also an interactive computer program that drives the disc, allowing flexible user control of the disc and follow-up computer activities (a Level III videodisc application). A touch screen and spoken instructions via a speech synthesizer make user control simple. Using the program is easy for students who have not had prior experience with computers.

A book or story is displayed on the screen one page at a time, while a voice reads the text aloud. The child listens and follows along in the text, advancing from page to page when ready. Using the program in its simplest form, a child may simply listen to the book from beginning to end, turning each page at will by touching the screen. There is time to look over each page and examine the text and illustrations at leisure, since the user controls the turning of the pages. Figure 2.1a and 2.1b show sample pages from Beatrix Potter's *Peter Rabbit.*

Computer control of the videodisc permits flexibility and interactivity, with overlay of computer text and graphics on the video image. Various

FIG. 2.1. Computer/videodisc display of pages from Beatrix Potter's *Peter Rabbit*.

options are made available to the user. For example, help is offered in "keeping the place," through highlighting the spoken portions on the page as the voice moves along, or displaying subtitles at the bottom of the screen, phrase by phrase, as the reader's voice proceeds through the text. Students can switch the highlighting or subtitles on or off at any time.

The menu screen for choosing highlighting or subtitles is shown in Fig. 2.2. Figures 2.3 and 2.4 show samples of pages with highlighting and subtitles, respectively.

Further, students may listen to the entire book or story from beginning to end, or move around in the book as desired. For example, a student may listen to a particular page several times before moving on, or may skip to any other page or portion of the story easily.

Follow-up activities on the microcomputer and videodisc are provided so that students may play with the story, check their reading or understanding, or investigate word meaning. These include vocabulary and comprehension games and exercises, analysis of story content, matching of text and illustrations, spelling practice, and the like. These activities are described in the section titled "Working and Playing With Stories and Texts."

For this project, the book we chose was Beatrix Potter's *Peter Rabbit,* although as mentioned earlier, the idea can be used with any suitable book or story. In this presentation, the feeling is somewhat like listening to a

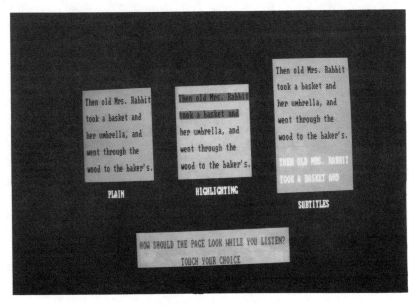

FIG. 2.2.   Menu for selecting how the book page looks on the screen: plain, with highlighting, or with subtitles.

FIG. 2.3. Sample page illustrating highlighting of spoken portion of text as the voice reads. On the computer screen the highlighted lines are clearly readable, although they appear obscured in this figure.

FIG. 2.4. Sample page illustrating "subtitles" on the lower portion of the screen. Each phrase is displayed in turn as the voice reads the page.

children's story record or audio cassette, with dramatic reading and music, but enhanced by seeing the book at the same time.

Before pressing the disc, we had some concern that mixing technology and reading aloud might spoil the warmth and charm that make reading aloud the personal and rewarding experience that it is. In fact, we suspected that it might not work at all and could deteriorate into a mechanical display. Fortunately this turned out not to be the case. The charm is retained to a surprising degree, and children react quite positively.

Although we used videodiscs for this experiment, other optical disc technology is also relevant. CD-ROM in a CD-I environment could be exploited for this same purpose, as could Digital Video Interactive technology (DVI). These are the potential entrants onto the laser scene that are under discussion at the moment, although by the time this book appears there may well be others. Either of these may be an entirely suitable medium for this type of "books-on-disc" presentation.

The important feature of using computer-driven videodiscs for presenting read-aloud material is that the book is pictured as it really looks when you hold it in your hands, with all its pictures and text. A good dramatic reading and music of course enhance the presentation. Overlay of computer text and graphics on the video image allows freedom of design and permits the inclusion of activities of many different kinds. The full power of the microcomputer is available for flexible presentation of a book and related play and instruction. The interactive aspect of computer-driven optical discs, and the ease of moving about on the disc, put the child in easy and smooth control of the listening.

The program as we have developed it in these early stages is suitable for use from kindergarten or first grade up through elementary school or later, depending of course on the book. It is appropriate for children with reading problems as well as for average and fluent readers. The idea is, as mentioned, applicable for use in the upper grades, as well for use in adult literacy programs and second language programs.

This program is experimental. It is still in the active development stage, in which we try it out with individual children, and revise according to their reactions. This is of course a time-consuming and critically important part of any software development.

But the development is far enough along to show that the idea is entirely workable, and we find the project promising. It has a sound theoretical basis in the recognized value of hearing books read aloud and the value of listening while reading. It captures the quality and charm of the real-life reading-aloud experience. And, we think, (or at least hope and expect) that it leads away from the computer and the screen to the real world of books.

Motivation to read "real books" remains to be examined. This examination awaits the completion of a full working prototype of the program, and the development of a variety of books on disc. With the program still in the development stage, and only *Peter Rabbit* available on disc, it is not yet possible to ask about effects of this kind of work on students outside of our laboratory sessions. So far we have observed only children who came in, one or two at a time, to work with the program in progress and give us their reactions.

We have learned a great deal from these sessions. One interesting thing is that children like to have a copy of the book available while they watch, for comparison. Some of them like to keep their place in the book as they "turn the pages" on the screen, making sure the book is always open to the matching page. Sometimes they follow the voice in the book rather than on the screen.

We have found also that the children enjoy working in pairs, discussing the story, pointing to the pictures, taking turns making the pages turn on the screen. They discuss whether to make the text highlighted, subtitled or plain, and switch from one format to the other frequently, by joint decision. They explore the program's capabilities eagerly, and they love the touch screen.

And then they can leave the computer lab, go home and read the book by themselves, any time. Children should clearly have a copy of the book to take home after a session like this. It is this tie to independent reading that matters, in our opinion. What's important is that children read, and expect to read, real books, the kind you hold in your hand and read on the subway, or while waiting for the bus, or when you climb into bed and night. This is, after all, the purpose of the project. To facilitate, to whet the appetite, to give access to reading and books out there in everyday life. For it is certainly true you cannot curl up with a keyboard or even a friendly touch screen, or get comfortable on the beach with the CD-ROM or DVI your best friend finally lent you.

WORKING AND PLAYING WITH STORIES AND TEXTS

These are activities we have been experimenting with, for additional work or play with a book or story.

Word-By-Word Reading

In this presentation, the text on the screen is read aloud, slowly, one word at a time. As each word is spoken, it is highlighted individually.

We tried this mode of presentation with a number of children, to see what their reaction would be. The students who liked this presentation, and chose it repeatedly, were slow readers who had trouble keeping up with the pace of the normal reading. This slowed-down version, in spite of its artificiality, was extremely welcome.

One 12-year-old slow reader regularly chose this type of presentation, to his tutor's surprise. It apparently was just what he needed, reported the tutor. He could finally follow!

Words on Request

With a text on the screen, the student may touch any word and hear it spoken. A second touch calls up a spoken definition or explanation of the word.

This option may be offered during the initial read-aloud session, or as a review activity. In the former case, students have the option available when the program pauses at the end of each page. Before proceeding to the next page, they touch those words they wish to hear again, with meanings if desired.

Games

These games have been popular with students.

Match Pictures and Text. An illustration from the story is shown on one half of the screen. The student finds the paragraph from the story that goes with this picture, by cycling through six or seven paragraphs offered on the other half of the screen, one at a time.

Alternatively, a paragraph from the story is shown on one half of the screen. The student finds the picture that goes with this paragraph, by cycling through a succession of pictures offered on the other half of the screen. Figure 2.5 shows a sample screen from this game.

Find the Word; Find the Object in the Picture. This game might follow the preceding one, in which the student has just matched an illustration and its text.

An illustration and its matching paragraph or story part are shown on the screen. There are three variations of this game:

1. The program highlights a word, and the student finds and touches the matching object in the picture.
2. The program highlights a part of the picture, and the student finds and touches the matching word in the text.
3. The student finds a word (in the text) and an object (in the picture)

FIG. 2.5.   Sample screen from the "Match Pictures and Text" game. This
game is in progress; the student has not yet found a match.

that match, and touches them both. Or if two students are playing, one
touches a word (or object), and the other must find the corresponding
object (or word).

Words on the Move. A paragraph is shown on the screen, with some
of its words removed. The missing words are listed at the bottom of
the screen. The student inserts each word where it belongs, by touching
the word and the blank space where it is to be inserted. The word
bounces up into place. Figure 2.6 illustrates the opening of this
game.

This game is particularly popular with children. One thing they like to
do is put the words in the wrong place and see the amusing outcome. Two
children working together have really had fun with this one, trying to make
the result as funny as possible. They then read it aloud with squeals of
laughter. Finally they put the words where they make sense, and complete
the game.

We encourage this playfulness by having the program accept any
placement of words during the game. At the end, when students have
put the words in their "correct" places, they may signal that they are
finished, and ask the program to check whether their choices match the
original text.

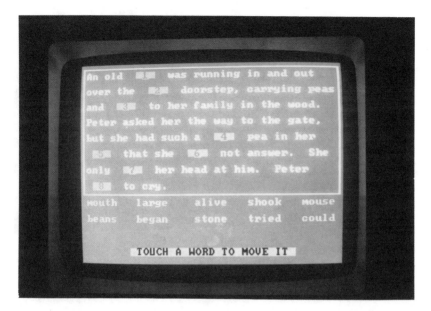

FIG. 2.6. Opening screen "Words on the Move" game. The student touches a word, and then touches a blank space in the text to insert the word. The word bounces up into place.

Students really enjoy making the words move around. Touching a word that is waiting at the bottom of the screen makes it move up into the text where they designate. Touching a word that has already been placed in the text makes it pop back down to the bottom of the screen. Once they discover this back-and-forth feature of the game, they like to experiment with a variety of placements. It is a "Let's try this one here" game, until they have the text exactly the way they want it. This reading and re-reading, considering the funniest combinations, deciding on the effect of putting a word in a particular place, is all excellent and valuable language play.

Word-Finder. A paragraph is shown on the screen, with certain words and phrases highlighted. The student identifies the relevant words or phrases in response to questions about their meaning.

This activity can be used to draw attention to vocabulary or to idioms. In the passage shown in Fig. 2.7, for example, one question is "Which word means *had in mind, planned?*" The student selects "intended" in response.

Figure 2.8 illustrates this same game with phrases rather than single words. In the passage shown, the phrase "just in time" answers the question "Which phrase means *before it was too late, at the very last minute?*"

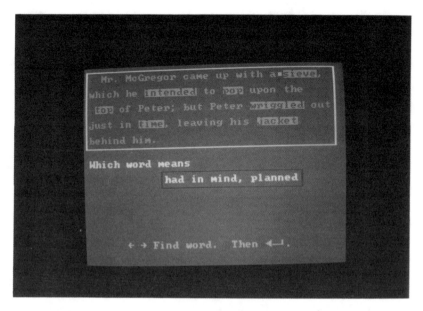

FIG. 2.7. Sample screen from the vocabulary game "Word-Finder." In answer to the question, "Which word means *had in mind, planned?*", the student selects the word "intended."

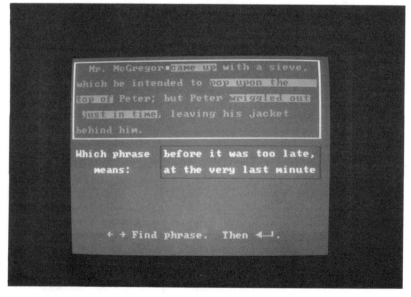

FIG. 2.8. Sample screen from the vocabulary game "Word-Finder." In answer to the question, "Which phrase means *before it was too late, at the very last minute?*", the student chooses the phrase "just in time."

SUGGESTIONS FOR USE

These are some suggested applications for books on videodisc. They are projections, not existing situations. They are entirely feasible, however, with current technology. What is required is only a budget for education and literature, and a priority system that places a high value on literacy. Neither is as readily available as the technological capability, unfortunately.

In School. A classroom, resource room, or school library has a books-on-disc installation, and a collection of videodiscs of relevant books. Students use the system prior to reading a book, as an introduction, or for review of a book they have read and enjoyed.

The in-depth work on a book is useful for both remediation and enrichment. The listening-while-reading aspect is good for students who need help with reading fluency; vocabulary help and comprehension games benefit all students; a read-aloud session, individual or for the whole class, is welcomed by all.

For example, the teacher projects an enlargement of the computer screen on the classroom wall, and presents a book to the class, one chapter a day. The class can go through an entire book, or hear the opening of the book as motivation to read it on their own.

The videodisc collections range from kindergarten read-aloud books and early elementary "easy readers" up through high school literature selections. Dr. Seuss' *Cat in the Hat* and Shakespeare plays can, with appropriate recordings, be presented with equal ease on videodisc.

Students can view/listen to videodiscs of authors or poets reading from their own works, and play-readings done by top actors. Well-prepared videodiscs using appropriate readings and beautiful editions of texts can provide a wealth of experience and exposure for students, right in the classroom.

In Libraries. A library has a videodisc system, in addition to existing facilities for listening to audiocassettes or videotapes.

Children choose a videodisc from the library's collection, and view and listen to a book either individually or in small groups.

Children also use the videodisc system for help in selecting a book to check out of the library. For this purpose, they use a "browsing disc," a videodisc containing many books, with only a short section from each one, perhaps a few pages. The child browses through this disc, stopping to listen to a page or two from books that look interesting. Or perhaps the child just skims through the browsing disc looking at the illustrations, without bothering to listen at all. Different children may use different criteria to identify a book of interest from the samples on the disc. They then get it from the shelf, and check it out.

This kind of browsing, where students can actually hear parts of the book, can help potential readers develop judgment about what they are going to enjoy reading. It gives more direct access to a book than many students can gain from just picking up the book from the library shelf. Many students are not yet adept at making such judgments from leafing through a book. On a browsing disc, the book in a sense meets them halfway.

Children also use the browsing disc for help in deciding what book they would like to listen to in its entirety. They start with the browsing disc, pick a book, and then request the full-length book on disc.

Adult Literacy. Books or texts of appropriate subject matter and level are prepared on disc. Adults view and listen to the discs at leisure, as a supplement to class work. Different rates of word-by-word reading with highlighting are available, so that students may work up to following along in the text at normal reading speed.

Texts may be presented on screen with no accompanying voice. Students read the text on their own. For difficult words, a touch feature is included so that students may touch a word and hear it spoken, as well as hear a definition or explanation of the word.

English as a Second Language. For ESL students, texts on videodisc supplement their language and conversation classes. Varied rates of reading are available, as described earlier for adult literacy applications. Definitions and explanations of words are available either in the native language or in English, according to the preference of the student or instructor.

Foreign Language Study. The entire system of books on disc can be used for listening and reading in a foreign language. Vocabulary help can be available in the foreign language directly or in English, by student or teacher choice. Spoken or written translations are available on the disc, and can be offered to students, if desired, in keeping with individual instructional needs and decisions.

SUMMARY

In summary, a "books-on-videodisc" presentation is suitable for children of early elementary school age, for older children who need extra practice with reading, or for any student who enjoys literature and drama. It can be used effectively for second language or foreign language students, and in adult literacy programs. Libraries might offer a collection of books on videodisc, to supplement their existing collections of books on audiocassette or videotape. Computer-driven videodisc offers particular flexibility with a book, including user control over pace of presentation, easy access to any portion of the book for review, help with keeping the place, and interactive follow-up activities that exploit both text and illustrations.

3

Computers and Videodisc Technology for Bilingual ASL/English Instruction of Deaf Children

Vicki L. Hanson
IBM Thomas J. Watson Research Center
Carol A. Padden
University of California, San Diego

It is nearly axiomatic for papers about the language of deaf children to begin with a litany of language problems. Lags in reading achievement, difficulties in comprehending and writing English syntax, and limited English vocabularies are cited in support of this position. These articles often proceed to talk about the "language deficiencies" of these children and the effect that this "lack of a language" might have on cognition. Such statements, however, neglect the fact that many deaf children possess competence in a human language, American Sign Language (ASL). As in the case of hearing children who are exposed in a normal way to a spoken language, these deaf children display the expected pattern: skill in the structure and content of the language of their community. Thus, these children exhibit not language deficiencies but rather gaps in their knowledge about English, the language of the cultural majority in the United States. In this chapter we describe our initial attempts to improve their written English skills, using their ASL competence and interactive video technology.

ASL has been variously characterized as derivative of English, or organized around properties of gesture, most likely because of its unusual mode of transmission—the visual–gestural mode. It is neither English nor gesture; its structure, although unlike English in a number of important respects, is not unusual given the class of human languages. At all levels of representation, from the internal structure of the sign (Padden & Perlmutter, 1987) to its rich morphological structure (T. Supalla, 1985) and its complex syntactic and discourse constraints (Lillo-Martin, 1986; Padden, 1988), the rules of the language conform to every constraint known for human languages. Children who have been exposed to ASL in a timely fashion acquire it in much the same pattern as hearing children acquire spoken language (Newport & Meier, 1985), without need for explicit or laborious instruction.

Until very recently, schools and programs for deaf children were not likely to recognize that competence in ASL might be a viable tool for teaching deaf children about English. Largely because of confusion about signed languages and how they compare to oral languages, many schools embarked instead on programs to alter signs in attempts to make them represent written English. The best known of such attempts are the artificial manual English systems (e.g., Seeing Exact English). The motive underlying the development of manual English systems is understandable: Because the deaf child does not hear well enough to access spoken English directly, why not instead use signs to represent English? Manual English systems use ASL signs and add invented forms to represent written prefixes, suffixes, and other grammatical elements of English. These forms are then produced in English word order.

There has been heavy criticism of such systems, among them, that invented forms violate structural rules of ASL and natural signed languages in general, resulting in forms that are unwieldy and unnatural (Baker, 1978; Charrow, 1975; Marmor & Petitto, 1979). S. Supalla (in press) has demonstrated that young deaf children fail to use certain manual English elements used frequently by their teachers presumably because they are not learnable. Furthermore, although the systems purportedly represent written English, they can do so only partially. The invented forms refer to elements of written English, for example by incorporating the first letter of a prefix or suffix into a sign, but these invented elements do not represent English elements in their full alphabetic form. Thus, children who learn manual English still need to learn how to match forms to their English translations for the reason that the forms are not themselves English words. Additional discussion of the difficulties of using manual English to represent written English can be found in Ramsey (1989). However, the urgency that underlies inventions such as manual English is a very real one: the need to introduce deaf children to written English.

Given that many deaf children are competent in ASL, it would seem logical to use competence in this language as a part of their education about English. But until very recently, there has been little effort to explore how to use ASL both to teach about various school subjects and to teach English. There have been calls for greater use of ASL in education of deaf children (e.g., Barnum, 1984; Johnson, Liddell, & Erting, 1989; Kannapell, 1985; Strong, 1988), but few concrete proposals have been made for how to use the two languages jointly. To date, the idea of bilingual instruction in ASL and

English has amounted largely to tacit recognition of ASL as one of several strategies available to teachers for explanation, but not as a central part of a teaching curriculum.

There have been, however, a few attempts to use the two languages jointly. Kannapell and Goodstein (1979) developed a set of videotapes for deaf adults in which ASL explanations were given for commonly used English expressions and idioms. The expressions appeared on captions underneath a signer's translation of them. Here the focus is on translation of specific expressions and phrases, to teach the meaning of specific English content. Another approach to using the two languages jointly has been to call students' attention to differences in the ways in which ideas are grammatically expressed in ASL and English (e.g., Akamatsu & Armour, 1987; Schneiderman, 1986; Strong, 1988). For example, Strong (1988) presented videotape versions of stories presented first in ASL then in strict manual English. Children were encouraged to look for differences in presentation in the ASL and English stories, with the goal of developing metalinguistic awareness. In a third approach, children at Kendall School in Washington, DC, review videotapes of their own stories before beginning to write (Mather, in press). Watching the videos helps the children to think about writing as recreating a story to be told to someone. In this approach, written English is not directly in the video, but takes place in the form of a separate task elsewhere.

There are at least two challenges in using ASL and English together as part of a bilingual[1] approach. First, how is English to be represented? Given the dissatisfaction with manual English systems, what are some alternatives? How else might English be taught to deaf children? Second, how should the two languages be used jointly as part of a concerted instructional approach? There are many possibilities for combining the two; what are the effects of the different combinations?

The advent of videodisc technology allows us to address these issues about a bilingual ASL/English instructional approach in a new way. This technology makes it possible to manipulate in traditional and unusual ways combinations

---

[1]The term *bilingual*, as we are using it here, differs from the typical usage of the term in that the situation involves only the primary (signed) form of one language, ASL, and only the coded (written) form of the other, English. As such, this approach is more consistent with the notion of a monoliterate bilingual approach rather than a true bilingual approach. The use of only signed ASL arises from the fact that there presently exists no system for writing ASL that has been developed for other than scholarly purposes. The use of only written English arises from the fact that deaf children cannot readily perceive English in its primary (spoken) form. The loss of hearing precludes normal auditory access, and lipreading, at best, presents only a partial representation of English to a hearing-impaired person. Lipreading is not the form of transmission for which English was developed; studies have indicated that English phonemes are not readily discriminable on the lips and that the absence of experience with auditory speech hinders deaf individuals in learning to lipread as evidenced by findings that hearing individuals lipread as well as or better than deaf individuals trained in lipreading (for a review, see Mogford, 1987).

of signed and written text. The technology not only makes it possible to present signed material and written text alternately, with the ability to switch easily and rapidly between ASL and written text, but also affords a novel possibility not otherwise available in real life: to juxtapose the two simultaneously, within the same visual field, using a rich variety of visual combinations.

We describe here an experimental project that uses videodisc technology to explore various possibilities for using ASL and English cooperatively in the instruction of deaf children. With it, we are able to examine theoretically different modes of presentation and different types of juxtapositions. The software, *HandsOn*, has been in use at a residential school for deaf children for approximately 1 year, and continues to undergo modifications based on user feedback and ideas for new possibilities of presenting the two languages. At this point, we are not able to offer conclusions about how the two languages might be most effectively used together to foster improvement in written English skills for deaf children. That is what we are currently investigating. We offer here, rather, a description of *HandsOn*, as it currently exists, and report on students' and teachers' reactions to the approach.

EQUIPMENT

HandsOn runs on an IBM InfoWindow™ system.[2] The hardware components of this system are an InfoWindow display monitor, an IBM personal computer, and a videodisc player. With this system, video can be overlaid with computer output, thus allowing both ASL video and English text to be simultaneously presented on one monitor, with the text appearing on top of the video. InfoWindow also makes available touch screen technology, thus allowing *HandsOn* to be accessible even to very young children. In most cases, students indicate their choice of task by touching the screen. The writing tasks require standard keyboard entry.

To date, two videodiscs have been developed for this project. Each contains several stories signed in ASL as well as signed feedback and questions for use with the questions component of *HandsOn* (see later). These materials have been signed by the second author, a third generation signer of ASL. To permit flexibility in developing tasks and changing the text, no audio was recorded on these first two discs. The materials on the first disc were stories, such as *Goldilocks and the Three Bears* and *J. J. Flournoy's Idea for a Deaf State* that were designed to be of interest to different ages. The story of *Goldilocks and the Three Bears* was chosen to be of interest to younger children, with the story of *J. J. Flournoy's Idea for a Deaf State* appropriate for the most advanced of the elementary school students. The stories ranged in length from 3–6½

---

[2]InfoWindow is a trademark of the IBM Corporation.

minutes. The second disc dealt with various science topics (e.g., plants, dinosaurs, planets). Again the goal was to provide a range of interest and difficulty levels. To make the stories appropriate to a wide range of reading abilities and interest levels, we developed both "easy" and "hard" versions of the signed stories. The students (or teachers) select, at the beginning of a session, whether they want an "easy" or a "hard" story. The difference in difficulty in the two levels is apparent at all levels—conceptually, as well as in English vocabulary and syntax. For example, in the story about *Dinosaurs*, the story begins by focusing on differences between plant-eating and meat-eating dinosaurs and discusses the fact that there are no longer any dinosaurs alive on earth. For students who have selected the "easy" version, the story ends at this point. For students who have selected the "hard" version, however, the story continues and presents theories about why dinosaurs became extinct. The stories on this second disc were shorter than the first, ranging from 2½ to 3½ minutes.

SOFTWARE

HandsOn is written in HANDY, an experimental authoring language developed at IBM. It provided us with the ability to easily control multimedia materials, specifically video, and to easily obtain user input in terms of screen touches and keyboard entries. In addition, HANDY allowed us to collect data on computer usage by the students. Perhaps most importantly for the design of research software, its incremental and iterative method of programming allowed us to rapidly test out ideas, and to constantly change our software based on user feedback.

When designing *HandsOn*, we were guided by the principle that at any point in time students should have various options available, rather than being presented with a pre-programmed instructional sequence. As a result, students using *HandsOn* make their own choices about which story and which activity option to use at each point in time. Thus, each student receives a unique instructional "sequence." Shown in Fig. 3.1 is an example of a computer screen from *HandsOn* that features the ASL video and the possible student choices at that point.

A goal in this project to explore ways that ASL and English can be used together in a bilingual instructional package without relying solely on word/sign translation. This motivation is prompted by the fact that, in some cases, there does not exist a one-to-one correspondence between an ASL sign and an English word; a concept that requires only one sign in ASL may require several words in English—or vice versa. We, therefore, are developing tasks that require students to interact with English and ASL in a story context, with translations between the two languages occurring at the sentence level.

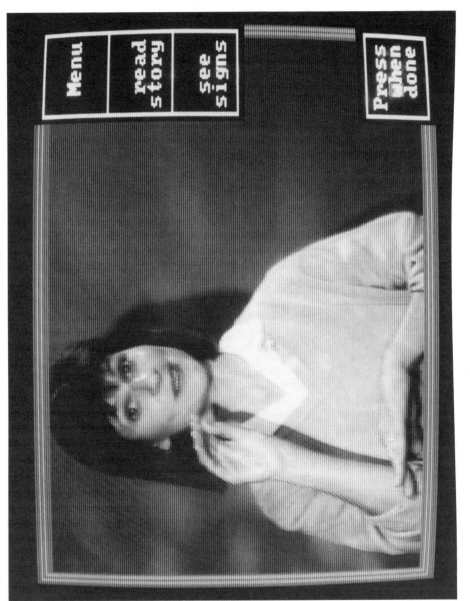

FIG. 3.1.   A sample computer screen from *HandsOn* in which touch boxes are graphically overlaid on

For example, in one component of the program, the students "subtitle" ASL stories in English. This combining of text and video also takes full advantage of videodisc technology, providing a simultaneous display of the two languages that is not possible in real life.

Our initial evaluations of *HandsOn* dealt with making the system easily usable, without intervention from us, by teachers and students. This required observations of students' usage of the system and discussions with teachers. Based on this feedback, *HandsOn* has gone through several iterations since its initial prototype (see Hanson & Padden, 1989). We have also tested a variety of activity options. Based on feedback from both students and teachers, we have added, deleted, and revised these options. We discuss here five options that have been tried and found useful. Of these, four (*Read a story, Answer questions about a story, Caption a story, Write about a story*) focus on English, with ASL providing "help." The fifth option (*Watch a story*) focuses on ASL.

Read a Story. With the *Read* option, students read English text and can request the ASL version of the English sentence by touching that sentence on the computer screen. Thus, the use of English and ASL alternate, at the students' request. The ASL versions can be used to aid story comprehension and vocabulary development.

Answer Questions About a Story. With the *Answer questions* option, students are asked questions, in English, about the stories and must respond by using the keyboard to type their answer (in English). When students need help with an answer, they can scan the English text. ASL is introduced into this task in several different ways: touching the question on the screen provides the ASL version of the question, the students can request the *Watch a story* option to scan the ASL story for the answer, and ASL feedback about answers is provided.

Write a Story. With the *Write* option, students write an English summary of one of the stories. Students may either scan the English text or the ASL story to support their writing of the summary.

Caption a Story. With the *Caption* option, students are able to write an English "subtitle" for segments of the ASL version of stories, one segment at a time. The ASL segments can then be played back with their English captions overlaid on the sign to create the effect of subtitling the video. For deaf students, the effect appears much like the closed-captioning of a TV show or movie that they watch. Thus, during playback the English and ASL are simultaneously presented on the computer screen. Students can get help with spelling or vocabulary by touching the screen to see the English version of the ASL segment to be captioned.

Watch a Story. With the *Watch* option, students watch one of the stories signed in ASL. The students have the choice, at any point in time, of touching the computer screen to get the English version of the ASL segment currently being signed.

Student Population

The target population for *HandsOn* was deaf children fluent in the use of ASL. For this reason, the first test site was a residential school with an extremely high proportion (about 50%) of students having deaf parents. These children of deaf parents learn ASL as a first, or native, language. Officially, for instructional purposes, teachers at this school uses a Total Communication or Simultaneous Communication approach, which involves the simultaneous signing and speaking of English. Students are encouraged to also simultaneously sign and speak English in class.

We initially designed *HandsOn* for use with children in approximately third through sixth grades. It assumes some basic reading ability on the part of the user. For example, all of the options (e.g., *Read a story* and *Caption a story*) as well as the touch buttons (with labels such as "see signs" "press for words") assume the user can read common English words. Despite our early targeting toward the upper elementary school grades, however, we found that teachers of the younger students, even kindergartners, were interested in using the program. For now, these youngest students use only the *Watch* option. Given the interest expressed by the teachers of these younger children, we would hope to be able to develop a range of tasks that could be used by these children.

Working With Students

HandsOn is effectively used by students working singly or in pairs. When working in pairs, we have observed that the students interact constantly: discussing which story to select, which activity option to select, and often debating about which one of them gets to touch the screen or type the responses. They also constructively interact by helping each other with vocabulary when reading, and with all aspects of the writing when, for example, captioning or answering questions.

Some familiarity with using computers was not assumed, although all students had some experience through the CAI program already in place at the school. This prior experience with computers, combined with children's natural inclination to use the computer, allowed students to be able to work through the stories by themselves. We note, however, that although the students were able to work by themselves, it was often beneficial to have a teacher present. The teacher was helpful not so much in moving students through software, but rather in adding supplemental information, for example, related to the story content. We return to this point later.

The program was used by students during class periods of 25 minutes. This time constraint, unfortunately, limited the amount of time that students could work at one sitting. In one class period, students would generally either watch a story, and then read the story or answer questions about it, or would read the story and then answer questions about it. Often there was not time to complete this reading or question answering component in the class period. We learned from our first videodisc, that the stories were too long to be practical within this time constraint. The shorter stories of the second disc were more amenable to the practical constraints of the school setting.

Working With Teachers

The teachers initially received *HandsOn* with somewhat wary enthusiasm. The teachers were receptive to the notion of using ASL for instructional purposes. But although they were fascinated by the technology and its potential for instruction, the new hardware was somewhat intimidating. Their enthusiasm for this new approach gradually persuaded many to try *HandsOn*. After trying it they came to realize that the equipment and software were easy to operate. Also, designation of one of the teachers as a local authority on the project has been extremely helpful in providing teachers with an on-site person who could answer questions and deal with any problems that might arise. As noted previously, *HandsOn* is still experimental, and the teachers are to be commended for their willingness to help test this software, despite its occasional "bugs," and for freely offering suggestions for its improvement.

Using *HandsOn*

Anecdotally, we can report that students enjoy using *HandsOn*, as shown in Fig. 3.2 They are excited that the computer can now include something that is central in their daily lives, their signed language, and they look forward to their time with the computer.

Significantly, we have also received enthusiastic feedback from teachers. Particularly relevant was one story told to us by a teacher about one youngster, fluent in ASL, who, despite being in upper elementary school, had never seemed to grasp reading. The teacher reports working with this student on

FIG. 3.2.   Students at the California School for the Deaf in Fremont using *HandsOn* (Photo courtesy of IBM Corporation).

the *Read a story* option, repeatedly demonstrating to the student how to go back and forth between the English and ASL version of a story. At one point, the youngster suddenly pointed to an English word on the computer screen and spontaneously made the sign for that word. According to the teacher, this was the first time that the youngster had actually understood the connection between the two languages.

The most effective joint use of ASL and English has been the *Read a story* option. With this option, students read the English text of a selected story, scrolling up and down through the story. At any point in time, they can request an ASL translation of an English word or sentence by touching that word or sentence on the computer screen. In all cases, the ASL version is of the entire English sentence for the word touched.

When reading a story, many of the students tend to sign the stories "aloud." This signing is not an artifact of our bilingual instructional approach, but rather a result of more general reading aloud in the classroom. Being able to observe students' "reading" in this way proved quite useful for us in terms of understanding how the children were progressing. We were able to observe that students would readily touch the computer screen to get the ASL version of the English text when they did not know an English word. Many new vocabulary items were learned this way. When these students asked for the ASL version, we then observed them using the ASL sign for the English text throughout the remainder of the story.

A teachers' presence is useful in correcting sign errors when students sign the stories aloud. These errors in signing occur because of the lack of complete one-to-one correspondence between ASL signs and English words. In this respect, English homographs are particularly problematic. For example, the English word "right" has different sign translations depending on whether the meaning of "right" refers to directionality, legal issues, or correctness. In this context, we observed that the children would sometimes translate an English homograph into the wrong sign, thus making their signed English sentence semantically incongruous. At this point, a teacher's input is useful, either in directly correcting the sign, or in instructing the student to request the ASL version of the sentence in question. It is notable that without this teacher intervention the students rarely questioned their own signed renderings of sentences, even though their own incorrect sign choices for particular words would result in nonsensical ASL and English sentences.

Probably due to its interactivity, the *Answer questions* option is the most popular option among the students. Students sometimes choose this option before they have either watched or read the story, and realize, once the questions are asked, that they will need to step back and go through the story before they can answer the questions.

With this activity option, students are presented with English questions about the stories, and must answer the questions by typing. The correct answer is programmed to be key words or key phrases. For example, in response to the following question about dinosaurs, "What did the dinosaurs who walked on two legs eat?" the program would accept as answers "flesh," "meat," or "dinosaur." Students' answers must contain one or more of these phrases to be correct. If the answer is correct, the ASL feedback is some type of positive statement, such as GOOD. If the answer is incorrect, the feedback suggests that the student either scan the text or search the signed story to help find the answer. Although feedback could easily have been given in English or some computer graphics, the students enjoyed getting the feedback in ASL. Students are not directly provided with the answer until they make two incorrect responses. At this point, the correct answer is printed for them on the computer screen.

Students are generally inclined to scan the ASL story when they need help to answer a question. This scanning generally works well. Problems arise, however, when students, after having learned the answer in ASL are then unsure about the English words or the spelling of the English words that they need for their answer. At this point, students can touch the screen and get the written English version of the ASL segment that contained the answer.

The two writing options are *Write a story* and *Caption a story*. The *Write a story* option is difficult to use within the constraints of students' keyboarding skills and class schedules. The *Caption a story* option was introduced to replace it. With the *Caption* option, students view an ASL sentence and then write that sentence in English. Given that the captions are each relatively short, limitations of class time and keyboarding skill are much less an issue than they were with the *Write* option. The ASL segment and its English version, overlaid on the signs, can be played back, allowing for the exciting ability to simultaneously display the two languages. It is possible to caption an entire ASL story in this manner and play back the story, from beginning to end, with its captions. The effect is that of a subtitled or "captioned" movie.

We noted earlier on that the students often had difficulty in knowing the English word for a particular sign and would have to ask a teacher for help. The software was modified so that students could get help with their vocabulary and spelling by touching the computer screen to get the English version for the signed segment they were to be captioning. To prevent students from copying the English version, the version disappears from the screen before they begin typing their caption. Thus, help is provided, but the students are not able to simply copy answers. Students take great care to correct their typographical errors and to work on their spelling and grammar.

The one case in which ASL is used as the dominant language is the case of the *Watch a story* option. With this option, students can watch one of the ASL stories from beginning to end, or, through the use of touch panels that use VCR symbols, can fast forward through the story or go in slow motion either forward or backward. Students, from time to time, make use of the capabilities for viewing the story at fast speeds or in slow motion. Many can still follow the ASL story at the fast speed, and prefer to view it at this speed in order to save time. Although the slow motion has potential for clarifying signs, students, when they choose to view the video in this way, do so because they find it "interesting" or "funny" rather than for any educational benefit. It could be pointed out, however, that many hearing nonsigners who have viewed *HandsOn* have noted the potential of the slow motion capability for teaching ASL to nonsigners.

We were initially concerned that the students might focus exclusively on the *Watch* option, ignoring the English options. Since their comprehension would be superior in ASL, this would seem natural. Students often, however, did not stay only with the *Watch* option, probably, at least in part, because the other activity options afford more interaction with the computer. These students continue on to a different activity option for the same story rather than choosing to watch another story. Other students, however, did tend to skip from story to story just watching the signing. This is one of the cases in which teacher intervention provides the needed direction for the purpose of using ASL and English together.

POSSIBILITIES FOR THE FUTURE

HandsOn is still under development. From a technical standpoint, the project has been shown to be feasible. From the enthusiastic reactions of teachers and students we are encouraged about the potential of such a bilingual approach with deaf students. At present, we are beginning evaluations of the effectiveness of *HandsOn* as a teaching tool. For this purpose, we have two procedures. The first involves recording students' frequency of usage of different options in the software. The second experimentally tests for gains in reading and writing related skills following usage of *HandsOn*.

In addition, we continue to explore new activity options. One goal in developing these new tasks will be to explore options that could be used by younger readers than the current options readily permit, such as kindergartners and first graders.

Also, we hope to be able to give the teachers flexibility to write their own English versions of the ASL stories. This would allow the signed stories to be readily adapted to different reading levels. We are currently at work on an extension of the program that will allow this capacity for teachers to create the English text and questions.

HandsOn, as described here, is still in an early state. It represents the beginning of a two-part research strategy. The first part explores the use of a bilingual ASL/English instructional approach for teaching written English to deaf children. The absence of adequate ability in reading and writing the language of the cultural majority presents formidable barriers to full participation in society. As mentioned at the beginning of this chapter, the idea of using deaf children's ASL language competence to improve their written language skills is an approach that has largely been ignored in deaf education. We are hopeful that our work can make a contribution in this area.

The second part of our strategy explores the potential of interactive video in meeting the special needs of deaf children. The system we describe here is fully interactive, using touch responses and activity options that range from being extremely open-ended (as in the *Write a story option*) to tutorial in nature (as in the *Answer questions* option). The video allows for presenting a real person on screen to give instructions and feedback and, importantly for this particular application, to present the ASL materials. People who have seen demonstrations of *HandsOn* are quick to see possibilities for applying this technology to meet their own needs in working with deaf populations. They are also quick to think of ways of extending *HandsOn*, such as in teaching ASL to English speakers, and, more generally, in second language instruction. This chapter describes just one application of interactive videodisc technology.

ACKNOWLEDGMENTS

We are grateful to the staff and students of the elementary school at the California School for the Deaf, Fremont, who have been participating with us in this work. We are grateful for their suggestions as to improvements and their patience in testing out this experimental software. In particular, we would like to acknowledge the contributions of Ed Copra who has devoted so much time to this project. In addition, we wish to thank Don Nix for his continuing support of this project, and Jeff Kelley and Guillermo Pulido for their help in producing the "ASL Science" videodisc. This work has been funded, in part, by a Small Grant from the Spencer Foundation to Carol Padden and by a Faculty Development Award to Carol Padden from the University of California, San Diego.

REFERENCES

Akamatsu, C. T., & Armour, V. A. (1987). Developing written literacy in deaf children through analyzing sign language. *American Annals of the Deaf, 132*, 46–51.

Baker, C. (1978). How does "Sim-Com" fit into a bilingual approach to education? In F. Caccamise & D. Hicks (Eds.), *Proceedings of the Second National Symposium on Sign Language Research and Teaching* (pp. 13–26). Silver Spring, MD: National Association of the Deaf.

Barnum, M. (1984). In support of bilingual/bicultural education for deaf children. *American Annals of the Deaf, 129*, 404–408.

Charrow, V. A. (1975). A linguist's view of manual English. *Proceedings of the VIIth World Congress of the World Federation of the Deaf* (pp. 78–82). Washington, DC.

Hanson, V. L., & Padden, C. A. (1989). The use of interactive video for bilingual ASL/English instruction of deaf children. *American Annals of the Deaf, 134*, 209–213.

Johnson, R. E., Liddell, S. K., & Erting, C. J. (1989). *Unlocking the curriculum: Principles for achieving access in deaf education* (Gallaudet Research Institute Working Paper 89-3). Washington DC: Gallaudet University.

Kannapell, B. (1985). *Language choice reflects identity choice: A sociolinguistic study of deaf college students*. Unpublished doctoral dissertation, Georgetown University, Washington, DC.

Kannapell, B., & Goodstein, A. (1979) *Building idioms through American Sign Language*. Washington, DC: Office of Educational Technology, Visual Communication Center, Gallaudet University.

Lillo-Martin, D. C. (1986). Two kinds of null arguments in American Sign Language. *Natural Language and Linguistic Theory, 4*, 415–444.

Marmor, B. S., & Petitto, L. (1979). Simultaneous communication in the classroom: How well is English represented? *Sign Language Studies, 40*, 16–21.

Mather, S. (in press). *Writing strategies for deaf children with English as a second language: Using glosses of signed narratives to aid written composition*. Washington, DC: Gallaudet Research Institute, Gallaudet University.

Mogford, K. (1987). Lip-reading in the prelingually deaf. In B. Dodd & R. Campbell (Eds.), *Hearing by eye: The psychology of lip-reading* (pp. 191–211). London: Lawrence Erlbaum Associates.

Newport E., & Meier R. (1985). The acquisition of American Sign Language In D. Slobin (Ed.), *The crosslinguistic study of language acquisition* (Vol. 1, pp. 881–938). Hillsdale, NJ: Lawrence Erlbaum Associates.

Padden, C. (1988). *The interaction of morphology and syntax in American Sign Language*. New York: Garland Press.

Padden, C., & Perlmutter, D. (1987). American Sign Language and the architecture of phonological theory. *Natural Language and Linguistic Theory, 3*, 335–375.

Ramsey, C. L. (1989). Language planning in deaf education. In C. Lucas (Ed.), *The sociolinguistics of the deaf community* (pp. 123–146). New York: Academic Press.

Schneidermann, E. (1986). Using the known to teach the unknown. *American Annals of the Deaf, 131*, 51–52.

Strong, M. (1988). A bilingual approach to the education of young deaf children: ASL and English. In M. Strong (Ed.), *Language learning and deafness* (pp. 113–129). Cambridge: The Cambridge University Press.

Supalla, S. (in press). Signed English: The modality question. In P. Siple & S. Fischer (Eds.), *Theoretical issues in sign language research: Acquisition*. Chicago: University of Chicago Press.

Supalla, T. (1985). The classifier system in American Sign Language. In C. Craig (Ed.), *Noun classification and categorization* (pp. 181–214). Philadelphia, PA: Benjamin.

4

Literacy as Search: Explorations Via Computer

John T. Guthrie
Mariam Jean Dreher
University of Maryland

Literacy for Schooling

We presume that literacy is central to schooling. Because schools are dedicated to transmission of knowledge and vicarious experiences, the written word is essential. As a technology for processing ideals and feelings, literacy enables us to transcend the limits of our historical period or geographical location. Furthermore, Boyer and the Carnegie Commission (1983) contend that literacy is not only "the essential tool for learning," but it is "the connective tissue that binds society together" (p. 85).

Despite its importance to the progress of students in school, and the functioning of adults in society, literacy is not universally acquired. The crisis is not simple, however. Very few adults are utterly incompetent in reading signs or sentences and writing their names. The problem exists at more complex levels. Among students who have graduated from high school, reading a newspaper commentary with full understanding is rarely possible. Effectively using a bus schedule, or comprehending employment benefits brochures are barriers for about 50% of the population (Kirsch & Jungeblut, 1986). This chapter is devoted to computer-based research that illuminates these more complex forms of literacy.

Computers for Literacy

Since the advent of computer-based instruction in about 1960, the technology has often been directed toward reading instruction. Mason, Blanchard, and Daniel (1983) point to 910 references that are at least vaguely relevant. The lion's share of instruction, however, has been atomistic. Reading has been viewed as word recognition and "teaching" has been raw repetition. A few ambitious programs have attempted to teach such skills as text comprehension, sequencing sentences, and drawing conclusions. The actual effectiveness of these programs, however, has been criticized and the efficiency of construction has been low. (A ratio of 250 hours of construction for 1 hour of instruction is common; Gilligham & Guthrie, 1987.) In view of these shortcomings, a new view of the role of computers for literacy is needed. We must progress beyond the previous constraints that limited the computer to an expensive delivery system for primitive instruction.

A Computer Language for Researchers

To learn about complex forms of literacy, it is necessary to represent tasks with multiple components and to gauge the performance of learners on each component. This chapter is an initial attempt to represent one class of literacy tasks on computer, and to study the interaction of students with the tasks. Our goal was to understand more fully how students process real world reading materials for purposes that are typical (Guthrie & Kirsch, 1987).

Writing computer programs that successfully represent the documents of the occupational or school environment, and that measure the performance of students on the cognitive subcomponents of reading these documents, is a formidable task. High-level authoring languages that are suited to this need are rare. Recently, however, HANDY, which is designed for environments of learning and instruction, has made the attempt feasible. Because its commands are in English and the syntax is sympathetic, the language can be used by psychologists of reading and literacy as well as computer scientists. The computer programs used in this research were composed by Guthrie, an electrical engineering undergraduate, a statistics graduate student, and an undergraduate in political science at various stages. Adaptability of the language for nontechnical users is high.

LOCATING INFORMATION IN DOCUMENTS

Literacy Levels

Being literate in today's society requires competence in complicated document reading tasks. The National Assessment of Educational Progress (NAEP) adult literacy study showed that over 96% of young adults are proficient at elementary tasks such as reading simple signs or notices (Kirsch

& Jungeblut, 1986). However, complex literacy tasks presented a challenge. Documents such as a lease, a health insurance form, or a bus schedule were problematic for a significant percentage of the population. Less than 50% of young adults were competent in literacy tasks that required associating three elements in the question and three elements in its corresponding document. In addition, less than 11% of high school graduates were capable of reading documents in which six pieces of information had to be located. Incompetence of young adults on such tasks may be due to the fact that the cognitive basis of this type of reading is poorly understood by psychologists or educators. Few attempts have been made to develop an understanding of locating information in documents.

A vast majority of the studies of reading comprehension have used prose recall as an operational definition in the research. Associations between performance or prose recall tasks and locating information in documents, however, are not necessarily high. Separate factors were reported for prose comprehension and locating details in prose, schematics, and manuals (Guthrie & Kirsch, 1987). In addition, the correlation among the prose, document and quantitative scales in the NAEP adult literacy study were only about .50, despite high reliabilities (Kirsch & Jungeblut, 1986).

A variety of distinctions between document search and prose comprehension has been proposed. Studies have shown that reading documents in occupational settings often involves different purposes than recall or knowledge acquisition that are usually demanded in classrooms (Kirsch & Guthrie, 1984). Document reading emphasizes reading to locate specific facts. Further, the contexts of document search and prose reading are often different. Contexts for document reading have been described as socially embedded (Heath, 1983) or, in the case of occupational settings, problem centered (Mikulecky & Winchester, 1983; Sticht, 1975). Although it has been suggested that memory for documents such as maps requires both spatial and semantic codes, studies of map-search processes have not been made (Kulhavy, Lee, & Caterino, 1985; Streeter & Vitello, 1986).

A critical difference between searching documents and reading prose for comprehension may be the nature of the goal. The goal of document search is usually to retrieve a specific subset of information. Recall of the full contents of the document is usually not a part of the reader's intention. Consequently, the cognitive processes needed for retrieval predominate in document reading tasks; and these processes are likely to differ from the knowledge and language-based processes needed for prose comprehension. This divergence is a probable reason for the moderate correlation of performance on document and prose reading tasks.

The purposes of this chapter are to outline a cognitive process model of search, and to present four studies that explore the model. These studies examine search using computer representations of a variety of texts—a plane schedule, a pay stub, and a science textbook chapter. The computer permits unobtrusive, simultaneous collection of data on the individual cognitive components of locating information in text.

Domain Definition

To examine the cognitive processes of search, it is necessary to define a domain of tasks. The domain examined in the first three studies is document search. Documents include tables, schedules, graphs, and notices. Although prose or connected discourse may be contained within one of these documents, the organization, structure, linearity, coherence, and macrostructure of prose that appears in texts or books is often different from prose in documents. In the final study of this chapter, the domain for examining the processes of search is extended to a textbook chapter.

The process of locating information, a second portion of the domain definition, requires the individual to search for specific meanings (verbal or quantitative) that are held as a goal of the reader. The entire document is usually not relevant. It must be searched selectively to obtain an optimal solution that maximizes accuracy and minimizes time. Declarative knowledge is not a constraining variable in the present model. The documents used here are universally familiar to the participants. Pellegrino and Glaser (1982) suggested that performance on figural analogies does not vary with declarative knowledge because the forms are familiar. A similar level of familarity is assumed for the tasks of the present study. Word recognition is obviously necessary, but it is not a limiting factor for these documents. The words, symbols, and numbers are nontechnical, and probably do not exceed the eighth-grade level of difficulty.

Examples of locating information are: (a) finding a desired accessory in a bicycle catalog, (b) looking up the name and telephone number of an organization that offers a certain type of job in an employment bulletin, or (c) reading an airplane schedule to locate a flight from New York to Los Angeles arriving at 7 p.m., costing less than $450, and serving a meal.

Document or textual search tasks differ from search and visual search tasks that have been used in studies of vigilance or memory in several respects. First, research on visual memory development in children requires the recall of objects that have been placed in arbitrary locations. Spatial cues, such as the location of adjacent objects are frequently used. Document and text search requires information extraction, but does not require recall as the criterion of task proficiency (Braine & Green, 1987; Miller, Haynes, DeMarie-Greblow, & Woody-Ramsey, 1986). A second distinction pertains to the selectivity of search. Some experimental paradigms require exhaustive search. For example, visually scanning air traffic patterns on CRTs requires scanning for targets that may appear in any location (Ellis & Stark, 1986). Although scanning is systematic and strategic, the total array must be examined. Search must be exhaustive. Vigilance for graphic symbols or flashing dots (Remington & Williams, 1986) and detection of alphanumeric characters (Dixon, 1985) also require inspection of the total visual array. This exhaustive search is similar to one phase of one component of the document search model that is presented, that is, the first attempt at information extraction. However, document and text-search processes that are necessary for "real world" literacy tasks are distinct from visual search by their emphasis on extraction rather than recall and their inclusion of selective rather than an exhaustive inspection.

Task Decomposition

To understand the nature of performance on complex tasks, Pellegrino and Glaser (1982) recommended a cognitive components approach. This strategy consists of identifying a significant task such as verbal analogies, spatial visualization or, in this case document and text search. The domain is first defined as precisely as possible. Task analysis is performed, in which the necessary and sufficient cognitive components are described. The relations among the cognitive processes are specified, especially if they are problematic. Measures are then constructed that estimate the contribution of each component to the total task performance. Chronometric measures are included, because the time to complete a complex task is, logically, the sum of the times to complete each of its components.

The cognitive approach to task decomposition is exemplified by Pellegrino, Mumaw, and Shute (1985) in their study of spatial aptitude. These investigators applied cognitive process theory to items from tests such as the Primary Mental Abilities Test. A study that used items from the Minnesota Paper Form Board illustrates their research strategy. In a typical item on this measure, the individual is given five pieces and five completed figures. The task is to determine which figure can be constructed from the pieces. The investigators devised a cognitive model that contained five processes. First, the person encodes one of the pieces. Second, the person searches for a match with a corresponding piece in a figure. Third, the person rotates the piece; and fourth, a comparison between the pieces and the elements of the figure is made. Finally, a positive or negative response is completed and the process recycles. The investigators reported that the model accounted for 94% of the variance in latency performance on the Minnesota Paper Form

Board items that require spatial visualization. The cognitive components approach is used in this chapter to decompose a complex task of document   reading.

A Cognitive Model for Document Reading

A cognitive processing model is proposed to account for performance on locating information in documents and texts. The model contains five components:

1. *Goal formation.* The goal is formed; the person must be able to verbalize an objective. Encoding the features of a question is one predominate type of goal formation.

2. *Category selection.* The person inspects an appropriate category of information. A category of information is a critical dimension in the organization of the material. It may be rows of a table, times on a chart, sections of a directory, or columns of a newspaper. Categories of information are structural features of the material. Because not all categories will be relevant to task performance, attention must be selectively directed to a pertinent one. Prior knowledge of the document structure or the information structure will contribute to the inspection of appropriate categories.

3. *Extraction of information.* Having selected an appropriate category, the person extracts information from a category that is useful to fulfilling the goal, or answering a question. If no relevant details are contained in the category, the decision to reject the category must be made expeditiously.

4. *Integration.* Information is integrated with previously obtained information or with the goal statement. That is, facts, concepts or numbers derived from the document are combined efficiently to construct an on-going synthesis of goal-relevant concepts.

5. *Recycling.* The person recycles through the first four components, until he or she fulfills the requirements of the goal. Efficient recycling requires selecting a sequence of categories that is optimal, with repeated extractions and accurate integrations.

This model describes a search process that is clearly valued by society and by individuals, but is not uniformly learned, in school or out, by a nationally representative sample of high school graduates. The first study examines the success of the model in predicting performance on searching a plane schedule (see Fig. 4.1).

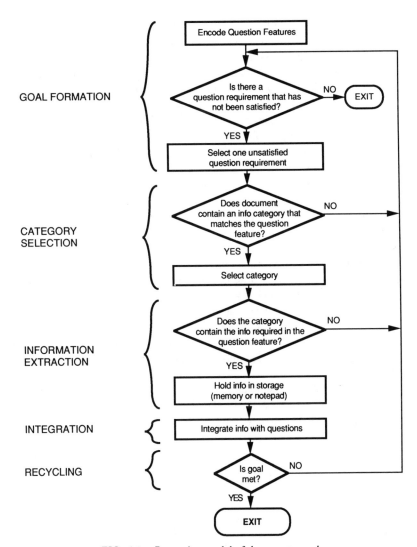

FIG. 4.1.   Processing model of document search.

AN EXAMINATION OF THE COGNITIVE MODEL
OF DOCUMENT SEARCH

A Task as a Scale Sample

A study of locating information in one document with one group of students may yield a finding that is idiosyncratic to the particulars of the experiment. To enhance the prospects for generalizing beyond the single task, we constructed a document-reading activity that is referenced against one of the scales in the young adult literary assessment of the NAEP.

The task in this study was designed to require a three-feature match. The questions given to the participants contained three informational requirements that had to be met through inspecting three sections of the document. In the NAEP adult literary assessment (Kirsch & Jungeblut, 1986), tasks requiring a three-feature match fell at the 300–350 level on the scale of 0–500. In the national sample of 18- to 25-year-olds, the 300 level was attained by 11% of individuals with 0–8 years of education, 22% of those with 9–12 years of schooling but no diploma, 50% of those with high school diplomas, and 82% of those with a postsecondary degree. By using a three-feature match task in this study we examined a type of document and type of question that are sensitive to educational effects, but are not fully learned by high school graduates.

Specifically, the three-feature problem in this study was an airline schedule reading task presented on a microcomputer. A section of the Official Airline Guide (OAG) was identified. The largest block of information that fit on the screen of an IBM color monitor was used. The material was altered in only one respect, by adding cost information to enable the screen to carry sufficient information to plan a cross-country flight. The representation displayed the following categories of information: flight numbers, flight times of arrival and departure, meals served, days of operation during the week, movies, and cost (see Fig. 4.2).

Expert review of this display was obtained. Two experienced travel agents (one an office manager) viewed the display and performed the experimental task. They reported the display looked highly similar to the arrays they use daily.

A menu was devised to permit access to the schedule in a selective, categorical mode. During the reading of a schedule, individuals do not inspect all of the array simultaneously. Indeed, eye-movement research with prose shows that sensitivity to graphic cues is limited to less than 20 characters on one line (Rayner, 1983). Therefore, we permitted people to inspect each category in isolation. The menu contained the following list: meals, entertainment, arrival and departure times, days of operation, flight class, cost, review the question, give an answer, end. The outline of the schedule was ever present on the screen. To observe a category, the person selected a menu choice, all of which were permissible on all occasions. As an aid, a notepad was available in the computer. The notepad was a window that appeared in an empty section of the screen. It was available at all times that a category of the schedule was visible; and it was presented automatically, when the person entered any menu choice. The readers could write anything they wished in a space of six lines of 20 characters. The entries were preserved in the notepad for later viewing.

Flights and Connecting Flights—New York to Los Angeles

FLT NO.	DEPART	TIME	ARRIVE	TIME	MEALS	DAYS	MOVIE	COST
11	N.Y.	10:20aED	CHIC	12:18pCE	—	1234567	N	$160.00
2	CHIC	2:10pCE	L.A.	7:35pPA	S	12345	N	$200.00
5	N.Y.	11:15aED	L.A.	4:08pPA	L	23456	Y	$425.00
27	N.Y.	11:35aED	DENV	2:14pMT	L	234567	N	$200.00
9	DENV	3:35pMT	L.A.	5:22pPA	—	1 7	N	$300.00
8	DENV	4:40pMT	L.A.	6:50pPA	D	23456	N	$210.00
52	N.Y.	12:40pED	K.C.	3:42pCE	S	123456	N	$220.00
90	K.C.	4:15pCE	L.A.	6:32pPA	S	123456	N	$210.00
3	N.Y.	1:02pED	L.A.	6:00pPA	D	1234567	Y	$450.00
6	N.Y.	1:15pED	DENV	3:23pCE	—	23456	N	$180.00
7	DENV	3:45pCE	L.A.	6:45pPA	D	23456	N	$210.00
45	N.Y.	1:35pED	L.A.	7:20pPA	D	1234567	Y	$380.00

Key   (1) "p" = p.m., "a" = a.m.
(2) Time Zones: ED = Eastern; CE = Central; MT = Mountain; PA = Pacific

FIG. 4.2.   Plane schedule document.

Reader—Task Interaction

The interaction between the reader and the task was initiated by a general orientation that requested people to enter their names. Next subjects were informed they would be given a question to answer using a "page" of information in the computer. The question was then presented within the border of the schedule. The versions of the questions are specified in a later paragraph. Following the question, the menu appeared. All of the options were open, including return to the question. Any category that was chosen appeared in a constant location of the screen. Simultaneously, the notepad appeared in an unfilled portion of the screen. It contained previous input from the reader in the top and open space in the bottom. After spending an indefinite amount of time inspecting the category, and/or writing in the notepad, the reader returned to the menu through the space bar. The category previously inspected disappeared; the notepad was hidden and the menu was presented. If the readers thought they could answer the question they chose "give an answer," which provided an "answer blank" display unit. A correct entry evoked a "thank you" from the computer; and incorrect entries were greeted with "sorry, keep trying." Feedback was supplied only for this menu choice. Otherwise, explicit feedback about right/wrong selections or good/poor strategies was not given.

There were three reading tasks given to each participant. Each task contained the same document with an identical menu, but the questions varied. All individuals were given Question 1 first; this was Task I. Then Questions 2 and 3 were counterbalanced such that half of the participants received Question 2 before 3 and half were vice versa. This permitted an examination of learning from Task II to Task III without confounding by question type. The three questions were:

QUESTION 1
Which direct flight or connection of two flights could you take to travel from NY to LA given the following considerations?
> Cost can not exceed $400 one way.
> You must arrive by 7 p.m. (PA time).

QUESTION 2
Which direct flight or connection of two flights could you take to travel from NY to LA given the following considerations?
> You must leave NY before 12 noon, Eastern time.
> You must fly on a Sunday.

QUESTION 3
Which direct flight or connection of two flights could you take to travel from NY to LA given the following considerations?

> You do not want to stop in Denver.
> Lunch much be served during the trip.

It may be obvious that each question contains three information requirement about: (a) flying from New York to Los Angeles; (b) traveling on a
certain time or day; and (c) an additional constraint of either cost, day of
operation, or meal. The tasks were constructed to be completed most quickly
by inspecting the non-times category of information first. Inspecting cost,
days, or meals first permitted elimination of a larger number of flights than
inspecting the times initially. Further, the non-times categories contained
less data. If participants learned the structure of information on the first or
second task, their sequences of inspecting categories might be expected to
be non-times, then times, or Task III. Thus, the tasks were designed to
permit us to observe the acquisition of document structure.

Interaction Records

The interactions of the participant with the task were tracked simultaneously
to form multiple records. The records were constructed to permit inferences
about the adequacy of the document-processing model.

First, the menu choices were captured. Each selection of a category of
information in the schedule was retained internally and stored in a hidden
display unit in the computer. This provided a record of which categories were
inspected, and the sequence in which they were viewed by the reader.

Second, the notepad was retained. Each entry was stored in the order in
which it was input. In addition, the category of information that was being
inspected at the time each entry was made was recorded. The computer kept
track of what the participants wrote in the notepad while they were inspecting
each category. The conjunction between inspection and writing permits us
to estimate what information was being extracted by the reader during the
inspection of any given category in the schedule.

Third, the time to solve each problem with the document was recorded.
The total time consumed inspecting the categories was calculated by adding
individual inspection times. The time spent viewing the menu, attempting
to input an answer, or reviewing the question were not included in this
measure. The amount of time to obtain the correct answer was the main
dependent variable in the study. Two participants who could not find the
right answer without help on one of the problems were not included in the
analyses of the data.

A typical set of output for one participant on the task follows:

T.A. Plane 4a

Times	27, 8
Question	
Question	
Times	9
Cost	
Times	6, 7, 3, 5
Cost	6, 7
Question	
Times	
Cost	
Question	
Correct Answer	586 sec.

Plane 4b

Times		11, 27
Days	11, 27	
Times	2, 7	
Days	9, 8	
Times		
Days	27, 9	
Times		
Question		
Correct Answer		361 sec.

Plane 4c

Meals	5, 27	
Times	5	
Correct Answer		90 sec.

Method

Subjects. The participants in the study were 26 undergraduates who volunteered. They were told they would learn about learning from computers, and were debriefed after their sessions.

Experimental Procedure. Each participant entered a computer laboratory in which two to three other individuals and an assistant worked. The assistant loaded the program, and oriented the person to the name entry task. He answered questions about the keyboard or the sequence of schedule, menu, or notepad appearances. Brief 2–3 minute breaks were taken between Tasks II and III. Sessions ranged from 30 to 75 minutes.

Measures of Cognitive Components. To examine the cognitive-processing model for locating information in documents, measures of the components in the model were needed. There are five parts of the model, and this study was intended to address four of them. The first component, goal formulation, was not measured. This process was necessary to performing the three tasks and it was incidentally assessed in several of the other measures, but it was not isolated. The capacity of the model to account for variance will be increased if this component is measured directly and entered into the analyses. However, this study did not attempt to incorporate it.

The second cognitive component of locating information is selecting a category of information for inspection. The most efficient reader will select the fewest categories that are logically necessary to solution. A reader who does not know which informational categories are required by the goal, or does not focus on the task analytically will select and inspect a larger number of categories. Because access to categories in the air plane schedule document was provided through the menu, the number of menu choices is a precise indicator of the number of categories the reader chose to view.

Indicators of the third component, information extraction, were designed to measure the completeness with which individuals detected and stored the details or facts within a category. For example, within the category of cost, when it was relevant to solution, a search for flights less than $450 would be facilitated by extracting all flight numbers that were less than that amount. The metric used to estimate extraction was the percentage of relevant data in a category that was entered into the computer notepad. Relevant data was defined as information that contributed uniquely with previously collected information accounted for. For example, if the person viewed the cost column as the first inspection of Task I, and entered Flights 6 and 7, which totaled $390, a score of .17 would be given. There were six possible and one was identified. Extraction efficiency scores could vary from .00 to 1.00 on any given extraction opportunity. The mean of extraction efficiencies on the first two categories that were inspected was the extraction score for a participant on a given task.

The fourth cognitive component is integration of information. Recently obtained information must be combined with prior extractions or with the goal requirements. Although this process may occur throughout the task, it is likely to be most intense following the attempt to extract details from a given category. A person who has failed to integrate at this point in reading is likely to be confused or disoriented. In this state of disintegration, it is reasonable to return to the original question. By making this move, the question may be instated in memory, or the match with accumulated information may be fostered. Thus, the measure of integration was the number of returns to the question that were chosen by the reader. This measure, like the category-selection measure is inverse. A high number of returns-to-question signifies a low level of integration capacity by the reader. The model of processing predicts that a low number of returns-to-question (i.e., high integrative skill) will be associated with efficiency of locating information in documents.

The final stage is recycling. As the reader addresses the document he or she iterates through the components of inspection, extraction, and integration until the goal requirements are met. Some theorists describe this as a *match* of the goal and solution. This term, however, denotes verbatim connection between the question and its answer, which is not realistic; the notion of a good fit between information extracted and goal requirements is more suitable. The estimate of recycling is the quality of the sequence of information choices. That is, an efficient reader will inspect a succession of categories (i.e., a sequence) that optimizes information gain on each trial. The quality of the sequence was measured by rating the sequence of menu choices. In addition to tracking the number of menu choices the computer recorded the sequence of these choices. A sequence that began with a non-times data set such as cost, meal, or day was more efficient than a sequence that began with the time of arrivals and departures. The quality of the sequence of categories was rated according to a weighted scheme. The first five choices were included. Five points were given for a sequence of: non-times, times, X, X, X; 3 points were given for: non-times, X, times, X, X; or times, non-times, X, X, X; 2 points were given for times, X, non-times, X, X; and 1 point was given for: X, X, X, non-times, times or X, X, X, times, non-times, or times, X, X, X, X.

Results

To examine the cognitive components of locating information in documents, a series of analyses was conducted to analyze both performance and learning. Performance was studied by performing multiple regressions of the measures of components on the task criterion that was the amount of time required to obtain the answer to the question. The analyses were run separately for Tasks I and II to determine the explanatory power of the model across three reading tasks. In addition, it was expected that the model would account for learning to locate information. If a set of cognitive operations is shown to contribute to proficiency levels on given tasks, evidence is obtained that individual differences among readers at one point in time are explained. On the other hand, if the model accounts for variance in performance of a group over three different occasions, then cognitive change as a result of task engagement, which is learning, is accounted for.

The regression procedure for the first analysis used time in seconds to answer the question as the dependent variable. The first independent variable was category selection, which was operationalized as total number of menu choices. It accounted for 58% of the variance ($p < .0001$). The second independent variable was extraction of elements, which accounted for an additional 8% of the variance ($p < .029$). The third variable was integration, which contributed 1% of the variance that was not significant. The fourth variable was recycling. Because it was operationalized as the sequence of inspections, and because the optimal sequence could not be determined by the reader on the first trial, it was not expected to contribute a significant increment in variance accounted for. It added 1%, bringing the total to 68%, and the increment was not significant (see Table 4.1).

The multiple regression was conducted with a forced entry procedure sequence of category, extraction, recycling. This procedure was used because we expected those variables to dominate the process model in that order.

Performance on Task II was analyzed with the same multiple regression procedure that was used for the first stage of the Task I analysis. Time to answer the question correctly was the dependent variable. The variables of category selection (total menu choices), element extraction (percent of available elements placed in the notepad), integration (number of question returns), and recycling (the sequence of category selections), were entered

TABLE 4.1
Effects of Four Cognitive Components on Performance
in Document Search of Plane Schedule

Indicators of Cognitive Components	R	R^2	R^2 Ch	Sig Ch
			Task I	
Category selection (no. of categories)	.76	.58	.58	.000
Extraction of elements (% of total)	.81	.66	.08	.029
Integration (no. ques. returns)	.82	.67	.01	.478
Recycling (inspect. sequence)	.83	.68	.01	.333
			Task II	
Category selection (no. of irrelevant)	.86	.73	.73	.000
Extraction of elements (no. of omissions)	.86	.73	.00	.958
Integration (no. ques. returns)	.86	.74	.01	.409
Recycling (inspect. sequence)	.88	.77	.03	.089

in that order respectively. The category selection variable accounted for 73% of the variance ($p < .0001$). The second and third components did not account for significant amounts of variance. The fourth component, recycling, contributed an additional 3% of variance, which was significant at .089 (see Table 4.1).

To examine the capacity of the cognitive model to account for learning, a multivariate analysis of variance (MANOVA) as conducted. The MANOVA included Task I and Task II as the independent variable and five dependent measures, consisting of (a) time to answer correctly, (b) category selection (total number of menu choices), (c) element extraction (percent of total entered in the notepad), (d) integration (number of question returns), and (e) recycling (the quality of category sequence). The MANOVA was significant [$F(5,21) = 14.20$, $p < .001$]. Subsequent univariate F tests were performed on each dependent measure. Time to answer the question reduced significantly from Task I (790.81 seconds) to Task II (258.61 seconds) [$F(1,25) = 79.69$, $p < .0001$].

The category selection improved because the number of categories that were inspected decreased from Task I (10.58) to Task II (4.00) [$F(1,25) = 37.57$, $p < .0001$]. The ability of the participants to extract elements from the categories improved significantly from Task I (39 percentage correct entries) to Task II (64 percentage correct) [$F(1,25) = 8.48$, $p < .007$]. The third component, integration, showed significant improvement from Task I to Task II [$F(1,25) = 29.74$, $p < .001$]. The efficiency of recycling did not significantly improve from Task I (3.27 quality rating) to Task II (3.58 quality rating) (see Table 4.2).

It should be noted that the data on Task III were omitted from this analysis of learning because performance on it was highly proficient for most participants and the resulting lack of variance precluded its inclusion.

TABLE 4.2
Means and Standard Deviations on Cognitive Components
of Learning to Search the Plane Schedule

Indicator of Cognitive Component		Tasks	
		I	II
Time	X	790.81	258.61
(seconds)	SD	347.26	237.05
Category selection	X	10.58	4.00
(no. of cats.)	SD	5.78	3.03
Element extraction	X	.39	.64
(% total)	SD	.35	.35
Integration	X	2.27	.69
(no. of return to ques.)	SD	1.51	.68
Recycling	X	3.27	3.58
(sequence of cats.)	SD	1.31	1.10

LEARNING TO SEARCH A DOCUMENT

Rationale

To examine whether the cognitive model predicts amount of learning, a transfer criterion was used in the second study. The model predicts that improvement from Task I to Task II will include the cognitive measures as well as the performance outcome measure. If time-to-solve is the dependent variable, performance on Task I should be reduced by completion of Task II, and vice versa. More vitally, the cognitive processes of category selection, information extraction, integration, and sequencing on Task I should facilitate those subcomponents of Task II and vice versa.

The model may be extended by examining it under tasks of different difficulty. Pellegrino and Glasser (1982) warned that difficult analogy tasks may require a different model from easier analogy tasks. Certainly, the generality of a model is reduced if it applies to restricted difficulty levels. It was expected that the proposed document-processing model would account for a significant amount of variance regardless of the task difficulty level. However, the weights, or relative contributions of the components were expected to be altered by task difficulty.

In this investigation, a paystub document was presented on a computer. It contained less information in each category than the plane schedule (see Fig. 4.3). This alteration was expected to decrease the performance time on this document and was expected to reduce the variance attributed to extraction, because the demand on extraction processes was virtually eliminated. Positive transfer from Document A to Document B permits a number of inferences. If category selection is improved, in the transfer paradigm, it is reasonable to suggest that the subjects (a) learned that a macrostructure was present in the first document; (b) identified the macrostructure in the second

CURRENT	625.00			625.00			459.88
YEAR TO DATE				4268.85			
HOURS					**REDUCTION**		
Regular	2nd Shift		Overtime	Total	State	Type	
50.0			none	50.0	12.73		
DEDUCTIONS					35.46		
		Federal	State		75.84		
CURRENT		108.94	13.75				
YEAR TO DATE		734.98	82.50		261.67		

FIG. 4.3.   Paystub document.

document; (c) associated question features with document features in both tasks; and (d) terminated the inspection of categories prior to an exhaustive search.

If the integration of information is improved under transfer conditions, the learners have increased their proficiency in: (a) extracting information from categories; (b) combining information with question requirements more efficiently; and (c) combining new information with previously extracted information more precisely.

To improve in sequencing from Document A to B the learners must: (a) learn that some sequences are more efficient than others in Task I; (b) detect the relations among categories and question features that enable a sequence to be superior; and (c) select a relatively efficient sequence in Task II. Lack of transfer on the outcome measure or any of the cognitive components could lead to the conclusion that the model is task specific, or that the measures were insensitive to the constructs under study.

Hypotheses

We expected positive transfer in document-reading performance from the first to the second task. We predicted positive facilitation for the global measure of proficiency, which was time to answer the question correctly. We predicted that the cognitive components of task performance would be improved from the first to the second problem. Both the plane schedule and the paystub tasks were expected to be facilitated by successful performance on the other task. We expected the paystub task to be searched more rapidly because its information density was lower.

Method

Subjects. The subjects were 24 undergraduates in educational psychology and early childhood education courses. They were rewarded with a $3 certificate to Roy Rogers for their participation.

Tasks. The paystub reading task was highly similar to an item from the NAEP adult literacy document scale. The item was a paystub accompanied by a three-feature question. It was designed to have specific relationships to the plane schedule. The question in both tasks contained three features. Number of categories and the amount of information within each category, however, were varied.

In the paystub document there were 11 categories of information, consisting of the following:

1. current information
2. year-to-date information
3. hours worked
4. pay amount
5. tax deductions
6. other deductions
7. gross pay
8. state deductions
9. federal deductions
10. overtime hours and
11. regular hours.

The plane schedule had six categories of information, about 55% of the paystub. The amount of information contained within each category was lower for the paystub than the plane schedule. The paystub had a mean of 2.8 elements per category, whereas the plane schedule had a mean of 15.5 elements per category. If number of categories increases processing time, the paystub should be more difficult than the plane schedule. Conversely, if more information in each category increases difficulty, the plane schedule should be more difficult than the paystub.

The question in this task was: "How much state tax has been withheld in the current check." Its three features were "state" because federal information was included; "tax," because other deductions were present; and "current," because year-to-date data were available.

The paystub reading task was presented on a microcomputer in a form similar to the plane schedule task. A menu was used to provide selective access to the categories of information on the simulated document. The menu contained the following categories: current, year-to-date, question review, give an answer, hours, pay amount, tax deductions, gross pay, state, federal taxes, overtime, regular. Any menu choice could be selected at any time. A selection caused the menu to disappear. Selected data appeared within the constantly visible outline of the paystub document. A notepad was present. When a category of information appeared, a vertical display unit titled NOTES occupied 10% of the screen on the right side. Any characters could be entered; and previous entries were visible. If the learner reached the bottom of the page the pad scrolled upward 10 rows. The notepad disappeared when the learner discontinued inspecting a category of information, but it was present when the learner chose to give an answer.

Reader–Document Interaction. The interaction was the same as the previous study. Orienting directions were given. The question was presented.

Upon request a menu appeared, accompanied by the outline of the paystub. Informational categories and data were omitted. The menu selections gave the learner unlimited opportunity to examine the document to answer the question. While the person was inspecting a category, the timer in the computer recorded the latency between onset and offset of each display unit. The notepad that was available during inspection contained instructions to enter an equal sign (=) to exit. This entry terminated the visible category along with the notepad and returned the menu to the screen. Data from the inspection were synchronized with the written note entries for later data coding. Feedback was given only for the learners attempt to give an answer. It consisted of "congratulations" or "sorry, keep trying."

Interaction Records. The interaction between the learner and the document was tracked in an identical form to that of the first study. Number and sequence of menu choices were recorded. This produced data for the number of category inspections, the integration of extractions, and the sequence of inspections. The notepad entries were preserved and their relationships to the inspected categories could be ascertained. The total time to solve the problem was computed from a summary of the inspection time.

Experimental Procedure. Participants were given both the plane schedule and paystub tasks in counterbalanced order. Assignment to order was random. The graduate assistant answered questions about the keyboard operations, but not about the task. A 2–3 minute break between tasks occurred; and sessions lasted from 12 to 45 minutes.

Measures of Cognitive Components. Category selection was measured with the same procedure that was used in the first study. Number of menu choices to informational categories in the document was used in both cases. Reviewing the question and attempts to give an answer were not included. Number of choices was expected to be negatively correlated with solution times.

Integration of information was measured by the number of times the learner inspected a category of information that had been previously inspected. We reasoned that a person who has failed to integrate a piece of information from a category, for example, year-to-date information, is likely to reexamine that category. Further, if the person has not compared the category with the question (i.e., determined that year-to-date information is not required in the question), the person may reinspect an inappropriate category. Reinspection of both question-relevant and question-irrelevant categories (i.e., all categories), including the question itself were counted.

Sequence of inspecting categories is a cognitive component in the model related to recycling. Sequencing may be viewed as the guidance system for recycling. As a person is finishing the integration of recently extracted information, a decision is made about the next category to be inspected. Because all categories cannot be examined simultaneously, a sequence is necessary. It is likely that some sequences will be superior to others in terms of facilitating the rapid collection of information. The quality of the sequence was estimated by rating the order of the menu choices.

The following criteria were used to rate menu choice order. If the first choice of the learner was a question feature, 3 points were awarded. For the plane this included the categories of times or cost. For the paystub it included the categories of current, state, and tax deductions. If the second menu choice was a feature of the question that was not used in the first selection, 2 points were awarded. If the third choice was a feature from the question that was not used in the first or second choice, 2 points were awarded. This award was made only if a question feature was not addressed in Choice 1 or 2. No points were given when the criteria were not met in a given choice. A maximum of 5 points was possible.

Goal information was not measured. The question served as the goal. Encoding the question was not recorded directly or estimated in isolation from other cognitive activities.

Extraction of elements from the selected categories was not measured or included in the data analysis of this study. In the paystub task the number of entries was extremely low. Only about 10% of the opportunities for entry were used by the learners. Because the use of the notepad was not compulsory, and the load on working memory was not high, entries were few. It is safe to infer that subjects were making extractions, because they, in fact, answered the question fairly quickly. The accuracy of these extractions, however, could not be estimated from their notes. This component of the cognitive model was not included in the analyses.

Results

To examine the hypotheses presented previously, a multivariate analysis of variance (MANOVA) was conducted. The design was 2 (group) x 2 (tasks) with repeated measures on tasks. Four dependent variables consisted of time to answer, number of category selections, number of category reinspections, and sequence quality. The results showed that the expected effect occurred. The group by task interaction was significant [$F(4,L9) = 2.64, p < .06$]. This showed that performance on the second task was facilitated by the first task for both documents. Univariate F tests were significant for time [$F(1,22) = 3.56, p < .07$], category selections [$F(1,22) = 10.36 \, p < .004$], and reinspections of categories [$F(1,22) = 7.29, p < .01$], but sequence was not significant. Performance transfer was confirmed by the time effect. Transfer on two cognitive components was confirmed by the category selection effect and the category reinspection effect.

Performance on both tasks was improved by successfully completing the complementary task. As Table 4.3 shows, when the plane schedule task was taken first, time to answer the question was about 514 seconds. When the plane schedule was taken second, following the paystub the mean time was about 392 seconds, which is a 30% improvement. Likewise, proficiency on the paystub improved from 262 seconds when it was taken first to 206 seconds when it was taken second, which is a 27% increase.

The cognitive model predicts that selection of categories of information will be facilitated in cases of positive transfer. The operational definition of this variable, number of menu choices, decreased from 8.42 to 5.58 for the plane schedule and from 10 to 4.54 for the paystub from the first to second in order. A decrease signifies improvement in selectivity of attention to critical document segments. Integration of information, which is necessary for rapid task completion improved significantly. The mean number of returns to previously inspected segments of the document, which was a measure of the inverse of integration, decreased for both documents. For the plane schedule the decrease was from 4.58 to 2.58; and for the paystub it was from 5.17 to 1.17. The quality of the

TABLE 4.3
Transfer of Learning on Plane Schedule and Paystub Search Tasks

| | Measures | | | |
| | Outcome | Cognitive | | Components |
Task Order	Time[a]	Category[b] Selection	Integration[c]	Sequence[d]
Plane first				
M	513.83	8.42	4.58	4.67
SD	158.30	6.13	4.64	.78
Plane second				
M	392.25	5.58	2.58	4.58
SD	182.27	2.47	2.02	.79
Paystub first				
M	262.25	10.00	5.17	3.08
SD	191.25	6.32	5.87	1.08
Paystub second				
M	206.17	4.58	1.17	2.83
SD	174.74	2.15	1.27	1.19

Note: $N=24$; n per condition $= 12$.
[a]Seconds.
[b]No. menu choices.
[c]No. menu returns.
[d]Rated quality.

sequence, as measured by the appropriateness of the first three choices did not improve across tasks I and II. The two groups, both of which received both tasks in counterbalanced order, did not differ significantly. Random assignment of subjects to group resulted in equal overall performance on the tasks.

Differences between performance on the plane schedule and the paystub were revealed by a task effect in the MANOVA. The multivariate effect was significant [$F(4,19) = 16.58, p < .0001$]. Univariate F tests revealed significant effects for time [$F(1,22) = 21.67, p < .0001$] and sequence [$F(1,22) = 31.42, p < .0001$], but no significant effects for category selection or integration. Mean time for the plane schedule was 453.04 seconds ($SD = 178.13$) and the mean for the paystub was 234.20 seconds ($SD = 181.43$). The mean number of menu choices for the plane schedule was 7.00 ($SD = 4.79$) whereas the comparable figure for the paystub task was 7.29 ($SD = 5.38$). Integration means were 3.58 ($SD = 3.64$) for plane schedule and 3.16 ($SD = 4.63$) for paystub, showing negligible differences. Sequence mean scores, however, were 4.62 ($SD = .77$) for the plane schedule, and 2.95 ($SD = 1.22$) for the paystub tasks.

To examine whether the cognitive components accounted for performance in reading the paystub as they did for the plane schedule in the first study, regression analyses were conducted. The regressions were similar to those of the prior study. Time was the dependent variable. Predictor variables of number of menu choices (category selection), number of returns to previously selected menu choices (integration), and quality of sequence were entered using a stepwise procedure. The use of both orders for both tasks introduced within-task variance on all variables and the predictability was expected to be lower for these data than the first study. The time to answer the question on the plane schedule was predicted by category selection ($R = .62, p < .001$). Although the other variables did not add significantly, the total R was .64, accounting for 41% of the variance. This replicated the effect of category selection found earlier. Performance on the paystub task showed a similar pattern. Time to answer the question was predicted by the number of menu choices (category selection) ($R = .61, p < .001$). The other two variables did not increment the multiple R significantly, but the three variables had $R = .65$, accounting for 42% of the variance. This similar level of predictability across two tasks of different surface features and different levels of difficulty is noteworthy. These regression analyses show that performance on the paystub task appears to be influenced by category selection in the same fashion as performance on the plane schedule task.

Discussion

The cognitive components that are proposed to account for document search performance reflected the positive transfer observed in overall task performance. Category selection showed significant increases for both tasks. A 52% improvement was observed for the plane schedule and a 118% increase occurred for the paystub. Integration showed improvements of about 80% and about 342% for the plane schedule and paystub tasks, respectively. These data suggest that these cognitive processes are mediators of performance on the tasks. Confirmation of the findings from the first study is provided by transfer across tasks for mental mediators as well as outcome proficiency.

What is learned when performance on document search improves? If a person searches a document in an optimal fashion, several knowledges and skills may be inferred. The person has encoded the features of the question accurately and completely. The person knows there is a macrostructure in the document and knows how to access it. The person matches features of the question to symbols or labels for categories of information within the document. A well-formed document contains categories of information that are mutually exclusive. The optimal reader presupposes this characteristic and searches the categories as though their contents were distinct.

Encoding the initial question and relating its features to the relevant dimension of the document were reasonably well accomplished. The sequence data reveal means of about 4.5 for the plane schedule and 3 for the paystub out of a possible 5. This shows that the appropriate categories were selected for inspection on at least two out of the first three opportunities. However, these well-chosen segments of the document were not scrutinized exhaustively and the information was not integrated into the question requirements on the first encounter with either task. The number of categories that had to be reinspected was 4.58 and 5.17. On the second task the learners did not improve in sequence quality. Initial question encoding and category identification remained reasonably high. What improved, however, were efficiency of extraction and integration. Subjects were less likely to reexamine the segments of the document a second, third, and fourth time. This implies that individual inspections were followed by more exhaustive extraction of information and deeper integration with the question in the second problem compared to the first.

Subjects examined fewer inappropriate categories in the second problem. The appropriateness of inspections can be estimated by relating the selection and integration data. On the first problem there were about two and three irrelevant categories examined for the plane schedule and paystub, respectively. These both reduced to only one irrelevant inspection on the second problem. Selectivity of category viewing improved across tasks, but selectivity did not attain an optimal level in either task. Subjects appear to assume that the categories are not well marked. They also appear to assume that the categories are not mutually exclusive.

The framework that is used in this chapter to examine the cognitive processes of document search may be related to models of analogical reasoning and visual search. As they are delineated by Pellegrino (Pellegrino et al., 1985) and Sternberg (Sternberg & McNamara, 1985), analogical reasoning models contain several cognitive characteristics. There is a goal to be encoded; stimulus features must be encoded, features must be compared, and their similarities or shared constituents must be inferred. These commonalities must be applied to a second stimulus set and a decision about the identity of relationships must be made; or a complementary stimulus element must be generated. There are encoding, inference, comparison, and decision processes required.

Visual search tasks usually differ from analogical reasoning tasks in several respects. In visual search, the task may consist of a relatively limited visual array with one to three categories of information. The task requirement is detecting a specified symbol or letter. Visual discriminability and familiarity have been shown to affect performance on these tasks (Dixon, 1985; Remington & Williams, 1986). In most document-search tasks neither visual discriminability nor familiarity are variables that could affect performance, because they were both high for all subjects. For visual search tasks in general, Cross and Wellman (1985) reported two broad strategies following their review of the literature. There is a "comprehensive search" in which the person plans to survey the entire space or distribute effort evenly across all parts of the space. Second, there is a "selective search" in which the person avoids inspecting certain areas, or at least defers them, in favor of a higher priority. The selectivity referred to by these authors is not related to the structure of the stimulus domain. It is an arbitrary delimitation for the sake of ordering an inspection. In document search, selectivity is important, but it is referenced to the structure of the document. A limited number of question-relevant dimensions is searched. The nature of the selectivity in vigilance tasks and document search tasks is not highly similar.

Visual search studies with children have emphasized recall of objects or information that are placed in arbitrary locations (Ackerman, 1985; Braine, & Green, 1987; Miller et al., 1986). The cues of spatial organization among objects, along with chronological age affect performance on this domain of task. However, document search is conditioned by the structure of dimensions in a document and the readers' knowledge of that structure rather than arbitrary spatial cues that are generated by the learner for purposes of recall. More similar to document search are tasks of locating familiar objects that are lost in a confined space. For example, Reeve, Campione, and Brown (1986) found that learning to be selective enhanced toy location in young children. However, the task of locating information in documents differs from object-search tasks in several respects. First, the locating task requires the encoding and/or immediate memory of a goal that is usually complex. As a consequence, document search imposes a cognitive demand for integration of extracted elements with prior knowledge. The proposed model allowed for this processing. Second, document search embodies a requirement for extracting key details or elements from a category of information. On the contrary, search research has used highly detectable targets, for the most part, such as a doll or boat. As a result, the proposed model for locating information in documents contained "extraction of elements" as a cognitive component, whereas visual search theory has not required this construct (Somerville & Haake, 1985).

The document-search tasks used in the present studies were drawn from the NAEP adult literacy scales to lend generalizability to the findings. Because approximately 50.2% of young adults with high school diplomas failed these tasks, it is reasonable to suggest that these young adults are not proficient in the cognitive processes found to influence task performance. Selecting appropriate categories from a document to delimit inspection, extracting critical details and integrating information into a question are not acquired to a fluent and transferable level. Reading documents such as an insurance form, or a legal regulation to answer realistic questions is a complex mental phenomenon that is not learned incidentally in 12 years of schooling.

Instructional implications of the proposed cognitive model are substantial. Effective teaching must extend beyond practice on the criterion task with corrective feedback. It should consist of engaging the learner with the task and facilitating each of the cognitive components. The processes in the model may be elicited by questions in the context of the task. Questions may activate the selection of categories, extraction of details, integration of data, and will sustain their operation until task completion. If teaching to these cognitive components enhances student proficiency on the criterion task of document reading, efficiency of instruction may be enhanced.

GENERALITY OF THE COGNITIVE MODEL
TO A FUZZY PROBLEM

Introduction

A cognitive model for reading documents was proposed and partially tested in the previous studies. This model consists of five mental operations that are likely to be necessary to the task of locating information in documents. The goal or purpose of reading that is most often studied in text-comprehension research is recall or acquisition of the body of knowledge in a text (Reder, 1985). On the other hand, most people read most documents for the purpose of locating specific information (Kirsch & Guthrie, 1984). Therefore, locating information rather than full recall of the total knowledge corpus is the use for document reading that is assumed in the construction of the cognitive model.

This study questions whether the cognitive model will predict performance on locating information in documents when the goal of the reading task is more general, and less well specified. In the field of problem solving, a useful differentiation is made between *fuzzy problems* and their converse, which are called *sharp problems* (Newell & Simon, 1972). In a fuzzy problem, the goal is unclear and vague; whereas a sharp problem has a precise goal or objective. In addition, in a fuzzy problem, the criterion for solution is not given or is not available. The learner may not know whether the fuzzy problem has any obtainable solution. The sharp problem has a stated or visible standard for solution that is external to the learner. An example of a fuzzy problem is: "what is the most comfortable hiking shoe"; whereas a sharp problem is: "what is the heaviest hiking shoe?"

In the previous study, the airline schedule task was a sharp problem. Only one solution was acceptable by the computer and the criteria for an acceptable solution were stated in the question. Does the model predict performance on a fuzzy problem, too?

It was expected that the components of the model that were found to be important in the sharp problem also would be important in the fuzzy one. The cognitive component of selecting the appropriate category of information for inspection was expected to be prominent. The directionality was expected to reverse, however. In the sharp problem, the criterion for good performance was a correct answer in a minimum period of time for which examining the fewest categories was optimal. In the fuzzy problem, a good solution depends on a large number of comparisons between different flights and therefore, examining a large number of appropriate categories will be helpful. The component of element extraction requires a consistent and complete retrieval of critical elements from each appropriate category that is examined. The directionality for this component is identical for both types of problems.

One basis for distinguishing between document reading and prose comprehension is psychometric. That is, if performance on the two tasks is not correlated, one may assume that the cognitive systems that govern the two systems are different. The way in which the systems differ is not defined by a modest correlation, but the fact of their mental independence is suggested. This psychometric standard for the independence of cognitive factors is not bidirectional. Although a low correlation suggests independence, a high correlation does not mean that the tasks are measuring the "same thing," because the correlation may be due to mutual association with a third variable. It was expected that the tasks of locating information in a document to answer a fuzzy question, and expository prose comprehension, would be moderately correlated. Specifically, it was expected that the components of the model would be more successful than a measure of prose recall in accounting for performance on document search.

Method

Subjects. The subjects were 18 undergraduates in a teacher education program who volunteered to participate.

Fuzzy Problem. The task in this study was designed to have the characteristics of a fuzzy problem. There was no explicit criterion for correct solution, and the specific objectives of the problem were open to amplification by the solver. The problem consisted of attempting to answer a question about planning a trip using an airline schedule. The document that was employed was identical to the document that was used in the previous study. The problem was varied, however, by altering the question. In this case the question was:

> Suppose you wanted to travel to visit a friend in Los Angeles. Which flight or connection of flights would you take and why? Provide an essay answer and give a full explanation for your choices.

This question differed from the question used in the study of solving a sharp problem with a document. In the sharp problem, the question was:

> Which flight or combination of flights could you take, if you wanted to fly from NY to LA given the following conditions:
> ⟩ the cost cannot exceed $450.
> ⟩ you must arrive by 7 p.m.

The reading task was presented on a microcomputer to enable the collection of data that would reflect on the cognitive model that was under study. The schedule was excerpted from the Official Airline Guide and has been verified as realistic by two expert travel agents during the prior study.

Access to the categories of information in the schedule was obtained by selecting choices from the embedded menu. The menu was a series of alternative choices superimposed on the image of the outline of the schedule. The choices consisted of columns in the schedule including: departures and arrivals, meals, days, movie, cost, class, and in addition, the following choices were displayed across the bottom of the screen: essay space, review question, help, and exit program. A small arrow moved to each of these choices, under the control of the solver through the space bar. A selection of a choice was made by pressing the enter key on the computer keyboard.

A person was able to read the schedule by viewing the outline with the embeded choices, selecting a choice, and examining the material displayed as a result of the selection. At the same time as the column of information was presented, a notepad was opened on the computer screen. The notepad consisted of a space with the title of NOTES about one quarter of the screen size. The cursor of the computer was placed in the notepad, and the reader was permitted to write anything he or she wished in the space. Limited word processing was available. To remove the screen containing the category of information and the notepad, the reader entered a plus (+) in the notepad. This act caused the embedded menu in the schedule to reappear and the previous screen to be hidden.

The notepad was present at all times when the reader had selected a category of information to inspect, except in the menu mode. The contents of the notepad were preserved, and were visible for the reader on each appearance. If the notepad filled up, which it occasionally did for writing-oriented readers, its contents were printed out on a connected dot matrix printer, and were given to the reader. A new, blank notepad was then supplied to the learner, according to the same system.

An essay space was supplied to the reader for the purpose of composing an answer to the question. The space consisted of a section about two thirds of the size of the screen, on the left side. The notepad appeared simultaneously on the right side of the screen. The cursor of the computer was placed in the essay space, with limited word processing available. Entries into the notepad were not possible in this condition. The solver could access the essay space through the menu mode at any time, and could return from it to the menu mode by placing an asterisk (*) in the far left column of the space and pressing the enter key. Although serial contributions to the essay were possible, all the participants chose to write the essay in one, uninterrupted period of time with considerable reference to the notepad.

Prose Recall. Following the trip-planning task, subjects were given a prose recall task on paper. A 385-word passage on sedimentary rocks was administered with instructions to read quickly and carefully. Written free recall statements were judged according to the number of propositions from the text that they contained.

Results

The results of the investigation are reported in terms of the cognitive model that has been proposed to account for performance on tasks of locating information in documents. The model predicts that the cognitive components of inspecting relevant categories of the document and extracting appropriate elements from the categories to fulfill the goal requirements will be positively associated with success in document search.

To examine the effect of category inspection and element extraction on the fuzzy problem used in this study, two multiple regressions were performed. The first included the quality of the essay on the plane trip as the dependent variable and the number of menu choices, the rated quality of entries in the notepad, and the prose recall score as independent variables. As displayed in Table 4.4, the number of menu choices, which was entered first, was significant at $p < .059$. Quality of notepad entries that was entered second, was significant at $p < .053$. Because directional hypotheses were being tested, one-tailed significance criteria were employed. The procedure of the regression was forced entry, because it was expected on theoretical grounds that category selection should precede element extraction in facilitating search performance.

To examine the relationship of reading comprehension and document search, the measure of expository prose recall was entered prior to the cognitive components of document search in a multiple regression. As shown in Table 4.4 prose recall did not account for a significant proportion of variance in the trip-planning essay when it was entered first. In addition, the cognitive components remain significant at nearly the same levels for category inspection ($p < .07$) and element extraction ($p < .05$). It appears that there is a uniqueness to document search that is not accounted for by paragraph comprehension and recall. This form of reading/literacy must be understood on its own terms, using cognitive components that are local to it; it is not easily subsumed under the rubric of prose comprehension.

The level of cognitive proficiency of the participants in the study may be observed by noting the means and variances on the measures in Table 4.5. The essay had a mean of 5.78 with a standard deviation of 1.53. The scoring system awarded 3 points for naming a flight that, in fact would go from the designated departure point to the designated arrival point. They were

TABLE 4.4
Prediction of Locating Information in a Document
with Fuzzy Problem

Variable	Mult R	RSQ	RSQCH	FCH	SigCH
No. menu choices	.38	.15	.15	2.74	.059
Notepad entry rating	.54	.29	.14	2.97	.053
Prose recall	.56	.31	.02	.49	.246
Prose recall	.18	.03	.03	.52	.24
No. menu choices	.41	.17	.14	2.46	.069
Notepad entry rating	.56	.31	.14	2.92	.055

Note: The significance levels for the change values are directional and one-tailed.

TABLE 4.5
Means and Standard Deviations of Variables in Locating Task
with Fuzzy Problem

Variable	X	SD
No. menu choices	8.94	4.58
Notepad entry rating	1.55	.51
Essay quality	5.78	1.43
Prose recall	7.50	4.82
Document reading time	927.89	556.46
Essay writing time	535.72	

awarded 1 point for each reason for their choice. Therefore, the scores imply that the typical participant gave three reasons for a choice that was plausible.

To attain this level, the average participant chose 8.94 menu selections for inspection; and 8 of 18 of these individuals were rated as efficient in their extraction strategies. The time spent by the participants in reading and writing during the search process was about 15 minutes (927.89 seconds) and their time spent composing the essay was about 9 minutes (535.72 seconds). Performance on the prose recall task consisted of a mean of 7.50 propositions, with a standard deviation of 4.83.

Discussion

This study examined the importance of category selection and element extraction on a document-search task with an ill-defined goal. These cognitive components were observed to account for performance in document reading when the goal was fuzzy and the criterion for successful solution was not specified. A single correct answer was not expected or available. Nevertheless, the task requirements elicited cognitive processing similar to that of a well-specified problem.

Investigators differ in their views of how people solve fuzzy problems. Greeno (1980) stated that although there are three varieties of problem solving (arrangement, transformation and induction), several critical processes are common to them all. Basic to them, are planning, which begins with global actions and proceeds to more detailed tactics, and knowledge representation, which may be more or less lawful (Chi, Feltovich, & Glaser, 1981). Unfortunately, the vagueness of the description of these processes prevents one from making precise predictions from them. Therefore, their role in a model is nominal and suggestive rather than quantitative and predictive.

In contrast to Greeno (1980), Gick (1986) asserted that reducing the specificity of the goal prevents the learner from engaging in means–ends analysis that leads to altered cognitive processing. A high amount of mens–

ends analysis, she claimed, mitigates the acquisition of the structural properties of the problem; and it precludes the learning of a schema for solution. However, in this study, the subjects rendered reasonable solutions in about 20 minutes of reading and writing; they justified their arguments and their choices. It appears that structural properties of the document were processed during reading, regardless of the vagueness of the goal.

INSPECTION AND EXTRACTION
IN TEXTBOOK CHAPTER PROCESSING

In this final study, search of textbook material is examined. Specifically, the success of the cognitive model in accounting for performance on a textbook-search task is examined. Although prose is used as the material of interest, the purpose for which it is used is to locate specific information rather than the more traditional prose recall task.

A task at the textbook chapter level was selected because the examination of processing in chapter length material is important but not common. As Calfee and Drum (1986) pointed out, most texts used in reading-comprehension research have been fewer than 1,000 words. Indeed, text-comprehension research has typically focused on the paragraph as the unit to be explained (Anderson & Pearson, 1984). Yet textbooks are a prevailing means of delivering knowledge to students (Godlad, 1976), and textbook chapters are a common unit of education used by students in applying study strategies and by teachers in planning curriculum, making assignments, and giving tests. Moreover, cognitive processing at the textbook chapter level may not be identical to the processing that occurs in paragraphs or short texts.

In addition to its use of a textbook chapter as the focus of study, this research differs from the typical text-comprehension research in the type of reading task that was examined. The reading purpose that is most often studied in text-comprehension research is recall or acquisition of the body of knowledge in a text (Calfee & Drum, 1986; Reder, 1985). In contrast, this study used a locating task in which all of the available information was not relevant. Instead of making a recall, students needed to use located information about five earth sciences terms to construct an essay explaining how the terms were related to one another. Thus, locating information in text involves detecting a specific subset of information within an array of information broader than what is needed to satisfy the goal.

Search of text merits research attention because of its pervasiveness in school and in the workplace. In school, examples include questions in elementary school basal reader manuals that ask students to read to locate an answer or to locate evidence supporting a conclusion, and the requirement from the intermediate grades on up that students locate information on a particular topic for reports. There is some research documenting the prevalence of such demands such as the work of Armbruster and Gudbrandsen (1986) who found that intermediate-grade social studies textbooks included the locating of information as a major objective. In addition, adults in the workplace have been found to spend more time on reading to locate information than reading for any other purpose (Kirsch & Guthrie, 1984).

Search tasks may appear to be easy because source materials are available to learners as they perform. In the current task, for example, students had access to chapter material and notes while assembling their answers. However, a locating task can be considered at least as challenging as a recall task. Indeed, locating tasks using much shorter documents than used here gave great difficulty to a high percentage of young adults (ages 21–25) in a National Assessment of Educational Progress study (see Kirsch & Jungeblut, 1986). The demands of the task used in the current study can be clarified in terms of Rohwer's (1984) two-dimensional classification of course and task characteristics that he proposed as part of a preliminary framework for research on studying. Rohwer advocated classifying task characteristics in terms of volitional latitude (opportunities for self-initiated study) and cognitive-transformational requirements. Volitional latitude is high in the current research because the task involves persistence in independence, self-paced studying. In other words, the task is student directed because neither a teacher nor a program provides the student with a decision on what to do next (Anderson, 1979). The task also falls at the high end of the cognitive-transformational requirements continuum. Although Rohwer referred to "courses" in the following statement, "tasks" could very well be substituted:

> Courses characterized by many cognitive transformational requirements are those where successful criterion performance presupposes autonomous student activity in selecting, organizing, processing, transforming and integrating the information to be learned. In contrast, courses having low-transformational requirements are those in which the criterion tasks are virtual copies of the information presented in resource materials. (Rohwer, 1984, p. 9)

In the current study, students had to select, organize, process, transfer, and integrate information without experimenter guidance.

When a learner is attempting to search, not all categories of a document are relevant. The proposed cognitive-process model holds that an efficient learner would engage in a selective search of categories likely to contain the required information rather than an exhaustive search of the entire document. According to the model, an efficient learner would first form a goal or objective regarding what information he or she will attempt to locate in the document. Second, the learner would select appropriate categories of information for inspection. Third, once a category is selected the learner must either extract information pertinent to the goal or make a determination to reject the category if it contains no relevant information. Fourth, as information is extracted from the document, the facts or concepts are integrated in an ongoing synthesis of information relevant to the goal. Fifth, the learner recycles through the prior components until the goal has been satisfied.

Searching to answer a question over a textbook chapter can be expressed in terms of the cognitive model (see Fig. 4.4). Students must decide what the needed information is (goal formation), determine which subset of the available chapter they need and locate pertinent sections of the text material (category selection), interpret and transform the available information (element extraction), remember or record the extracted information, and combine individual pieces of information prior knowledge (integration) in order to infer and explain the relationship among the pieces of information. They

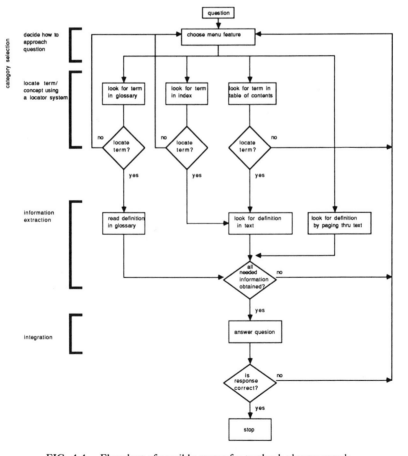

FIG. 4.4.   Flowchart of possible routes for textbook chapter search.

must also repeat these steps to develop a complete set of information needed for constructing an answer (recycle).

In this study, the goal is represented by the question. The task is to answer the question, which contains references to the content. The processing could be considered question driven, or goal initiated. As a result, the nature of the question is important. In this study the question was neither as broad as "read to recall the text" nor as narrow as "locate fact x." Instead, the question required both the identification of propositions and across-paragraph integration.

The purpose of the study was to examine which components of the proposed cognitive model account for performance in reading to answer a question over a textbook chapter.

Method

Students. The students in this study were 23 undergraduate student volunteers. All were enrolled in a course required for a teaching credential and received extra credit for their participation. At the end of the study, the students were given an overview of the results.

Materials. In addition to paper and pencil for recording the answers to the questions, the materials in this study consisted of a chapter on erosion from an eighth-grade earth science textbook (Brown & Anderson, 1977). This chapter was presented to the students on a color video monitor via an IBM AT microcomputer. Although illustrations were not included, all other features of the chapter such as italics, headings, and review questions were transferred to floppy disk for computer display. Only minor changes were made in the text in order to remove references to other chapters or to the eliminated illustrations. In addition to the chapter, the computer display also made available those sections of the textbook's table of contents, glossary, and index that were pertinent to the chapter. The chapter text was 6,863 words long and consisted of 41 pages or screens. The display area for these screens was approximately 5 x 8″ or 25 lines x 40 spaces. Each screen was designed to present the information in a readable and pleasing manner. The index for the chapter consisted of 6 such screens with 161 entries and the glossary of two screens with 15 entries. The table of contents, presented on one screen, contained 7 headings and 21 subheadings.

Students were able to access the material by using a menu with the following eight choices.

1. To see Table of Contents
2. To Scan Chapter
3. To Browse Page by Page
4. To see Particular Page

5. To see Glossary

6. To see Index

7. To Review Your Assignment

8. End of Session

Table of Contents provided students with the seven section headings for the chapter; with the exception of the heading for the brief introduction to the chapter, each of these headings was accompanied by three or four subheadings. From *Table of Contents*, students could go directly to a chosen section. The *Scan Chapter* feature simulated a reader's flipping through a text by scanning the entire chapter including the table of contents, index, and glossary at a rate of 2 seconds per screen. Unlike the *Scan* feature which was not under the subject's control once it started, *Browse Page by Page* allowed a subject to go through the chapter at whatever pace was desired. Although *Browse Page by Page* started at the beginning of the chapter, once in the *Browse* choice, a student could go backward or forward at will and could exit at any time. However, if he or she wished to do so, a subject could use *Browse Page by Page* to simply start at the beginning of a chapter and read all of the way through. The *Particular Page* allowed students to go directly to any chosen page; as in *Browse*, students could then proceed backward or forward at will from the chosen page. By choosing *Glossary*, students went directly to the two screens containing the 15 glossary entries for the chapter. Students could move back and forth between the glossary screens. When *Index* was chosen, students first accessed an index menu that indicated the first and last words on each of the six index screens. Students then selected the index page they wanted; once on that page, students could examine the entries and type in the number of the text page they wished to see. The index feature went directly to the specified page. Students could repeat the cycle as often as needed before leaving the *Index* feature. The *Review Your Assignment* choice allowed students to review the question that they were to answer. Finally, when students were ready to answer the question, they selected *End of Session*.

Procedure. Students engaged in the task individually. A research assistant informed each subject that he or she would be using material on a microcomputer to answer earth science questions. Students were told that they would be receiving a sample question followed by the assignment, that they should work as quickly as possible keeping in mind the importance of accuracy, and that they should write their answers on paper when they were ready. They were also told that they could use all available information in whatever manner they chose. Paper was also available for any notes that students wished to make.

After explaining the procedure, the research assistant then loaded the program. Students first encountered the sample question: "What is the meaning of the word talus?" The program informed students that the answer to the question could be found by using the menu before the main question. When students chose *End of Session* in order to answer the sample question, the computer presented the assignment.

Assignment. Students received the following assignment: "Explain how the following terms are related to each other: *bacterial, humus, lichens, mechanical agents, solute.*" The program provided no instructions on how to proceed in completing this assignment. Students were free to work as long as they needed before writing their answers.

This assignment required locating and integrating information from two of the seven sections of the chapter. These two sections, one on weathering and the other on soil formation, each contained six screens. However, only three of the screens in the first section and four screens in the second section were key screens containing information directly related to the assignment. In addition to these seven key screens in the text of the chapter, the two glossary screens were also key screens because they each contained one of the terms in the assignment.

Inspection Records. The computer recorded the sequence of chapter elements (or menu choices) used by each student and the time in seconds spent on each choice. An excerpt from a student's record is shown in Table 4.6.

TABLE 4.6
Sample Computer Output of Student Process Record
in Chapter Processing

Computer Output		Key
GLOSSARY		student selects glossary from menu
48.0769	GLOSSARY—1	choses glossary p. 1, spends 48 seconds
85.2197	GLOSSARY—2	choses glossary p. 2, spends 85 seconds
INDEX		selects index from menu
20.3046	INDEX—1	selects p. 1 of index and from there
89.0659	PAGE—30	accesses pp. 30, 31, 32 of chapter
171.8681	PAGE—31	
77.5824	PAGE—32	
24.5604	INDEX—3	selects p. 3 of index and from there
38.1868	PAGE—3	accesses pp. 3, 4, 5 of chapter
32.9670	PAGE—4	
28.8462	PAGE—5	
7.7473	INDEX—5	selects p. 5 of index and from there
180.4396	PAGE—5	accesses p. 5 of chapter
23.0219	REVIEW ASSIGNMENT	reviews assignment and ends session

Measures Used

Essay Scores. Students' written responses to the assignment were evaluated on a 15-point scale. These 15 points were distributed evenly over three categories. First, 1 point was awarded for each of the five terms that was correctly defined. Second, 1 point was awarded for each of the five terms that was related to the central concept in a simple way. The terms are related in that they all have to do with soil formation, that is, the break up of rock and the subsequent formation of soil from the broken up rock. Thus, a subject might make an unelaborated statement that a term was related to soil formation. It was permissible to relate all the terms to the central concept in the same statement. In addition, it was possible for a response to give the relationship among the terms without defining them. Third, 1 point was given for each term that was related to the central concept in a complex way. A response was judged to go beyond a simple statement of relationship if it described *how* the term was related to soil formation. Scoring instructions provided detailed information on acceptable responses.

All essays were scored by two independent judges. The interrater correlation between scores for the two judges was $r = .88$. A third independent scorer was used to resolve disagreements.

Category Selection. Category selection was estimated by the number of text screens inspected before a student selected a relevant or key text screen. Key screens were those that contained information directly related to one or more of the five terms listed in the main assignment. There were seven key screens in the text of the chapter. (Text screens could be accessed directly from *Table of Contents, Browse, Particular Page,* and *Index.*) In addition, the two glossary screens each contained one of the terms. Thus, there were a total of nine key screens. To obtain a measure of screens examined before getting to a key screen, key screens were marked on each student's inspection record. Returns to key screens were not considered. Then the number of non-key screens students inspected before getting to a key screen was counted. These numbers were summed for each key screen to produce a total score. A subject who went directly to key screens would have a score of zero on this measure.

Extraction Efficiency. In order to compute a measure of a student's efficiency in extracting the necessary information, it was first determined which key screens a student had examined. If students correctly defined in their essays the term that occurred on a key screen that they examined, then they were given 1 point. The resulting figure was then used as the numerator in a ratio with the number of key screens examined as the denominator. In other words, extraction efficiency was the number of key screens examined for which the subject correctly defined the term divided by the total number of key screens viewed.

It should be noted that only one third of students' essay scores involved defining the terms in the assignment (see the section on scoring the essays). Overall, the assignment can be characterized as high on volitional latitude and cognitive-transformational requirements (see Rohwer, 1984). However, that portion of the assignment pertinent to extraction efficiency is low in cognitive-transformational requirements because it requires only copying definitional information. In addition, a major component of extraction efficiency, the total number of key screens examined was in no way dependent on the essay score.

Integration. The number of returns made by students to screens that they had already examined was used as an index of confusion or nonintegration. Thus, the number of returns to both the key screens and non-key screens was computed to produce an inverse indicator of integration.

Quality of Sequence (Recycling). The quality of the sequence of access systems was measured by rating a subject's first three choices. Ratings could range from 0 to 14, with the higher scores indicating a more efficient sequence. Sequences were evaluated according to the following scheme:

Position	Access System	Rating
1	glossary	6
	index	4
	table of contents	2
	other	0
2	index	6
	table of contents	4
	glossary	2
	other	0
3	glossary	2
	index	2
	table of contents	2
	review assignment	2
	other	0

This method of rating sequence of choice was based on the assumption that the more efficient method of obtaining the information to complete the assignment would be to access systems that would define the terms and then to gather other broader information to establish the relationship among the terms. Consequently, the most efficient route would be first to consult the glossary, because it is the most specific access system. Next, the index would be used both to locate information on terms that were not in the glossary and to locate areas in the text that might extend or clarify the glossary information. Thus, the highest rating was given to students who chose *Glossary* followed by *Index*. Although none of the students chose *Index*, then *Glossary*, this reverse order would have been rated less efficient. The *Table of Contents*, although less specific than either the *Glossary* or the *Index*, might also be expected to provide helpful information. However, the *Table of Contents* was considered to be a better choice in the second position than in the first because the ideal first choice should provide more specific information. Once a more specific information system is accessed, then consulting a more general source of information such as the *Table of Contents* would seem reasonable.

Students who made the third choice were given credit for accessing or returning to the *Index, Glossary,* or *Table of Contents*. In addition, choosing *Review Assignment* was also considered appropriate as the third choice. The rationale for scoring the third position was that students might need to review or extend the definitional and relational information they located in their first two choices. Students might also wish to verify that they had obtained all necessary information before they wrote their responses.

A penalty of 3 points was subtracted for more than four choices. No points were given if students chose *Scan Chapter, Browse Page by Page,* or *Particular Page;* although these less-specific access systems can lead to successful completion of the task, students did not receive points for using these systems because they were not efficient choices.

Results

Table 4.7 lists the means and standard deviations for the measures of the cognitive model components and for other measures not used in the model but nevertheless helpful in characterizing the performance of the students on the task. Table 4.8 reports the intercorrelations among the variables in the cognitive model. Students' performances on each component of the cognitive model are reported first, followed by the results of the test of the model. Finally, other descriptive measures of students' performances are reported.

Easy Performance. The essay task produced considerable variation in students' performance. Students' essay scores ranged from 1 to 12 out of a possible score of 15; the mean essay score was 6.04 with a standard deviation of 3.38.

Category Selection. The mean number of text screens that students inspected before identifying key screens was 2.61 with a standard deviation of 4.59. Performance on this measure, which was used to estimate category

TABLE 4.7
Performance on Essay, Cognitive Components, and Other Descriptive
Measures of Textbook Chapter Reading

Variable	Mean	Standard Deviation
Essay	6.04	3.38
Category selection	2.61	4.59
Element extraction	.46	.32
Integration	2.39	2.35
Recycling	6.65	4.27
Number of key pages examined	7.00	1.28
Average time on key pages (seconds)	95.91	44.43
Average time on non-key pages (seconds)	26.17	20.17
Number of different information routes chosen	3.74	1.91
Number of returns to key pages	2.13	2.12
Number of returns to non-key pages	.26	.54

selection, ranged from no non-key screens inspected before selecting key screens to 22. The high standard deviation was explained by an examination of the frequency distribution for this measure. Of the students, 78% looked at 0,1, or 2 non-key screens before selecting key screens. However, the remaining students examined 3 to 22 screens. Thus, although most students were fairly efficient on this measure of category selection, a few had considerable difficulty. Category selection correlated $-.18$ with essay score ($p = .40$).

Extraction Efficiency. The mean proportion of key screens inspected, which the students identified and extracted definitional information for a term, was .46 with a standard deviation of .32. In other words, when students examined a key screen, they extracted the key information an average of 46% of the time. There was a considerable range in extraction efficiency, from 0 to .89. Even within one standard deviation of the mean, the range was from 14% to 78%. It is striking that 22% of the students received a 0, indicating

TABLE 4.8
Correlation Among Cognitive Components of Textbook
Chapter Reading

	Category Selection	Element Extraction	Integration	Recycling
Essay	−.18 (.40)	.56 (.01)	−.41 (.05)	.43 (.04)
Category selection		.30 (.17)	−.11 (.63)	−.50 (.01)
Element extraction			−.12 (.59)	−.20 (.35)
Integration				−.40 (.06)

Note: Results of tests of significance for each correlation are given in parentheses.

that they were unable to extract the necessary information even when they inspected an appropriate page. Of the students, 61% in the experiment scored at or below an extraction efficiency score of .50. Extraction efficiency and essay performance had a .56 correlation (p = .006).

Integration. The mean number of returns to previously inspected screens, an inverse indicator of integration, was 2.39 with a standard deviation of 2.35. Of the students, 22% made no returns to previously inspected pages, whereas 39% engaged in one or two returns. The remaining 39% made three to eight returns. This measure correlated -.41 with essay performance (p = .053).

Recycling. Recycling was estimated by the quality of students' inspection sequences. Scores ranged from 0 to the highest possible score of 14. The mean score was 6.65 with a standard deviation of 4.27. A good or adequate performance on this measure would require a score of at least 8 (see the rating system discussed earlier), which only 35% of the students obtained. Moreover, of the remaining students who scored at 7 or below, 47% received the penalty for excess number of choices suggesting difficulty in finding information in the chapter. Recycling and essay had a correlation of .43 (p = .04).

Testing the Cognitive Model. A stepwise regression procedure was used to analyze the data. This procedure was chosen because as students attempted to deal with the multiple terms in the task, they most likely did not do so in separate linear execution of cognitive components for each term. Instead, students were most likely at different points in the processing of information for each term resulting in some degree of simultaneous processing of the various components. A stepwise regression was judged to fit this situation better than other alternatives.

Table 4.9 presents the results of a stepwise multiple regression with essay performance as the dependent variable. The measures representing four of

TABLE 4.9
Multiple Regression of Cognitive Variables on Essay Performance

Variable	R	R^2	Change in R^2	F for Change	Significance Level for Change
Extraction	.555	.308	.308	9.348	.006
Recycling	.784	.615	.307	15.921	.001
Category selection	.793	.628	.014	.698	.414
Integration	.812	.657	.029	1.499	.237

Note: Probability of entry into the stepwise regression was set to permit entry of all variables.

the components of the cognitive model produced a multiple correlation of .81, thus accounting for 66% of the variance in essay performance. The overall F test for the regression equation was statistically significant ($F = 8.62$, $df = 4/18$, $p = .0005$). However, only two of four components contributed at a statistically significant level. Extraction efficiency and recycling each accounted for 31% of the variance in essay performance. Category selection and integration added 2% and 3%, respectively, to the prediction of essay variance but these were not statistically significant increments. Because the correlation matrix in Table 4.3 indicates that the measure of category selection had a low, nonstatistically significant zero-order correlation with essay, the small contribution of category selection is not surprising. In addition, however, category selection is correlated with recycling ($r = -.50, p < .01$) so that a good deal of any potential contribution of category selection was most likely subsumed by recycling. Similarly, although integration has a $-.41$ zero-order correlation with essay, its potential contribution was probably also subsumed by recycling with which it had a $-.40$ correlation.

Other Descriptive Data. Out of a possible nine, the mean number of key screens examined was seven with a standard deviation of 1.3. (This figure does not include returns to key screens.) The mean proportion of time spent on key screen was .88, with key screens receiving an average of 96 seconds while non-key screens were allocated an average of 26 seconds.

There were few returns to non-key screens: 78% of the students made no returns to non-key pages whereas the remaining students made only one or two returns. The number of returns to the nine key pages varied from zero to seven with a mean of 2.13 (standard deviation 2.12). Returns of either kind were negatively correlated with essay performance, returns to non-key screens at $-.26$ and returns to key pages at $-.39$.

To complete the assignment, students could select from seven information routes (e.g., index, glossary, scan). The mean number of information systems accessed was 3.74 with a standard deviation of 1.91. The frequency distribution indicated that 43% of the subjects selected four or more choices, although the most efficient route to obtaining the information required accessing only two systems.

Discussion

This study examined the ability of a cognitive-process model of locating information in written documents to account for textbook chapter processing. The need for a separate process model for "search" written documents springs from the fact that locating needs to be distinguished from the more commonly investigated task of prose recall. It is argued that the two cannot be accounted for by identical cognitive variables. For example, a factor-analytic study indicated a clear distinction between a traditional text comprehension construct and a locating construct (Guthrie & Kirsch, 1987). Yet other currently available theoretical models do not adequately address this dimension of literacy. The inadequacies of the other formulations with regard to locating tasks are discussed at length by Guthrie and Mosenthal (1987). Briefly, however, problem solving and studying models are too general to allow specific predictions and locating in documents, whereas schema theoretic explanations of reading comprehension emphasize knowledge schemata useful in explaining text recall but neglect procedural schemata that are more pertinent to locating.

The current research provides a processing account of how students go about answering a complex question at the textbook chapter level. How efficiently and effectively did students use this textbook chapter to locate the information they needed? The variables of extraction efficiency and recycling each accounted for approximately 31% of the variance in the quality of the answer to an essay question. Adding the variables of category selection and integration, the combined components of the model accounted for 66% of variation in the outcome measure.

Results indicated striking deficiencies in extraction efficiency and in the sequence of inspection (recycling) used by many students in attempting to gather information to answer the question. Extraction efficiency scores indicated that students were successful in extracting the relevant information from a key screen less than half the time on the average. Indeed, 61% of the students performed at or below a 50% extraction efficiency level. Yet there was apparent recognition of the importance of these key screens in contrast to the non-key screens because almost four times as much time was spent on key screens as on non-key. But despite the selective attention to key screens in contrast to non-key screens, most students were not particularly successful in element extraction. In fact, 22% of the students received a 0, indicating that they were unable to extract the necessary information even when they inspected an appropriate page.

Difficulties are also apparent when the quality of the sequence of choices students made is examined. Although writing a quality essay was a difficult task, getting started on finding the necessary information should have been fairly straightforward because it would involve only locating the terms in the assignment. Thus, it would seem reasonable to assume that most students should have been able to at least initiate their search for information efficiently. Instead, many students seemed to have little idea how to approach the chapter. Two thirds of the students failed to attain at least 8 points that was the lowest score that could be loosely described as adequate. Moreover, approximately half of those students received the penalty for an excessive number of menu choices, highlighting their unplanned, uninformed approach to locating chapter information.

Although the chapter used in this study was from a junior high school text, it is apparent from the essay performance that the task was nevertheless challenging. What made the task difficult? Aside from any problems with the text itself, at least three possibilities are likely. First, the students had limited knowledge of the content. The assumption was verified by giving the question without the chapter to 20 undergraduate students who were enrolled in a similar course but who did not participate in the study. Although 14 students made general comments such as "They are all science terms," none of these students was able to even approximate a correct answer. Second, the characteristics of the task made it difficult. In terms of Rohwer's (1984) classification, the task was high on both volitional latitude and cognitive-transformation requirements. The difficulty of the task may have been heightened by its dissimilarity to typical assignments. For example, one study indicated that over 90% of precollege science teachers use textbooks in a traditional "read/discuss/answer the question" manner (National Science Teachers Association, 1981), which involved teacher direction and a preponderance of factual level questions. Third, the task was challenging because many students did not know how to use the available material efficiently (Garner, 1987). The third point merits expansion.

Although it might be argued that students may have had difficulty simply because the task involved a microcomputer rather than an actual textbook, we hypothesize instead that many of these students were rather unfamiliar with how to approach a chapter for a locating task. By the time they reach the college level, students have presumably had years of experience with textbooks because they are the prevailing means of delivering knowledge to students (EPIE, 1974; Goodlad, 1984; Mikulecky, 1982; National Science Teachers Association, 1981). However, other research findings raise questions about the nature of students' content area textbook exposure. First, use of textbooks in school may be rather narrow in scope. For example, in one study, high school students reported that their overwhelming purpose when using their textbooks was to read to learn the content. They reported that their major strategies in accomplishing this purpose were to reread and take notes; there were only rare references to using such strategies as problem solving or relating new ideas to what is known. Moreover, there were no reports of using text material in any kind of reading to judge or evaluate and very few reports of reading in order to accomplish a task (Mikulecky, 1982). In another study, high school students reported a rather restricted range of study strategies. The most common pattern was to engage in a single reading of a chapter with an eye to memorizing portions of it (Tierney, 1982). Second, although content-area textbooks are pervasive, students may not actually be reading them to the extent that has been assumed (Anderson & Armbuster,

1984). At the high school level, apparently little reading occurs in class—less than 5% of class time (Goodlad, 1984). Therefore, one would assume that most textbook reading occurs outside of school. However, Smith and Feathers' (1983) ethnographic study of secondary content-area classrooms suggested that little reading is actually assigned and that many students view their teachers' lectures as of equal or greater importance than their textbooks for obtaining information. Similarly, in a study of junior and senior high school classes, Ratekin, Simpson, Alvermann, and Dishner (1985) found that the teacher, not the textbook, was the primary information source for students. Because students could rely on the teacher to develop new concepts, it was possible to perform adequately without reading the textbook. Observation indicated that instruction did not include teaching students to read and learn from their content-area textbooks. Dolan, Harrison, and Gardner (1979) and Rieck (1977) reported similar findings. In short, many students may have had little initiation into the use of features such as an index, glossary, or table of contents that the current task required (Mayer, Dyck, & Cook, 1984).

Thus, research evidence on the type and amount of content-area reading that actually occurs in pre-college education appears to explain why so many of the students in the current study approached the task in an inefficient manner. Despite years of exposure to textbooks, they may have used those texts for very narrow purposes or have actually used those texts minimally, relying instead on teacher lectures for information.

Future research, taking advantage of the computerized approach used in the current study, can further examine the skills students have. Data on what students do, including information on effective and ineffective routes in approaching differing types of tasks, would be valuable not only to researchers but to teachers for diagnosis and instruction. Future work should also investigate whether effective locating processes can be taught. For example, can effective locating be taught by using questions based on the components of the cognitive-process model? In addition, the components of the model need to be explored with regard to the effects of the type of reading goal or question. With the current question, integration and category selection were not statistically significant contributors to the prediction of performance. However, with broader or narrower questions the importance of the components in the model may shift. With a narrow question, such as locating a particular fact, category selection may increase in importance, whereas integration and sequence of inspection diminish. In contrast, with a broad goal, such as remembering the next five pages read, integration would seem likely to be critical.

To summarize, this last study located two cognitive operations that are vital to locating information in a textbook chapter: sequence of inspection (recycling) and element extraction. The data suggest deficiencies in the inspection and extraction processes of many college students as they attempted to write an essay answer to a question using an earth sciences textbook chapter. The complexity of the question as well as students' lack of prior knowledge of the topic and their apparently limited knowledge of how to use a textbook, made the task a challenging one. The processes of sequencing the inspection of sections of the chapter, and extracting critical details from a screen of text accounted for high proportions of variance among students and warrant further exploration.

SUMMARY

This chapter proposed a cognitive-process model of document and text search and examined the model in four exploratory studies. The first three studies offer evidence that the proposed model accounts for both performance and learning in search tasks using a plane schedule and a paystub. In addition, the model was shown to account for both fuzzy as well as sharp search tasks. In a fourth study, the search model was extended to a locating task using a textbook chapter. Taken together, these studies demonstrate the value of the proposed cognitive model and illustrate the rich possibilities for studying document and text search via computer representation.

REFERENCES

Ackerman, B. P. (1985). The effects of specific and categorical orienting on children's incidental and intentional memory for pictures and words. *Journal of Experimental Child Psychology, 39*(2), 330–325.

Anderson, R. C., & Pearson, P. D. (1984). A schema-theoretic view of basic processes in reading. In P. D. Pearson (Ed.), *Handbook of reading research* (pp. 255–292). New York: Longman.

Anderson, T. H. (1979). Study skills and learning strategies. In H. G. O'Neil, Jr. & C. D. Spielberger (Eds.), *Cognitive and affective learning strategies* (pp. 77–98). New York: Academic Press.

Anderson, T., & Armbruster, B. (1984). Studying. In D. Pearson (Ed.), *Handbook of reading research* (pp. 657–681). New York: Longman.

Armbruster, B. B., & Gudbrandsen, B. (1986). Reading comprehension instruction in social studies programs. *Reading Research Quarterly, 21*, 36–48.

Boyer, E. (1983). *High school*. New York: Harper & Row.

Braine, L., & Green, L. (1987). Effect of stimulus configuration on spatial judgments in search tasks. *Journal of Experimental Child Psychology, 43*(1), 1–12.

Brown, W. R., & Anderson, N. D. (1977). *Earth science: A search for understanding*. New York: Lippincott.

Calfee, R., & Drum, P. (1986). Research on teaching reading. In M. C. Wittrock (Ed.), *Handbook of research on teaching* (pp. 804–849). New York: Macmillan.

Chi, M.T.H., Feltovich, P. J., & Glaser, R. (1981). Categorization and representation of physics knowledge by experts and novices. *Cognitive Science, 5*, 121–153.

Cross, D. R., & Wellman, H. M. (1985). Mathematical models of search. In H. M. Wellman (Ed.), *Children's searching: The development of search skill and spatial representation.* Hillsdale, NJ: Lawrence Erlbaum Associates.

Dixon, P. (1985). The category effect in visual detection and partial report. *Perception and Psychophysics, 38*(3), 286–295.

Dolan, T., Harrison, C., & Gardner, K. (1979). The incidence and context of reading in the classroom. In E. Lunzer & K. Gardner (Eds.), *The effective use of reading* (pp. 108–138). London: Heineman.

Ellis, S., & Stark, L. (1986). Statistical dependency in visual scanning. *Human Factors, 28*(4), 421–438.

EPIE Institute. (1974). *Fits and misfits: What you should know about your child's learning materials.* Columbia, MD: National Committee for Citizens in Education.

Garner, R. (1987). *Metacognition and reading comprehension.* Norwood, NJ: Ablex.

Gick, M. L. (1986). Problem solving strategies. *Educational Psychologist, 2*(1 & 2), 99–120.

Gillingham, M. G., & Guthrie, J. T. (1987). Relationships between CBI and research teaching. *Contemporary Educational Psychology, 12,* 189–199.

Goodlad, J. I. (1976). *Facing the future: Issues in education and schooling.* New York: McGraw-Hill.

Goodlad, J. I. (1984). *A place called school: Prospects for the future.* New York: McGraw-Hill.

Greeno, J. G. (1980). Trends in the theory of knowledge for problem solving. In D. Tuma & F. Reif (Eds.) *Problem solving and education.* Hillsdale, NJ: Lawrence Erlbaum Associates.

Guthrie, J., & Kirsch, I. (1987). Distinctions between reading comprehension and locating information in text. *Journal of Educational Psychology, 79*(3).

Guthrie, J. T., & Mosenthal, P. (1987). Locating information in documents: A computer simulation and cognitive model. *Educational Psychologist, 22,* 279–297.

Heath, S. B. (1983). *Ways with words: Language, life and work in committees and classrooms.* Cambridge: Cambridge University Press.

Kirsch, I. K., & Guthrie, J. T. (1984). Adult reading practices for work and leisure. *Adult Education Quarterly, 34*(4), 219–238.

Kirsch, I., & Jungeblut, A. (1986). *Literacy: Profile of America's young adults.* Princeton, NJ: Educational Testing Service.

Kulhavy, R., Lee, J. B., & Caterino, L. (1985). Conjoint retention of maps and related discourse. *Contemporary Educational Psychology, 10,* 28–37.

Mason, G., Blanchard, J. & Daniel, D. (1983). *Computer applications in reading.* Newark, DE: International Reading Association.

Mayer, R. E., Dyck, J. L., & Cook, L. K. (1984). Techniques that help readers build mental models from scientific text: Definitions pretraining and signaling. *Journal of Educational Psychology, 76*(6), 1089–1106.

Mikulecky, L. (1982). Job literacy: The relationship between school preparation and workplace actuality. *Reading Research Quarterly, 17*(3), 400–419.

Mikulecky, L., & Winchester, D. (1983). Job literacy and job performance among nurses at varying employment levels. *Adult Education Quarterly, 34,* 1–15.

Miller, P., Haynes, F., DeMarie-Greblow, D., & Woody-Ramsey, J. (1986). Children's strategies for gathering information in three tasks. *Child Development, 57*(6), 1429–1439.

National Science Teachers Association. (1981). *What research says to the science teacher* (Vol. 3). Washington, DC: Author.

Newell, A., & Simon, H. A. (1972). *Human problem solving.* Englewood Cliffs, NJ: Prentice-Hall.

Pellegrino, J., & Glaser, R. (1982). Analyzing aptitudes for learning: Inductive reasoning. In R. Glaser (Ed.), *Advances in instructional psychology* (Vol. 2, pp. 269–336). Hillsdale, NJ: Lawrence Erlbaum Associates.

Pellegrino, J., Mumaw, R., & Shute, V. (1985). Analyses of spatial aptitude and expertise. In

S. Embretson (Ed.), *Test design: Developments in psychology and psychometrics* (pp. 45–76). New York: Academic Press.

Ratekin, N., Simpson, M., Alvermann, D. E., & Dishner, E. K. (1985). Why content teachers resist reading instruction. *Journal of Reading, 28*, 432–437.

Rayner, K. (1983). *Eye movements in reading: Perceptual and language process*. New York: Academic Press.

Reder, L. M. (1985). Techniques available to author, teacher and reading to improve retention of main ideas of a chapter. In F. S. Chipman, J. W. Segal, & R. Glaser (Eds.), *Thinking and learning skills*. Hillsdale, NJ: Lawrence Erlbaum Associates.

Reeve, R. A., Campione, J., & Brown, A. (1986). Remember the right locations: Factors affecting young children's logical search ability. *Cognitive Development, 1*, 239–251.

Remington, R., & Williams, D. (1986). On the selection and evaluation of visual display symbology: Factors influencing search and identification times. *Human Factors, 28*(4), 407–420.

Rieck, B. J. (1977). How content teachers telegraph messages against reading. *Journal of Reading, 20*, 646–648.

Rohwer, W. D., Jr. (1984). An invitation to an educational psychology of studying. *Educational Psychologist, 19*, 1–14.

Smith, F. R., & Feathers, K. M. (1983). Teacher and student perceptions of content area reading. *Journal of Reading, 26*(4),348–354.

Somerville, S., & Haake, R. (1985). The logical search skills of infants and young children. In D. Wellman (Ed.), *Children's searching: The development of search skill and spatial presentation*. Hillsdale, NJ: Lawrence Erlbaum Associates.

Sternberg, R., & McNamara T. (1985). The representation and processing of information in real-time verbal comprehension. In S. Embretson (Ed.), *Test design: Developments in psychology and psychometrics* (pp. 21–45). New York: Academic Press.

Sticht, T. (1975). *Reading for working: A functional literacy anthology*. Alexandria, VA: HUMRRO.

Streeter, L. A., & Vitello, D. (1986). A profile of drivers' map-reading abilities. *Human Factors, 28*(2), 223–239.

Tierney, R. J. (1982). Learning from text. In A. Berger & H. A. Robinson (Eds.), *Secondary school reading: What research reveals for classroom practice* (pp. 97–110). Urbana, IL: National Conference on Research in English/ERIC Clearinghouse on Reading and Communication Skills.

5

Anchored Instruction: Why We Need It and How Technology Can Help

John D. Bransford
Robert D. Sherwood
Ted S. Hasselbring
Charles K. Kinzer
Susan M. Williams
George Peabody College of Vanderbilt University

Most educators agree that we must help students learn to think for themselves and to solve problems (e.g., Feuerstein, 1979; Linn, 1986; Mann, 1979; Segal, Chipman, & Glaser, 1985). This emphasis on thinking has prompted educators to focus their attention on *processes* involved in thinking rather than only on the contents of thought. Nevertheless, research demonstrates that knowledge of important content—knowledge of concepts, theories, and principles—empowers people to think effectively. Without appropriate knowledge, people's ability to think and solve problems is relatively weak (e.g., Bransford, Sherwood, Vye, & Rieser, 1986; Newell, 1980; Simon, 1980).

An important challenge for educators is to teach relevant content in a way that facilitates thinking. This chapter discusses some possible approaches for meeting this challenge. Our discussion focuses on the concept of *anchored instruction;* we explore why we need it and why it is advantageous. We also argue that, although anchored instruction can be implemented without the use of technology, it becomes more powerful when used in conjunction with microcomputer technologies and videodiscs.

WHY WE NEED NEW APPROACHES TO INSTRUCTION

Before introducing the concept of anchored instruction, we consider some problems with many traditional approaches to instruction. The purpose of this discussion is to explore the need for change. The basic problem is that

115

traditional instruction often fails to produce the kinds of transfer to new problem-solving situations that most educators would like to see.

Illustrations of Effective Instruction

In his *Psychology for Teaching*, Lefrancois (1982) begins with a story that provides a powerful illustration of the importance of education. The story begins with an imaginary archeologist who uncovers some stone tablets in a cave. The tablets tell the story of Oog.

> Oog writes that it occurred to him that a great many children of the People did not know very much. They did not know that they should walk on the top of the hills where their scent would be carried away into the skies; rather than at the bottom where the scent would find its way to the beasts that lie on the hillsides. They did not know that the huge Bela snake hides among the branches of the Kula berry bushes, not because the snake likes the berries, but because he likes the children. Of this they were ignorant, even as they were ignorant of the skills required to fashion the houses of the People so that the rain would not come in, and of a thousand other things that the People should know. (p. 5)

The story continues with an account of how Oog became a teacher and taught the People, and of how the People flourished because of the information they learned.

Lefrancois' story about Oog is fiction. Nevertheless, it helps us appreciate the importance of education. In today's terminology, it illustrates some basic ways in which "information is power." We can imagine that people in Oog's time would go out of their way to acquire the information he supplied because it was so important for them; it empowered them to achieve important goals such as avoiding dangerous animals, protecting their children, and building effective shelter. Under conditions such as these, the teacher is revered.

An Analogy to the Oog story

An analog to the fictitious Oog story involves a true story about astronomers who lived in the 1600s. They were struggling to understand the nature of the stars and the planets. In order to achieve these goals they were frequently required to work with extremely large numbers. When these numbers had to be multiplied and divided, the calculational complexities were immense.

Imagine how the astronomers felt when they first learned about the new mathematical invention called *logarithms*. They were elated. The relevance of this information to problems that concerned them were clear. In 1624, the English mathematician Henry Briggs wrote the following:

> Logarithms are numbers invented for the more easy working of questions in arithmetic and geometry. By them all troublesome multiplications are avoided and performed only by addition. . . . In a word, all questions not only in arithmetic and geometry but in astronomy also are thereby most plainly and easily answered.

Like Oog's students, the astronomers actively sought particular types of knowledge because it had direct relevance for important problems—problems that they experienced daily and that were important to them.

Illustrations of Less Effective Instruction

In many educational settings there is an absence of features that were present in the case of Oog and of the astronomers. In particular, students often have not had the opportunity to experience the types of problems that are rendered solvable by the knowledge we teach them. They treat the knowledge as ends rather than as a means to important ends.

Sherwood, Kinzer, Hasselbring, and Bransford (1987) asked college students to explain how knowledge of logarithms might make it easier to solve problems. Why were they invented, and what good do they do? The vast majority of the students had no idea of the uses for logarithms. They remembered learning them in school but they thought of them only as math exercises that one did in order to find answers to logarithm problems. They treated them as difficult ends to be tolerated rather than as exciting inventions that allowed a variety of problems to be solved.

There are hundreds of additional cases in which information is understood as ends rather than as tools for effective problem solving. In algebra, many students fail to appreciate the power of using variables to prove that various principles apply to all cases and not just a few cases (e.g., see Bransford, Hasselbring et al., 1988). In science, students often do not appreciate how new concepts and theories can render perplexing problems solvable and make previously puzzling sets of data cohere (e.g., Hanson, 1970; Sherwood, Kinzer, Bransford, & Franks, 1987). In the humanities, students often fail to see how sets of classic writings provide important perspectives on current problems. The common denominator in all these cases is that new information is treated as facts to be learned rather than as knowledge to be used.

SOME CONSEQUENCES OF ACQUIRING
INFORMATION AS FACTS VERSUS TOOLS

It is useful to explore some of the disadvantages of educational experiences that encourage the acquisition of mere factual content rather than tools for problem solving. A major disadvantage is that information stored as facts often is not spontaneously used to solve problems. Instead, as Whitehead (1929) suggested many years ago, the knowledge will remain inert.

In educational settings, failures to access and use potentially relevant information result in failures to transfer. Bereiter (1984) described an excellent case in point. He discussed a teacher of educational psychology who gave her students a long, difficult article to read. The students were told that they had 10 minutes to learn as much about the article as they could. Almost without exception, the students adopted a familiar strategy: They began with the first sentence of the article and read as far as they could until the time was up.

Later, the students were asked to discuss their strategies. All acknowledged that they knew better than to simply begin reading the article. They had all had classes that taught them to skim for main ideas, read main headings, and so forth. However, they did not spontaneously think to use this knowledge when asked to perform the reading task.

In recent years, a number of researchers have begun to explore the inert knowledge problem by using laboratory experiments that allow effective control over a variety of variables. Examples include Asch (1969); Brown (1986); Gick and Holyoak (1980, 1983); Ross (1984); Stein, Way, Benningfield, and Hedgecough (1986); and Weisberg, DiCamillo, and Phillips (1978). Limited space precludes exploring all of these studies in detail, but we can illustrate the nature of their findings by considering some work conducted at Vanderbilt.

In a series of experiments, Perfetto, Bransford, and Franks (1983) asked college students to solve word puzzles such as the following:

1. Uriah Fuller, the famous Israeli superpsychic, can tell you the score of any baseball game before the game starts. What is his secret?
2. A man living in a small town in the U.S. married 20 different women in the same town. All are still living and he has never divorced one of them. Yet, he has broken the law. Can you explain?

Subjects in baseline groups simply saw the problems and were asked to solve them. Across several studies, performance in these groups was poor, ranging from 18% to 25% correct. Experimental subjects were provided with answers to the problems before trying to solve them. For example, during the *acquisition* phase that began the experiment, subjects rated the general truthfulness of statements such as:

1. A minister marries several people each week.
2. Before it starts the score of any game is 0 to 0.

Experimental subjects who were then given problems to solve and informed of the relevance of the previous acquisition information performed quite well. In Perfetto et al. (1983) they averaged around 80% correct.

For our purposes, the most important data involve subjects who received the correct answers during acquisition but were not explicitly informed that these answers were relevant for problem solving. Initially, it seemed obvious to Perfetto et al. that these subjects would use the acquisition statements as clues because they were closely related to the subsequent problems. Much to their surprise, the problem-solving performance of subjects in this uninformed group was not significantly better than the performance of baseline subjects. In short, relevant knowledge was available to the uninformed subjects but this knowledge remained inert. The other researchers mentioned earlier have found similar examples of failures to utilize available and potentially valuable knowledge when subjects are not explicitly informed about its relevance for a particular task.

Transforming Facts Into Conceptual Tools

Differences between information as facts and information as tools are illustrated by an experiment conducted by Adams et al. (in press). These researchers compared two different types of acquisition conditions. One involved a repetition of conditions used in the previously described study by Perfetto et al. Recall that, in the Perfetto study, uninformed subjects rated acquisition statements such as "The score of a game before it begins is 0 to 0" or "A minister may marry several people each week" for their plausibility prior to seeing the verbal puzzles.

In the second acquisition condition, Adams and colleagues changed the structure of the clue statements so that they evoked a simple problem-solving process. Thus, subjects heard statements such as "It is easy to predict the score of any game before it begins; the score is 0 to 0." and "It is common to marry several people each week; if you are a minister." The goal was to first help students experience a problem (e.g., "It doesn't seem easy to me to predict the score of games"). Students were then able to experience how information functioned as a tool that enabled them to solve each problem (e.g., "Oh, I see, I'm suppose to predict the beginning score of the game, not the final score").

Subjects who received the problem-oriented acquisition statements were much more likely to use this information during uninformed problem solving than were subjects who initially received the simple factual statements. The format of allowing participants to first experience a problem and then see how information permitted a solution to that problem resulted in greater spontaneous use of relevant information in new problem-solving settings. In subsequent work reported by Adams et al. (in press), data indicated that this effect was knowledge specific rather than the result of a general set effect such as "catching on" to the structure of the experimental task.

A THEORETICAL FRAMEWORK THAT EMPHASIZES CONDITIONALIZED KNOWLEDGE

In his article on problem solving and instruction, Simon (1980) provided a theoretical framework that is useful for thinking about the issue of access failures and for clarifying what it means to acquire knowledge as tools. Simon argued that the knowledge representation underlying competent performance in any domain is not based on simple facts or verbal propositions but is instead based on productions. Productions involve "condition-action pairs that specify that if a certain state occurs . . . , then particular mental (and possibly physical) actions should take place" (Anderson, 1987, p. 193). Productions thus provide information about the critical features of problem situations that make particular actions relevant. Knowledge-based theorists such as Newell and Simon (1972) and Anderson (1983, 1987) provide important insights into the need to help people conditionalize their knowledge—to acquire knowledge in the form of condition-action pairs mediated by appropriate goal-oriented hierarchies rather than as isolated facts.

Simon noted that many forms of instruction do not help students conditionalize their knowledge. For example, he argued that "textbooks are much more explicit in enunciating the laws of mathematics or of nature than in saying anything about when these laws may be useful in solving problems" (p. 92). It is left largely to the student to generate the condition-action pairs required for solving novel problems. Thus, students may learn the definition of statistical concepts such as "mean," "median," and "mode" and learn how to compute them. This knowledge is important, but it provides no guarantee that students will know if a particular statistic is the most appropriate one to use.

As a similar example, imagine that a person learns proverbs such as "Too many cooks spoil the broth" and "Many hands make light work." Knowledge of these proverbs is quite different from knowing when each is most applicable. Indeed, when they are taken out of context many proverbs seem to contradict one another (e.g., Bransford & Stein, 1984). Wise individuals have conditionalized this knowledge. For example, they know when each proverb is applicable and when it is not.

The concept of production systems can clarify the results found in the previously discussed experiment by Perfetto and colleagues (1983). Recall that, in their studies, participants were first asked to rate the general truthfulness of a variety of clue statements such as "Before it is played the score of any game is 0 to 0." This processing activity presumably resulted in the encoding of these sentences in the form of condition-action pairs. However, these pairs were not helpful for later, uninformed problem solving.

As an illustration of the preceding argument, consider the goal of specifying the general truthfulness of "Before it is played, the score of any game is 0 to 0." Given this goal, an appropriate action is to retrieve general information about games from memory and to check to see if they all begin with no score. This type of condition-action pairing is very different from what is needed to solve the superpsychic problem under uninformed conditions. In contrast, for the informed problem-solving condition, the instructions specify the goal of using what was just learned to solve the problems. Under these circumstances, subjects have an opportunity to first reconstruct their initial learning context and then find the relevant answers for each problem that they see.

The concept of production systems can also clarify why Adams and her colleagues did find spontaneous access when they presented information in a problem-oriented rather than a factual format. Consider problem-oriented statements such as: "It is easy to predict the score of any game before it begins; the score is 0 to 0"; "It is commonplace to marry several people each week, if you are a minister." Subjects who received information in this form may have generated productions such as "Given the goal of predicting the score of any game, check to see whether the problem involves the initial score rather than the final score." or "Given the goal of understanding why it might be commonplace to marry several times per week, check to see if the interpretation of marry can be 'conduct a marriage ceremony' rather than 'get married.' " If subjects tended to form these problem-specific productions, this would account for the findings that, when factual versus problem-oriented statements are manipulated as a within-subjects variable, access is facilitated only for those problems whose initial answers appeared in a problem-solving format (see Adams et al., in press). In general, the way in which individual concepts and theories are initially learned seems to play an important role in the degree to which this information is used later on.

Perceiving the Value of Information

It is also useful to see how problem-oriented acquisition helps students appreciate the value of information. Imagine that college students are asked to rate a series of statements on a scale of 1 to 7, where 1 stands for information that "is not useful—I knew it already" and 7 stands for information that "is extremely useful." Assume that the statements to be rated mirror the acquisition information provided in the original experiments conducted by Perfetto and colleagues (1983). For example,

1. Before it begins, the score of any game is 0 to 0.
2. A minister may marry several people each week.

As you can imagine, students who see these statements in isolation do not rate them as useful. They knew the information before entering the experiment so it seems of little use.

Contrast the preceding situation with the ratings from students who have first tried to solve problems such as the superpsychic problem and the marriage problem. They are unable to solve most of these problems, so the introduction of relevant information (e.g., "The score of games before they begin is 0 to 0") provides an insight into problem solving. These students rate the experimentally provided information as extremely useful. They knew the information before entering the experiment but had not accessed it when it was needed. When it helped them solve problems, the information was valued rather than dismissed as "something I already knew."

There are many everyday examples in which the information presented often seems "old" and even "trite." For example, on a videotape designed to help teachers teach thinking, an expert teacher advised that one should "pay attention to the children and listen to their thoughts on various subjects." Everybody knows that this can be important to do, so it is easy to perceive the information as "trite."

As previously noted, there are large differences between knowing something and spontaneously thinking to do it or use it when one is engaged in an actual problem-solving situation. For example, information about listening to children can be perceived as insightful when a student teacher is receiving feedback about a lesson in which he or she did much too much lecturing and not enough listening. Under these conditions, people are able to compare what they did spontaneously with what they might have done had they acted from the perspective suggested by others. This comparison allows people to experience changes in their perception and comprehension of situations and hence increased the likelihood they will value the new perspectives.

Summary of Relationships Between Facts and Access

Our discussion so far has emphasized that, in many instructional settings, students acquire only facts rather than acquire tools for problem solving. They often have not experienced the kinds of problems that make information relevant and useful, so they do not understand the value of this information for problem solving. They therefore fail to conditionalize their knowledge in ways that specify when information should be used. To return to an earlier example, imagine telling students that they will win prizes depending on the number of large-number multiplication problems they can complete in 1 hour. They cannot take a computer, calculator, or slide rule with them, but they can take anything else. Most of the students interviewed by Sherwood, Kinzer, Hasselbring, and Bransford (1987) will never think to take tables of logarithms. Because they do not understand the functions of logarithms, they will fail to use this concept to solve problems. Their knowledge of logarithms will remain inert.

THE CONCEPT OF ANCHORED INSTRUCTION

Our goal in this section is to discuss a model for instruction that we call *anchored instruction*. The model is designed to help students develop useful knowledge rather than inert knowledge. At the heart of the model is an emphasis on the importance of creating an anchor or focus that generates interest and enables students to identify and define problems and to pay attention to their own perception and comprehension of these problems. They can then be introduced to information that is relevant to their anchored perceptions. The major goal of anchored instruction is to enable students to notice critical features of problem situations and to experience the changes in their perception and understanding of the anchor as they view the situation from new points of view.

Varieties of Anchors

Anchored instruction begins with a focal event or problem situation that provides an anchor for students' perceptions and comprehension. Ideally, the anchor will be intrinsically interesting and will enable students to deal with a general goal (e.g., planning a trip to the South American jungle, improving the efficiency of a business) that involves a variety of related subproblems and subgoals. Effective anchors should also help students notice the features of problem situations that make particular actions relevant. For example, imagine creating a general problem-solving context that always requires the calculation of the perimeter of areas of land. Students could learn to perform well in this context yet fail to differentiate the conditions that require information about perimeters from those that require information about the area of various land segments. In order to appropriately conditionalize their knowledge, the anchors for instruction must help students focus on the relevant features of the problems that they are trying to solve.

Case-based approaches to instruction provide one illustration of anchored instruction. They have been used in business schools for some time, and for many of the reasons that were discussed earlier. In 1940, Gragg lamented that traditional forms of instruction failed to prepare business students for action. The students knew a lot of facts and concepts but failed to use them to make effective business decisions. In case-based approaches, students first begin with cases that represent problems-to-be-solved. As they are introduced to new concepts and frames for thinking, they see the effects of this information on the problems they confront.

Programs such as Lipman's (1985) "Philosophy for Children" and Wales and Stager's (1977) "Guided Design" are also excellent illustrations of anchored instruction. Lipman's program is centered around novels involving children who encounter a number of problems in their everyday lives and at school. They learn to use a variety of methods from philosophy for exploring these problems. In "Guided Design," students are introduced to interesting problems plus a general framework for solving problems. Students generate their own strategies for solving the problems and then work with others to develop a group consensus. Each group's solution is then compared to the strategies used by experts in particular domains.

In these programs, the focal events or anchors are almost always presented in a verbal format. This format is fine for a number of purposes. However, there are also advantages of providing video-based anchors rather than relying on a purely verbal mode.

One advantage of using video-based anchors is that they contain much richer sources of information than are available in the printed media. Gestures, affective states, scenes of towns, music, and so on always accompany the dialogue. Therefore, there is much more to notice than is true for books. This increase in opportunities for noticing is especially important for increasing the possibility of finding relevant issues that are embedded in the movie— it provides an opportunity to encourage problem finding and problem representation (e.g., Bransford & Stein, 1984) rather than to always provide pre-set problems to students. In addition, the richness of information to be noticed increases the opportunity to help students appreciate how their perception and comprehension change as they are helped to view the video from multiple points of view.

A second advantage of using video-based anchors is closely related to the first. Often, the ability to perceive dynamic, moving events facilitates comprehension. Young children may need to see waves and strong winds in order to deeply understand these concepts; older students may be helped by viewing moving scenes that illustrate acceleration versus constant velocity. A recent study conducted by Johnson (1987) provided a powerful illustration of the advantages of video versus purely verbal forms of information transmission. He worked with young 4- and 5-year-old students from the inner city who teachers felt were at risk for school failure because of a lack of language skills and other preschool experiences. Some of the students were instructed in a verbal format; others were instructed in the context of video stored on videodiscs. The video-based instruction resulted in much greater retelling scores and comprehension scores than did the instruction that was conducted in verbal form.

A third advantage of using video is related to our previous discussion of the importance of conditionalizing one's knowledge. Without knowledge of the appropriate "triggering conditions," relevant knowledge will not be accessed and applied. Simon (1980) noted that, often, our educational systems fail to develop the pattern recognition abilities necessary to specify the condition side of condition action pairings. It is often difficult to develop skills of pattern recognition when one teaches in a primarily verbal mode.

As an illustration of the preceding argument, imagine a student in clinical psychology who learns to diagnose based on verbal descriptions such as "The client is *slightly anxious, mildly defensive*," and so on. Verbal labels such as "slightly anxious" and "mildly defensive" represent the output of an expert's pattern recognition processes. If students do not develop similar skills of pattern recognition, their ability to diagnose based on verbal labels will be of little use in the real world environment. Here, pattern recognition depends on visual and auditory cues rather than on already labelled events (see Bransford, Franks, Vye, & Sherwood, 1986; Bransford, Sherwood, & Hasselbring, in press).

The advantages of using video are enhanced by the capabilities of videodisc technology. In this format, each of the 54,000 frames that make up the 30 minutes of video on one side of a disc has a unique number and can be located in seconds (compared to the extremely slow and cumbersome methods of access available on videotape). Frames can be played in slow motion or frozen clearly for detailed study so that students can take advantage of this rich source of information, or the video can be scanned rapidly looking for important events (these features were previously available on only the most expensive videotape players). This ease of access to any part of the video changes its function, from a linear element used to introduce or enhance instruction to an integral resource that can be explored and analyzed in detail. Teachers can locate and replay scenes in order to illustrate particular points or to invite class discussion. Segments of video that are not contiguous can be easily juxtaposed and contrasted to develop pattern recognition skills. This type of access can be accomplished using only a videodisc player and a simple hand-held remote control device, an inexpensive system comparable in price to an ordinary videotape player.

Computers can also be used to control videodisc players. With a word processor, a teacher can build a database that includes a descriptive name and frame numbers for every segment on a disc. Then using simple programs such as one developed at Vanderbilt, segments can be accessed randomly by name. Computer control provides faster, more error-free access than hand-held remote control, allowing a teacher to catalog and store many illustrations in advance and retrieve them in any order. Authoring software such as HANDY, an experimental language developed at IBM's Thomas J. Watson Research Center and PRODUCER developed at Vanderbilt are designed especially to be used by students. Using this software, students can create their own productions by choosing segments of video and overlaying computer generated graphics and text on the video.

Scores of productions are not available on videodisc at a reasonable cost (major movies and plays are often less expensive than the videotape version). We should also note that it is legal to use existing video as long as (a) one buys it rather than rents it, and (b) one uses it for educational purposes rather than for pure entertainment (Becker, 1985).

INITIAL STUDIES OF ANCHORED INSTRUCTION

During the past several years, we have conducted a number of studies that were designed to explore aspects of the concept of anchored instruction. Our initial work made use of existing video segments from *Raiders of the Lost Ark*, *Swiss Family Robinson*, and so forth. Recently, we have begun to produce our own video in order to create anchors that facilitate students' abilities to learn.

Anchors for Facilitating Mathematical Problem Solving

Consider first a study involving mathematical problem solving. This work was motivated by a concern with traditional approaches to instruction in this area. In particular, it is commonplace to assume that instruction in solving word problems involves instruction in problem solving, and it does to some extent. Nevertheless, the word problems tend to be treated as ends-in-themselves rather than as means to more general ends.

Figures 5.1a and 5.1b illustrate two different types of relationship between word problems and problem solving. In Fig. 5.1a, the relationship between "mathematics" and problem solving is one of set to subset. Figure 5.1b illustrates a different relationship. Here, mathematical thinking is viewed as an important component of general problem-solving skills.

We believe that both sets of relationships depicted in Fig. 5.1 are important. However, those depicted in Fig. 5.1b are especially relevant because they focus on the goal of helping students understand the function of mathematical tools for simplifying problem solving. As noted earlier, students often do not view mathematical concepts from this perspective. They see them as

A.   PROBLEMS AS ENDS IN-AND-OF-THEMSELVES

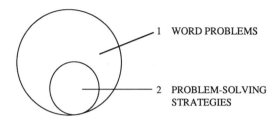

1   WORD PROBLEMS

2   PROBLEM-SOLVING
    STRATEGIES

B.   PROBLEMS AS MEANS TO LARGER ENDS

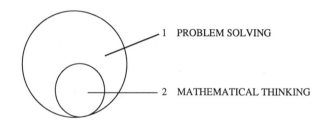

1   PROBLEM SOLVING

2   MATHEMATICAL THINKING

FIG. 5.1.   Different approaches to teaching word problems.

facts and procedures that have to be learned rather than as exciting inventions that make problems easier to solve.

It is useful to consider how approaches to teaching word problems might differ if one emphasized the relationships depicted in Fig. 5.1a and 5.1b. As an illustration of Fig. 5.1, imagine that students receive word problems such as the following in math class:

> A waterboy for a softball team brings 1 quart of water for each player. If there are 9 players, and each quart of water weighs 2 pounds, what is the total weight of the water?

It seems clear that the ability to answer this word problem requires problem solving. The relationship between the problem and problem-solving skills is the one illustrated in Fig. 5.1a. We argue that, in this approach, problem solving is emphasized only in a restricted sense.

In order for Fig. 5.1b to become applicable, individual word problems would need to be incorporated into a larger context that provides richer experiences with problem solving. In our studies, we used the first 10 minutes of *Raiders of the Lost Ark* (e.g., Bransford et al., 1988). It provides an excellent anchor for teaching mathematical thinking. In this segment, Indiana Jones goes to South America in the hopes of finding a golden idol. A lesson using this segment could focus on the idea of planning for a trip to the South American jungle that is similar to the trip taken by Indiana Jones. In order to plan for the trip, students need to anticipate problems that they might encounter. In short, one can help them generate word problems that they need to solve.

Our work with fifth- and sixth-grade students (all were at least 1 year behind their peers in mathematics achievement) involved the following goal: Assume that we want to return to the jungle to explore the region or to get the golden gong that Indiana left behind. If so, it could be important to know dimensions of obstacles such as the size of the pit one would have to jump, the height of the cave, the width of the river and its relationship to the size of the seaplane, and so on. Because this information is on film, it does no good to measure sizes directly (e.g., the pit is only several inches wide on the screen). However, one can use known standards (e.g., Indiana Jones) to estimate sizes and distances that are important to know.

The general goal of learning more about important dimensions of potential obstacles and events guided the selection of mathematically oriented problems that were based on scenes from the 10-minute movie segment. Through the use of random access videodisc we were able to isolate and quickly access the sequence of frames that specified each problem situation. For example, at one point Indiana comes to a pit and must attempt to get over it. He jumps. How wide is the pit? Could humans possibly jump something that wide?

The width of the pit can be estimated by finding another, earlier scene where Indiana uses his bullwhip to swing over the pit. By freezing the frame of the video we are able to show a scene of Indiana swinging and extending halfway across the pit. Measurement on the screen (either by hand or through the use of computer graphics) allows students to see that the pit is two Indiana's wide. If Indiana is 6 feet tall, the pit is 12 feet wide. Students can be helped to determine this information for themselves and, subsequently, to see if they could jump something that was 12 feet wide.

In our initial studies, the problems that we worked with involved finding the length or width of an object given its proportional relationship to a standard with a known length or width. Our aim was to facilitate children's comprehension of the problem situations and thereby improve their motivation to solve various problems plus increase their understanding of the relationships between the known and unknown quantities expressed in the problems. The use of the video provided an especially rich macro-context from which to begin. The video was supplemented with effective teaching (mediation). For example, students were encouraged to create visual and symbolic representations of problems, and they received individualized feedback about the strengths and weaknesses of their approach to each problem. All instruction was one-on-one.

Effects of learning in the video context were compared to the effects of learning in a control condition in which students received teaching that was similar in format but more individualized than the teaching they received in school. For example, in one-on-one sessions that included a great deal of encouragement, students in the control group worked on problems and were shown correct solution strategies after attempting to solve each problem. They therefore received more attention and more immediate feedback than they received in class.

Overall, the results of our mathematics study were very encouraging. Students in the control condition showed very little improvement. In contrast, those who received the anchored instruction showed a great deal of change. They improved not only on problems that referred to the Indiana Jones context; they improved on out-of-context problems as well. In addition, in several instances we observed students who had received the video-based instruction spontaneously using what they had learned in class to better understand events in their everyday environment; they used themselves and their friends to estimate the height of buildings, trees, and the like. In these instances, students were spontaneously defining their own problems and using knowledge that they had acquired in class.

Anchors for Science Instruction

A study conducted by Sherwood, Kinzer, Bransford, and Franks (1987) demonstrates some advantages of anchored instruction in the domain of science teaching. As in the mathematics study, the video-based anchor involved the first 10 minutes of *Raiders of the Lost Ark*. The materials consisted of 13 short passages that might be encountered in middle and high school science classes. Examples included topics such as (a) kinds of high carbohydrate foods that are healthy versus less healthy; (b) the use of water as a standard for measuring the weight of liquids (e.g., "A pint of water is a pound the world around") and as a standard for measuring the density of other liquids; (c) the density of metals such as gold, lead, and so forth; (d) ways to make a bronze-age lamp from clay and olive oil.

College students in one condition simply read about each of the 13 topics with the intent to remember the information. Those in the second condition read the same information, but in the context of problems that might be encountered during Indiana Jones' trip to the South American jungle. For example, students in the second condition were first asked to consider the kinds of foods one should bring on a trip, and then asked to read the passage about different types of high carbohydrate foods. Similar introductions were used with the other passages. The goal of this type of presentation was to help students understand some of the kinds of problems that the science information could help them solve.

Following acquisition, all participants received one of two types of tests. One half of the students in each group were simply asked to recall the topics of the passages that they had just read. As expected, students who learned in the context of the trip to South America were able to remember a greater number of topics than were students in the no-context group.

The remaining half of the students in each group received a test designed to assess whether they would spontaneously use information that they had just read to solve a new problem. The test they received was disguised as a filler task to be completed before memory questions would be asked about the previously read topics. Students were asked to imagine that they were planning a journey to a desert area in the Western part of the United States in order to search for relics in Pueblo caves. They were asked to suggest at least 10 areas of information and to be as explicit as possible (e.g., instead of just answering "you would need food and supplies" they were asked to describe the kinds of food and supplies).

The results indicated large differences in students' spontaneous use of information. Students who had simply read facts almost never mentioned specific information about the material they had read. Their answers tended to be quite general. However, students in the second acquisition condition made excellent use of the information they had just read. For example, when discussing food, most of them focused on the importance of its nutritional contents. Overall, students who received information in the context of problem solving were much more likely to remember what they read and to spontaneously use it as a basis for creating new sets of plans. Similar results on the recall of science information were found with seventh- and eight-grade students in an earlier study (Sherwood, Kinzer, Hasselbring, & Bransford, 1987).

Additional Studies With Science Information

In a recent study, Sherwood, Kinzer, and Carrick (1987) conducted an experiment with six-grade students that was similar to the preceding experiment with college students. Six rather than 13 science passages were used, and students read them either in isolation or in the context of problems to be solved by Indiana Jones during his trip to the South American Jungle. Tests included free recall for the topics and students' abilities to say why the science information was useful to know.

Students in the anchored instruction group recalled an average of 3.94 topics compared to 3.67 for those in the isolated reading conditions. These differences were not significant, in part we think because there were too few topics to be helped by the advantage of the retrieval context (in contrast, in the college study we used 13 topics). In addition, many of the sixth graders may not have spontaneously used the memory strategies necessary to use the video segment as a complex set of retrieval cues (see Adams, 1985, for a discussion of retrieval strategies).

The most important part of the study with the sixth graders involved the students' abilities to state how various types of science information might be useful to them. Students in the anchored instruction group were much better in this test (mean number of uses: 4.72) than were students who received the traditional approach to instruction (mean number of uses: 1.72). An example answer of a student in the anchored instruction group to the question of why the weight of liquids is important was "If you go on a hiking trip and carried water with you, you would need to know how much you can carry." We argued earlier than the opportunity to view information as means to important ends helps students learn about the conditions under which knowledge is useful (Simon, 1980). This increases the chances of spontaneously using that knowledge to solve new problems that are confronted later on.

Students as Producers of Knowledge

In the preceding discussion we focused on situations in which we as teachers helped students identify and define important problems. An important part of problem solving involves the ability to identify and define one's own problems (e.g., Bransford & Stein, 1984; Sternberg, 1985). These aspects of problem solving are often overlooked in schools, in part because they are difficult to teach.

Computer programs such as IBM's HANDY and the Vanderbilt Learning Technology Center's PRODUCER provide an opportunity for students to create their own products that combine text-plus-video images. The computer programs are very easy to learn and use.

In our work with middle school students in Nashville (e.g., Sturdevant, Johnson, Kinzer, & Bransford, 1987), we find that the creation of computer-plus videodisc products is highly motivating to students. One reason is that the products are professional looking because they include high-quality video from professionally made videodiscs. This increases the interest of the audience, which in turn increases the quality of their feedback with respect to product quality. Students therefore take a great deal of interest in creating products that are of high quality.

One product created by three fifth-grade girls was called "Snake Shop." It was a very creative "advertisement" for a mythical snake shop that the girls supposedly owned. In producing the computer-plus-videodisc product the girls had to find appropriate scenes of snakes (they used scenes from the *Raiders of the Lost Ark* segment where the ark is found in a tomb containing snakes), as well as create written text to go with the scenes. The final product is a very engaging production that humorously describes the snakes in their shop, how to take care of a snake from the shop, and how they will package and deliver the snake.

The preceding example of a student-produced product involved a creative story. Teachers can also focus the assignments so that students' products are related to particular academic content. In this way, students can learn information in their texts and readings while combining this information in a way that is unique. For example, in one of our studies students created a program about light. By using segments from the movie *Star Wars* they were able to illustrate some important concepts about light (e.g. that our sun is a star that gives off light). Although this fact could be read in a science text book, the use of a very short video segment, tied with text, appears to make the learning of this type of information more meaningful and interesting for the students who produced the video and for the other students who watch the production.

DESIGNS FOR THE FUTURE

We are currently beginning to work on several different projects that are based on the concept of anchored instruction. All involve the use of computers and videodiscs.

A major goal of our projects is to provide conceptual anchors that enhance motivation to learn and permit students to integrate information across traditional subject areas. This emphasis on integrating knowledge seems to be particularly important. In middle school and high school, students take separate courses in mathematics, science, history, social studies, and so forth. In college, even students studying the liberal arts tend to develop encapsulated knowledge because their philosophy courses involve one set of examples, their science courses involve other examples, their literature course involve still other examples. In everyday problem solving, we often need a combination of knowledge from areas such as history, literature, science, philosophy. Traditional ways of teaching seem to make a great deal of potentially relevant knowledge inert.

The Young Sherlock Project

Several of our current projects begin with anchors that involve films that are available on videodisc. Risko, Kinzer, Vye, Barron, and Williams are heading a project based on *The Young Sherlock Holmes*. Just as Sherlock is a master at attending to significant details in order to solve crimes, students in this middle school project are encouraged to "play Sherlock" and check the details of the Sherlock movie for authenticity. Students will then use either PRODUCER or HANDY to provide presentations for other class members and other classes as well.

Early in the Sherlock film, a young Watson notes that he is in London in December in the middle of the Victorian Era. This 10- second scene contains a number of clues that students can explore in more detail. For example, where is London? (Ideally all middle school students know, but unfortunately many do not.) Does it really snow in London, and if so, does it snow in December? (Students can read the geography sections of many of their texts to find out about climate.) What was the Victorian Era and when was its height? (This brings in relevant information about history.) Assuming that the date is the 1880s to 1890s, is it accurate for Watson to be riding in a horse-drawn carriage rather than using other transportation such as a car?

Other scenes invite inquiry into the nature of dress in England in the 1880s, the type of lighting (when was electric lighting invented?), the types of schools (Watson attends a boarding school). Still other scenes show a pedal-powered airplane (clearly a fantasy but a nice prompt for reading about the history of aviation plus about modern pedal-powered planes), a chemistry lesson (which according to our expert is factually and historically accurate), a gym class that involves fencing, scenes just outside of London that involve mountains, and so forth. The movie provides a wealth of issues that can be explored.

By looking for interesting issues, students should learn to find and define their own problems. And once they have identified particular issues, the students should develop important information finding skills (including ways to use computer-based databases) plus presentation skills. Eventually, we hope to help these students bridge from England at the turn of the century to other places such as New York City in the 1890s (this is recreated with considerable accuracy in the movie *Hello Dolly*), the western part of the United States (the movie *Oklahoma* provides interesting turn-of-the-century information), and other areas of the world. With strong historical anchors that link events around the world in a very vivid manner, we think that students' abilities to integrate knowledge within a historical perspective will be considerably enhanced.[1]

---

[1]For more recent and detailed information on the *Young Sherlock Holmes* project, see Bransford (1988); Bransford, Vye, Kinzer, and Risko (in press); Risko, Kinzer, Goodman, McLarty, Dupree, and Martin (1989).

The Multidisciplinary Thinking Project

A second project that we are developing involves college students. Recent books by Bloom (1987) and Hirsch (1987) argue that today's students are not aware of important ideas and concepts that come from the study of history and literature. People often assume that this type of information is taught in schools and that students acquire it in ways that enable them to adopt a variety of informed perspectives on problems they may encounter later in life. For example, most people would agree that instructors in the natural sciences, the social sciences and the humanities introduce students to powerful ideas that have the potential to guide decisions and set the stage for lifelong learning. Ideally, students are exposed to ideas from all three of these areas rather than from only one or two of them. Breadth as well as depth of knowledge is important for making decisions that are wise and just (this is a major argument for the value of a liberal arts education).

Currently, most students who take courses in the humanities, social sciences, and physical sciences learn about each area as a separate entity. They rarely have the opportunity to apply ideas from one area to a problem that is also being addressed from the perspective of the other areas. Students therefore lack a common ground for comparing the effects of adopting different perspectives. Because of the specialized nature of their training, most college professors share a similar fate.

As it is currently planned, our college project will be organized around a classic movie: *The Third Man*. It is an exceptionally well-produced movie that illustrates a variety of issues that can be approached from many perspectives. It is also available on videodisc.

Students' understanding of *The Third Man* can be enriched by drawing on information from a number of different areas. For example, it takes place in Vienna after World War II. Why is Vienna occupied by so many different countries? The history of World War II is relevant here.

The movie also provides many illustrations of how the Austrians dealt in black market activities plus other activities that they would probably not engage in under normal circumstances. Information about economics is relevant here. So is information about psychological research on people's behavior as a function of social pressure.

Scores of additional issues can be found in the movie. What kinds of technology were available to build Vienna initially and to rebuild it after the war? Who managed the rebuilding task? How important was the discovery of new drugs such as penicillin to people's lives, and what kinds of attempts were made to protect the quality control of the drugs (the film focuses on the scheme of Harry, one of its main characters, to get rich by selling diluted penicillin). How might one analyze Harry's ethics when he notes that the war killed so many individuals that a few more won't matter, and what does one say about Harry's friend who, in the end, kills Harry? What were the special types of filming techniques used to give the movie its disturbing quality? These are just some of the issues that could be explored from the perspective of the humanities and the social and natural sciences. There are many more.

In our initial project we plan to focus on seven different areas:

1. philosophy (including classical concepts of "the good life"),
2. history,
3. science and technology,
4. psychology,
5. sociology,
6. the performing arts and the film media, and
7. literature.

The model course will be conducted as a one-semester seminar and will be overseen by one or two faculty members. Groups of two to four students will choose one of the seven areas of focus just noted and, by working with designated professors, will become the resident experts in their respective areas. They will then share their expertise with the rest of the class.

Each of the seven "designated faculty" members who work with a group of students will have access to a videotape of the focal events (e.g., *The Third Man*). The students in the seminar will also have seen the movie so they and the faculty member will begin with a common ground.

Through a series of meetings, the students and the faculty expert will identify potential issues. Students will be helped to find references that they can consult in order to prepare a presentation for the rest of the class. Each "designated faculty" member will be present for his or her group's presentation to the class. Students will be encouraged to use videodiscs to enhance their presentations (videodisc players and videodiscs will be made available to students throughout the semester). Presentations will also be videotaped for future use.

Students in the class will not begin immediately to work with designated faculty experts. Instead, they will be encouraged to articulate their own perspective on the movie so that they are better able to appreciate ways their personal viewpoints can be enriched. Several activities are anticipated that should help this comparison process.

First, after viewing the movie students will be asked to write a paper that describes the major issues that they noticed.

Second, students will compare their perspectives on the movie with the perspectives of other students in their class.

Third, the students in the class will be helped to choose one of the seven "specialty areas" and to compare their perspective with the appropriate resident professor.

Fourth, students will be able to compare the perspective gained from the area in which they have become a resident expert with the perspective from other areas as discussed by the classmates. They will also be asked to write critiques of other groups' presentations, and individual critiques will be shared as a group.

Fifth, the class as a whole will attempt to forge a synthesized perspective that provides the basis for a class presentation that will be videotaped and can eventually be shared with other classes and other schools.

Finally, students will be asked to prepare a final paper in which they discuss the ideas that they found most relevant. They can then compare this paper with the one they wrote at the beginning of the course and with their fellow students. Depending on time, students may also be asked to watch a movie from a different period in history and be asked to reflect on the ideas, issues and values that persist over time versus change.

The Invitations to Thinking Series

Our third project in anchored instruction involves the production of videodisc-based materials rather than the use of existing movies. The use of movies has been valuable for conducting research that has provided important information. Our Invitations to Thinking series is designed to make use of existing research to design our own video. These products will also be researched so that general design principles for anchors can be developed. Initially, we plan to create prototypes discs that are produced by simple, VHS recorders and filmed by us (amateurs). After we research our prototypes, we plan to create professional videodiscs.

The first video for our series is a river adventure. The adventure is especially designed for teaching mathematical thinking, although it can also be used to teach about a number of additional topics. The previously mentioned work with *Raiders of the Lost Ark* as an anchor for teaching mathematical thinking played a major role in the design of this disc.

The video begins with a group of students who win a contest that allows them to use a houseboat for a week. They will travel approximately 50 miles from a lake through a lock at the dam to a boat dock on the river. They will then travel back up the river and must return the boat within a week. All the video on the disc is accurate with respect to the river travel.

Students must do all the planning for the trip, including plans for water, food, gasoline. They must also tell the people at the boat dock the size and height of their boat plus the time of day they plan to arrive, the amount of time they will stay, and whether they will need water and fuel.

Included on the video are pictures of the boat the students will use, examples of another group using the boat to go down river, illustrations of charts for navigation and so forth. After seeing a video introduction, the students must determine the types of problems they need to solve in order to plan effectively. They are therefore encouraging to identify and define problems of their own (e.g., Bransford & Stein, 1984).

A number of interesting problems are relevant to this adventure. One involves learning about the boat. How long is it? How wide? How tall? Information such as this is necessary to arrange for a slip that is the right size. But the only information available is on video. The video about the boat includes scenes of a person who is 6 feet tall either standing or lying on the deck. This information can be used to estimate dimensions of the boat (analogous to using Indiana Jones as a standard in our *Raiders'*-based adventure).

In addition to measuring length, width, and height in order to find valuable information, students also need to solve other problems. How much gasoline will the boat hold? This can be determined by measurements of the two gas tanks on the boat. The gas mileage can be calculated by information provided during the video of a river trip.

How much water can the boat hold, and how much water tends to be used during normal activities such as taking a shower, washing dishes, drinking a glass of water, and so on? The water tank is not visible so it cannot be measured directly. However, one can use other strategies such as timing the number of seconds to use a hose to fill one gallon of water, and then timing the total fill time for the tank. Data are also provided about typical uses of water. Thus, a shower on the boat takes a gallon of water every 40 seconds, filling the sink three quarters full takes 1 gallon, drinking a glass of water takes either 9 or 12 ounces, and so forth.

There are a host of other problems that are available on the river adventure. How much gas does the canister for the gas grill hold? How much extra weight will be added when the water and gasoline tanks are filled? How does one estimate the length of the anchor rope without a ruler available? How much water does the lock hold and what is the rate of discharge in order to empty it in 11 minutes? There are a variety of problems, and the answers to them are empirically real. In addition, there are often a variety of ways to arrive at the same estimate, so that the students can use "converging operations."

Overall, the river adventure is designed to help students learn to identify, define, and solve a variety of problems that people actually have to solve in order to accomplish particular goals effectively. Ideally, the students will also develop skills and knowledge that will transfer to new situations. For example, a second adventure that we would like to create involves flying cross country. Many of the issues found in the river adventure are relevant here, but the details also include new twists. The weight of water and gasoline is much more critical for flying than being on the water, aerial maps differ from river maps, and so on. By learning the similarities and differences in a number of complex situations, students should acquire knowledge in a form that is useful rather than inert.[2]

SUMMARY AND CONCLUSIONS

Our goal in this chapter has been to discuss the concept of anchored instruction. We argued that new approaches to instruction are necessary because effective problem solving requires a great deal of specific knowledge, yet traditional forms of instruction tend to produce knowledge that remains inert.

The overall goal of our approach to anchored instruction is to overcome the inert knowledge problem by allowing students to experience changes in their perception and understanding as they are introduced to new bodies of information. Students may realize that, initially, they failed to identify important issues, failed to define them from a more fruitful perspective or failed to come up with strategies that were the most efficient and accurate. We want to help them experience the usefulness of information and treat it as means to important ends. As we have argued, this leads to a greater appreciation of the value of information plus a greater tendency to use it when it is appropriate in new situations.

We have also argued for the advantages of using video-based anchors that are on videodisc and controlled by computer. This increases the amount of information available for students to notice plus makes it possible to help students develop the pattern recognition abilities necessary to function in particular environments. Because of the ability to use video in their class presentations, students should be in a better position to learn by teaching. Furthermore, their peers should be better able to learn from the students because the presentations are clearer and more interesting to watch.

ACKNOWLEDGMENT

Research reported in this article was supported in part by grants G0083C0052 by the Office of Education, by the Army Research Institute, and by grants from the Spencer Foundation and the IBM Corporation.

---

[2]For more recent research with the *Invitations to Thinking* video series, see Cognition and Technology Group (1989); Van Haneghan, Barron, Young, Williams, Vye, and Bransford (1989); Vye, Bransford, Furman, Barron, Montavon, Young, Van Haneghan, and Barron (1989); Young, Van Haneghan, Barron, Williams, Vye, and Bransford (in press).

REFERENCES

Adams, L. T. (1985). Improving memory: Can retrieval strategies help? *Human Learning, 4*, 281–297.

Adams, L., Kasserman, J., Yearwood, A., Perfetto, G., Bransford, J., & Franks, J. (in press). The effects of facts versus problem-oriented acquisition. *Memory and Cognition*.

Anderson, J. R. (1983). *The architecture of cognition*. Cambridge, MA: Harvard University Press.

Anderson, J. R. (1987). Carnegie-Mellon University, skill acquisition: Compilation of weak-method problem solutions. *Psychological Review, 94*(2), 192–210.

Asch, S. E. (1969). A reformulation of the problem of associations. *American Psychologist, 24*, 92–102.

Becker, G. (1985, November–December). A question of copyright. *Electronic Education*, p. 19.

Bereiter, C. (1984). How to keep thinking skills from going the way of all frills. *Educational Leadership, 42*, 75–77.

Bloom, A. (1987). *The closing of the American mind*. New York: Simon & Schuster.

Bransford, J. D. (1988, December). *Designing invitations to thinking*. Paper presented to the National Reading Conference, Tucson, AZ.

Bransford, J. D., & Stein, B. S. (1984). *The IDEAL problem solver*. New York: Freeman.

Bransford, J. D., Franks, J. J., & Vye, N. J., & Sherwood, R. D. (1986, June). *New approaches to instruction: Because wisdom can't be told*. Paper presented at the Illinois Conference on Similarity and Analogy, Champaign, IL.

Bransford, J., Hasselbring, T., Barron, B., Kulewicz, S., Littlefield, J., & Goin, L. (1988). The use of macro-contexts to facilitate mathematical thinking. In R. Charles & E. Silver (Eds.), *The teaching and assessing of mathematical problem solving* (pp. 125–147). Hillsdale, NJ: Lawrence Erlbaum Associates.

Bransford, J. D., Sherwood, R. S., & Hasselbring, T. S. (1988). Effects of the video revolution on development: Some initial thoughts. In G. Forman & P. Pufall (Eds.), *Constructivism in the computer age* (pp. 173–201). Hillsdale, NJ: Lawrence Erlbaum Associates.

Bransford, J. D., Sherwood, R., Vye, N. J., & Rieser, J. (1986). Teaching thinking and problem solving: Suggestions from research. *American Psychologist, 41*(10), 1078–1089.

Bransford, J. D., Vye, N., Kinzer, C., & Risko, V. (in press). Teaching thinking and content knowledge: Toward an integrated approach. In B. F. Jones & L. Idol (Eds.), *Dimensions of thinking and cognitive instruction*. Hillsdale, NJ: Lawrence Erlbaum Associates.

Brown, A. (1989). Facilitating transfer in young children. In S. Vosniadou & A. Ortony (Eds.), *Similarity and analogical reasoning* (pp. 369–412). Cambridge: Cambridge University Press.

Cognition and Technology Group at Vanderbilt. (1989). *Anchored instruction and its relationship to situated cognition* (Tech. Rep.). Nashville, TN: Vanderbilt University, Learning Technology Center.

Feuerstein, R. (1979). *Instrumental enrichment*. Baltimore, MD: University Park.

Gick, M. L., & Holyoak, K. J. (1980). Analogical problem solving. *Cognitive Psychology, 12*, 306–365.

Gick, M. L., & Holyoak, K. J. (1983). Schema induction and analogical transfer. *Cognitive Psychology, 15*, 1–38.

Gragg, C. I. (1940, October 19). *Harvard alumni bulletin*, pp. 78–84.

Hanson, N. R. (1970). A picture theory of theory meaning. In R. G. Colodny (Ed.), *The nature and function of scientific theories* (pp. 233–274). Pittsburgh: University of Pittsburgh Press.

Hirsch, E. D. (1987). *Cultural literacy: What every American needs to know*. Boston, MA: Houghton Mifflin.

Johnson, R. (1987). *Uses of video technology to facilitate children's learning*. Unpublished manuscript, Vanderbilt University, Nashville, TN.

Lefrancois, G. R. (1982). *Psychology for teaching.* Belmont, CA: Wadsworth.

Linn, M. C. (1986). *Establishing a research base for science education: Challenges, trends, and recommendations* (Report of a National Science Foundation national conference). Berkeley, CA: University of California.

Lipman, M. (1985). Thinking skills fostered by philosophy for children. In J. Segal, S. Chipman, & R. Glaser (Eds.), *Thinking and learning skills: Relating instruction to basic research* (Vol. 1, pp. 83–108). Hillsdale, NJ: Lawrence Erlbaum Associates.

Mann, L. (1979). *On the trail of process: A historical perspective on cognitive processes and their training.* New York: Grune & Stratton.

Newell, A., & Simon, H. (1972). *Human problem solving.* Englewood Cliffs, NJ: Prentice-Hall.

Newell, A. (1980). One final word. In D. T. Tuma & F. Reif (Eds.), *Problem solving and education: Issues in teaching and research* (pp. 175–189). Englewood Cliffs, NJ: Prentice-Hall.

Perfetto, B. A., Bransford, J. D., & Franks, J. J. (1983). Constraints on access in a problem solving context. *Memory and Cognition, 11,* 24–31.

Risko, V. J., Kinzer, C. K., Goodman, J., McLarty, K., Dupree, A., & Martin, H. (1989, April). *Effects of macro-contexts on reading comprehension, composition of stories, and vocabulary development.* Paper presented at the meeting of the American Educational Research Association, San Francisco, CA.

Ross, B. H. (1984). *Remindings and their effects in learning a cognitive skill.* New York: Academic Press.

Segal, J., Chipman, S., & Glaser, R. (Eds.). (1985). *Thinking and learning skills: Relating instruction to basic research* (Vol. 1). Hillsdale, NJ: Lawrence Erlbaum Associates.

Sherwood, R. D., Kinzer, C. K., Bransford, J. D., & Franks, J. J. (1987). Some benefits of creating macro-contexts for science instruction: Initial findings. *Journal of Research in Science Teaching, 24*(5), 417–435.

Sherwood, R., Kinzer, C., & Carrick, D. (1987, April), *The use of video-based technology to develop contextually rich instruction in science.* Paper presented at the annual meeting of the National Association for Research in Science Teaching, Washington, DC.

Sherwood, R., Kinzer, C., & Hasselbring, T., & Bransford, J. (1987). Macro-contexts for learning: Initial findings and issues. *Journal of Applied Cognitive Psychology, 1,* 93–108.

Simon, H. A. (1980). Problem solving and education. In D. T. Tuma & R. Reif (Eds.), *Problem solving and education: Issues in teaching and research* (pp. 81–96). Hillsdale, NJ: Lawrence Erlbaum Associates.

Stein, B. S., Way, K. R., Benningfield, S. E., Hedgecough, C. A. (1986). *Constraints on spontaneous transfer in problem-solving tasks.* Cookeville, TN & Tampa, FL: Tennessee Technological University.

Sternberg, R. J. (1985). *Beyond I.Q.: Toward a triarchic theory of intelligence.* Cambridge, MA: Cambridge University Press.

Sturdevant, T., Johnson, R., Kinzer, C., & Bransford, J. D. (1987, April). *Students as producers.* Paper presented at the annual meeting of the American Education Research Association, San Francisco, CA.

Van Haneghan, J. P., Barron, L., Young, M. F., Williams, S. M., Vye, N. J., & Bransford, J. D. (1989). *The Jasper series: An experiment with new ways to enhance mathematical thinking* (Tech. Rep.). Nashville, TN: Vanderbilt University, Learning Technology Center.

Vye, N., Bransford, J., Furman, L., Barron, B., Montavon, E., Young, M., Van Haneghan, J., & Barron, L. (1989, April). *An analysis of students' mathematical problem solving in real world settings.* Paper presented at the meeting of the American Educational Research Association, San Francisco, CA.

Weisberg, R., DiCamillo, M., & Phillips, D. (1978). Transferring old associations to new situations: A nonautomatic press. *Journal of Verbal Learning and Verbal Behavior, 17*, 219–228.

Whitehead, A. N. (1929). *The aims of education.* New York: MacMillan.

Wales, C. E., & Stager, R. A. (1977). *Guided design.* Morgantown, WV: West Virginia University Center for Guided Design.

Young, M., Van Haneghan, J., Barron, L., Williams, S., Vye, N., & Bransford, J. (in press). A problem-solving approach to mathematics instruction using an embedded data videodisc. *Technology and Learning.*

6

Should Computers Know
What You Can Do With Them?

Don Nix
IBM, Thomas J. Watson Research Center

DIGNITY AND PREDICTABILITY

Machines in general, and in particular computers, can pose a threat to one's dignity. The following bit by Woody Allen (1965) exemplifies this:

> My father was fired. He was technologically unemployed. My father worked for the same firm for 12 years. They fired him. They replaced him with a tiny gadget that does everything my father does, only it does it much better. The depressing thing is that my mother ran out and bought one.

In this bit, the distinction between machines and humans is blurred. It makes the machine and machine-like qualities attractive in a way that triumphs over the human. As an indication of a final triumph, one could imagine adding the comment, "And my father went out and bought one too."

The notion of dignity vis-à-vis machines (computers) is central in this chapter. In educational circles, dignity is often associated with being able to perform well on educational tasks. In such circles, a child feels stupid, inferior, undignified, if he or she cannot read, or do math or science or social studies. This ties the notion of self-worth to a predefined level of performance on preset skills. But the notion of dignity that is a desideratum in the type of computer explorations to be described is a reversal of this. If a child has

143

a sense of dignity, then reading, for example, is important or unimportant in terms of what he or she thinks about reading. Math, reading, science, and social studies are epiphenomena of the world of classroom attendance—rather than being the basics. What is basic is how the child relates to these areas. It is presumptuous to define a concept such as *dignity* within the confines of thinking about computers in education, when the concept has already been inconclusively developed and debated by more humanistic disciplines. However, there is an aspect of dignity that is particularly relevant to computers in general, and to computers in education specifically. This is the aspect of differentness from computeristic predictability. What *dignity* means for the purposes of discussion here is based on a child's experience of him or herself as intrisicially different from the way a computer functions, specifically by being able to actively consider his or her processes and feelings, and to be unpredictable in a creative way. Many of the ways computers are used in education pose a threat to the dignity of children. This is a problem.

As a way of focusing on this problem that computer pose, the following metaphorical question is considered: *"Should computers know what you can do with them?"*[1] By discussing it in this context, the notion of creativity in the sense of unpredictability is highlighted.

In current applications in education, the computer to a considerable extent *knows* ahead of time what the student will learn in some content domain. That is, the computer as experienced by the child is structured so that one can predict to an important degree what the child will learn, specifically because of what the computer is programmed to do. This predictability in fact is commonly used as a measure of the success of both the computer and the child. A successful author of a clearly designed instructional package can refine the materials to the extent that a significant number of children who interact with the materials will get to a certain level of knowledge. Advertisements that are persuasive to school personnel are built on the convincing representation of such predictability. This problem is one of mediocrity of knowledge.

In addition to predictability in a given content domain, such as math, programming, or history, there is the possibility in a higher, metacognitive way, given an effectively designed and programmed course of instruction. For example, based on the structure of the interaction between the computer and the child, the child can learn a certain way of learning, or of problem solving, or of behaving in the role of one who is being taught. The experience can contribute to the child's development of a picture of what learning is, and what his or her role is with regard to it, in terms of both cognition and modes of feeling. Not only what the child learns about social studies can be

---

[1]Computers do not actually *know* anything. However, computers can be programmed so that one can predict what the user will in some sense know, as a result of using the computer. The term *know*, when applied to computers in this chapter, is used in this sense.

predicted, but what the child learns about how to study social studies can be predicted as well. The problem involved here is the threat to dignity.

These somewhat exaggerated concerns assume that it is true that computers actually can have an effect on cognitive processing and on feelings. This is a common and strategic assumption made both by people who are skeptical of computers (e.g., Weizenbaum, 1976) and ones who see computers as at least potentially having a positive and liberating impact (e.g., Papert, 1980). The truth of this assumption in general has not at this point been empirically supported in terms of the experimental paradigms of psychology and educational psychology. However, a general hypothesis of this type, which involves complex issues of human functioning, is not likely to be approachable using such paradigms. Social studies Program A may be shown to teach specific social studies facts. But to show that Program A teaches strategies of thinking and problem solving, and even further, that these strategies extend to domains outside the purview of Program A, and further still, that Program A is responsible for a child's developing a certain attitude about him or herself as a person, and further, finally, that the fact that the child learned something, whatever it is, via using a computer program of a certain type, are simply inaccessible to "experimental" proof. Yet, arguments for and against computers, including the ones herein, are based on assuming that such claims can be shown to be true, or at least to make sense.

As a matter of faith, based on experience with computers, and many encounters with children and others who have spent large amounts of time engaged in working with and playing with and thinking about computers, it will be assumed here that, yes, prolonged and/or critically important interaction with a computer can and does, in a somewhat Whorfian way, cause predictable changes in both cognition and affect in children. As mentioned, this is a common starting point for agitated arguments for and against the use of computers in education, and society in general (Papert, 1980; Sloan, 1985).

In typical current applications of computers to education, then, computers know in an important sense what the child will learn. That is, the designers can predict what their creations will do to the children who interact with them. This predictability applies both to the content domain involved, and to the way a child is influenced to think of and feel about learning and his or her role regarding it. The one poses the problem of mediocrity of knowledge, and the other constitutes a threat to dignity.

WAYS COMPUTERS KNOW WHAT YOU CAN DO WITH THEM

The most familiar and pervasive uses of computers in education are the often derided, scorned, and ridiculed drill and practice and the tutorial modes. These originated in traditional computer assisted instruction (CAI) days, over 30 years ago, and closely resemble programmed instruction technology, as well as the world of print workbooks and ditto sheets. Over the years, the philosophy of these modes has not altered fundamentally, although the sophistication with which they are algorithmetically conducted has.

In these modes, the degree of predictability is high, to the extent that the program is successful. The child learns prepackaged information such as addition, decoding, history facts, science facts, and so on. The information to be mastered is relatively simplistic, due to the exegiencies of teaching it in this mode of instruction. Simplistic here means unambiguous, rule based, rather than necessarily easy. The syntax of modern Russian is simplistic in the manner intended here, and succeptible to drill and practice techniques for mastery, but is not particularly simple to learn and remember and use. At the level of learning about learning, drill and practice and tutorial modes embody the notion that learning involves the notion that the concepts of right and wrong are central to thinking about learning, and that these concepts can be and should be unambiguously defined. The child also has the experience that he or she as a person is irrelevant to the process of learning. What is to be learned is out there, defined ahead of time by someone else. Learning is finding what has been defined, remembering it, reproducing it. It is a form of hide and seek. The computer knows something you do not know but need to find out. Learning is not basically to be thought of as a process whereby the child explores, creates, and owns. In these modes, the computer knows what you can do with it. That is, the student's learning outcome is predictable in a meaningful sense.

The CAI modes are relatively clear examples of outcome predictability. Many objections to traditional and updated CAI have been expressed. Different authors find different features to excoriate. One particularly formidable objection is Papert's (1980). A significant focus of his objection is the passive role the child is constrained by play in the drill and practice, tutorial, CAI mode. Such a role is undignified. At best it ignores human potential. At worst it represses it.

An alternative plan for computers and education is exemplified by work by Papert. An early and still popular embodiment is the LOGO language for children. In a LOGO environment, the intention is for the child to program the computer, rather than to be programmed by it. The focus is not on presenting a set of facts that the child must master. Instead, the child creates something with the computer. What is created can be a picture, or animation sequence, or, in principal, any kind of program that can be written with a general programming language. The computer is not pre-programmed to teach a certain set of facts about a certain content area. At this level, the computer cannot know what the child can or is doing with it. The language is rich enough so that, for example, the set of pictures the child can draw (program) is greater than the set that can be realistically defined ahead of time.

At the processing level, however, the situation is different. LOGO is a tendentious language. The language is designed so that, as an ideal, a child will learn a type of problem-solving technique that is deemed to have special value in itself. The type of problem solving envisioned has been described and defended in detail in various publications (e.g., Papert, 1980). A significant goal of the LOGO orientation is to have an impact on creative, self-expressive, problem-solving strategies. The goal is not for the child to learn unambiguous facts, but to learn processes that will be used to solve problems in subsequent LOGO and LOGO-like environments, and that can be used to generalize to other domains in the life of the child. The problem-solving technique is computeristic. The domain of expression is defined basically in conceptual schemes related to computers, such as algorithmic thinking, procedural thinking, logical debugging, and modularization.

Supporters of this type of role for the child at the computer define an important aspect of success in terms of the child's becoming an active problem solver of the type described. An ideal is for the child to master and become proficient at this type of creativity and problem solving in a wide range of domains beyond the specific computer setting that fosters it. It is at this processing level of predictability that the computer knows what the child will do. At the level of what specifically is predictable, this environment is radically different from the traditional drill and practice and tutorial modes of computers in education. The content is not very predictable. The process is. Thus, the fact that something significant about the outcome of the child's experience with the system is predictable, generates some of the same concerns as the other modes.

A final example is sketched here. It is based on a recent development in computer-based instruction, which can be characterized as being more than modifications and amalgamations of what has gone before. This genre of computers in education comes from a noneducational field noted for its extravagant claims: artificial intelligence. Proponents of artificial intelligence CAI (ICAI) view the computer as "knowing" something literally. In theory, the computer would, for example, understand the content to be learned, the goals of the student, and the ongoing cognitive states of the student, with regard at least to his or her progress in learning what is to be taught. In a sense, then, the computer's knowing what the child can do with it is an explicit design goal. Again, success of the ICAI system can be measured in terms of a certain type of predictability. The student would learn certain facts about arithmetic, or about rain forests, or some other content area under consideration.

From the standpoint of technology, the ICAI approach and related "expert systems" (or, more accurately, "para-professional" systems) approaches are radically different from the two genres referred to previously, the drill/practice/tutorial and the creative programming approaches. The software design and implementation of a typical para-professional system may include thousands of rules, an "inference engine," and many lines of code for managing the system, keeping a database, processing input, and so on. Such systems represent significant advances at the software technology level. They are basically creations from the domain of computer science.

In terms of the educational outcome, there are clear similarities to traditional teaching systems. At the content level, the computer knows the material to be taught, not in the same way a human teacher might know it, but in terms of a database of facts and clearly specified relationships between and among these facts. At the content level, then, the computer knows what the child will learn if the system is successful, similar to the situation with drill and practice, even though the teaching methodology may be quit different.

At the level of having an affect on the way a child might learn to think about problems, ICAI is basically an empirically unexplored area. It is easy to consider ways in which, for example, para-professional systems could be designed to teach either overtly or implicitly a manner of approaching some domain of problems, rather than or in addition to specific success in solving problems in that domain. However, the basis of such systems so far consists of explicit rules and algorithms for combining them. Given this deterministic type of system, no matter how complex, it is likely that the way in which a child learned to think and solve problems like the "expert" would be predictable. The computer would know. In fact, the goal of such a system would be to transfer an explicated version of expertise from the computer to the child. This in many cases could be valuable, assuming considerable progress will be made in the complexity of para-professional systems. But it would also be predictable.

In the examples just given, arguments can be made that what the systems teach is worth teaching. It may be that such systems teach what they teach, in terms of content, in an ideal manner. This is not the issue. Most if not all content material can be taught in a variety of ways. Children could be supported in exploring ideas and feelings that go beyond what is comprehensible to computers. This could be done in a manner that goes beyond the information processing style of problem solving embodied in computers. The issue is whether the tutorial and programming genres of computer interaction limit this, and have side effects that are inimical from the point of view of this goal.

This outline of several computer uses in education is intended to stress that those uses do not exploit the computer's potential, as far as encouraging the children who use them to think and feel in productive ways that are not circumscribed by the lighted circle of computeristic concepts. Whether these uses of computers are a boon, bust, or Big Brother, they are not conceptualized in terms of the type of creativity that is based on unpredictability. This is not an argument for replacement. The point is that there is considerable room in exploring the uses of computers in education for a different type of system with different starting assumptions, and different effects. There is room for the type of computer in education where the computer does not and cannot know what you can do with it.

EXAMPLES OF THE COMPUTER NOT KNOWING WHAT YOU CAN DO WITH IT

A paradigm that we are exploring is intended to fit into the "computer-doesn't-know" category. The term *Making-a-Scene* is used to refer to the general environment and point of view we are implementing. This *Making-a-Scene* paradigm has not as yet been explored in detail. It is based on the use of a child-controlled multimedia computer system, including voice, videodisc and ver, audiocassette, animation, graphics, and a language named HANDY. HANDY refers to the fact that the language and its environment are intended to be handy to use for the exploration of ideas. The focus of our paradigm is on how the child can use the technology in an expressive way. The focus is not on the technology itself. The goal is to enable the child to be creative and self-expressive using the computer, but in areas that are not intrinsically related to computeristic concepts, and that cannot be expressed computeristically. These are ways that, in short, are not bound by computeristic limitations.

This paradigm differs from the traditional drill and practice and tutorial systems, and the aspirations of ICAI and para-professional systems, in that our stress is on self-expression. Our intent is not to teach a particular part of a content area. In general, we do not teach anything that is predictable in a specific, detailed sense. Our paradigm also differs from the programming oriented systems such as LOGO in a significant way, even though such systems at least theoretically are enablers of self-expression. The difference is that we are dealing or attempting to deal with areas of self-expression that are more experientially familiar to humans. These areas include, for example, fun, humor, passion, satire, aesthetics, and interpersonal negotiations, in such topics as civil rights, rock 'n roll, political campaign advertisements, soap operas, and television game shows.

The *Making-a-Scene* computer application uses the computer as a decentered participant, in contrast to most computers in the classroom. That is, activities involving the computer are just one of a range of activities that are not computer based. The computer as we have programmed it does not know anything about a specific content area. The computer language does not intentionally embody a specific style of problem solving. The decentered role the computer plays at least minimizes a significant source of predictability. This is technology and clutter in the style of Max Headroom. It is an attempt to get closer to Papert's metaphor of the computer as pencil.

MAKING-A-SCENE WITH HANDY

In order to explore ways that children could try out ideas using a computer, we created an experimental computer language. The language, HANDY, is briefly described here for the purposes of illustrating the feel of the language. After the description, several case studies of using it are sketched.

HANDY enables a child (or other person as an author) to construct interactive scenes presented on a computer. The scenes can integrate videodisc, videotape, audiotape, synthesized voice, digitized voice, touch panel, animation, and graphics.

The child can make the scene interactive according to a plan he or she has in mind. Examples of scenes include animating stories of interest, telling jokes, making a rock video or a play, and constructing an essay consisting of video and voice-over and text and touchable menus of questions that enable the reader–listener–viewer to browse this multimedia event as one can browse a printed essay.

Using HANDY, the child creates the "script" and "objects" that are to be visible to whomever will subsequently interact with the scene or scenes. A script is a program written in the HANDY language. The objects are individual elements that can be displayed on the computer screen. Objects can be pictures or text created by the child, or windows onto videodisc or videotape segments. Objects can also be audio segments from a cassette player, voice synthesizer, or digitized voice. Once the child has created all or part of a script and its associated objects, he or she can try them out in an interactive, iterative manner. Thus, once a scene or part of a scene has been created, it can be run, interrupted, revised, and continued. Scenes can be simple in the case of a small set of objects and a single script, or complex in the case of hundreds of objects and scripts that call other scripts, or programs written in standard programming languages.

To take a relatively simple *Making-a-Scene* example, suppose a child wanted to comically annotate a few scenes from the movie, *Ghostbusters*, and then to show it to his or her class. The child might use a scenario as follows. A robot would come out onto the stage (the computer screen), and ask the user what he or she wanted to see—the school library, or the librarian. The robot would speak the question using the voice synthesizer, and also show two boxes for touching to indicate the choice. If the viewer touches the box indicating the library, the script would move the robot offstage, and then play (using the videodisc) the scene from *Ghostbusters* that shows the front of the New York City Public Library. While this scene was playing on the computer monitor, the script could move an object onstage that had the text in it, "This is the modest PS 233 School Library." When the scene ended, the text would disappear, and the robot would return and present the two choices again.

If the user touches the box indicating that he or she wants to see the librarian, the robot might be moved offstage, and the script would play the scene from *Ghostbusters* that shows a ghost drifting through the card catalog area. The label, "Our Librarian," could be superimposed on the video. The video would then be scripted to freeze on a closeup on the ghost's face. A box would shrink down to frame just the face, blanking out the rest of the video image. The robot would come out. A text balloon would appear above the ghost's face with the words, "I don't know why the children are afraid to check out books." Then once the user touches the screen, the box framing the ghost's face would close all the way up so that no video was visible, and the robot would ask the choice question again.

In this example, which is based on a project done by fourth graders, the video scenes would be from the *Ghostbusters* movie videodisc. The objects (robot, text balloons, frames, voice synthesis, and so on) would be created by the child, and superimposed on the video material.

An example of a script written to perform the aforementioned is shown in Fig. 6.1. The words in uppercase in the following description are names the child has given to the objects he or she created. The picture objects are not shown in Fig. 6.1. What each picture object shows is as follows: ROBOT is the robot; LIBRARY contains the text, "I want to see the library"; LIBRARIAN contains the text, "I want to see the librarian"; LIB contains the text, "This is the modest PS 233 School Library."; FRAME is a box for outlining the

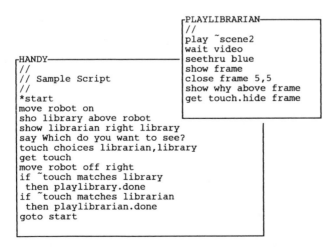

FIG. 6.1.   Sample script written in HANDY.

ghost's face; and WHY contains the text, "I don't know why the children are afraid to check out books."

Most of the script is self-explanatory. The statement, "~touch," however, needs explanation. This statement is a variable that is automatically replaced by the word, "library," or "librarian," once the person interacting with the scene has made a choice and touched one of the objects, LIBRARY, or LIBRAR-IAN. So, if the LIBRARY object is touched, for example, then the script determines that "~touch" matches the word, "library," and so the script runs the subscript labeled "playlibrary" via the statement, "then playlibrary." The "playlibrarian" scripts is run if the LIBRARIAN object is touched.

The variables, "~scene1" and "~scene2" contain the videodisc frame numbers for the two scenes the script will play. These are set by the child by viewing the video, and then telling HANDY what sections of the video are to go by those names. Any names could be chosen.

The example in Fig.6.1 is relatively simple. HANDY itself has hundreds of additional commands and facilities, and can be used for quite sophisticated programming. The application of HANDY in Fig. 6.1 uses only a small subset of the system. It is presented here to indicate the type of language HANDY is. The commands are based on English word order and vocabulary; the environment is interactive; a variety of media is supported.

At the programming or scripting level this example is straightforward. However, in other ways, this example shows the necessity for considerable initiative, design, and iteration for the children. The child has to study the movie; analyze it; reconceptualize it; create a mode of presentation, including a mode of interaction, for the audience he or she intends to show it to; plan and create the objects; and write and try out and revise the script. The creativity involved in doing this is not circumscribed by computeristic concepts. It involves a wider range of issues, many of which are "real-world" issues that are unrelated to computers—such as humor, satire, and a challenge to authority. This is the point of the *Making-a-Scene* paradigm.

On the other hand, the child does deal with computer concepts quite directly in order to create his or her production. The script in Fig. 6.1 *is* a computer program. It is not English. It is written in an artificial language that has to be learned, using where possible what one knows about English as a guide. Once the script is written, or some of it is written, it has to be debugged.

The design goal of HANDY was to create a language that would facilitate a type of noncomputeristic self-expression. The intention was to make the language itself as decentered as possible. As a result of children using the language over a range of projects, we have created other HANDY-based languages as well. The different languages have different focuses. Some of the examples of projects discussed in the next section use HANDY, and others use

HANDY derivatives. It should be noted that other chapters in this book illustrate projects done in HANDY itself.

EXPLORATORY STUDIES

We have conducted a series of exploratory studies in which children create scenes with HANDY and its derivatives, for children and others. Although there are many questions that can be experimentally studied using this environment, at this early stage the focus is on providing children with the facility, and seeing what they do, and where they have problems. Several examples are outlined. I am grateful to children and staff at the Dalton School, New York City, and to children from the Tarrytown, New York, School District, for these examples, and the experiences we had working on the projects.

Video Essays

One class of uses of HANDY is that of creating interactive *video essays*. In general, a child creates an "essay" that, instead of being written on paper, consists of video segments chosen by the child to make his or her point, combined with superimposed annotation or extended text, and voice-over from the child. The person who "reads" the essay actually reads and listens and watches the essay, and can make choices about what he or she wants to see next, or see again. The *Ghostbusters* example is a simple example of this type of essay.

A more elaborated example is a project in which kids (in 10th grade) created mock political advertisements for a presidential candidate, using video tape footage from *The Video Encyclopedia of the 20th Century* (available from CEL Educational Resources, New York City). The *Visual Encyclopedia* consists of 75 hours of news reel footage containing news clips from 1893 to 1985. This project was part of a course being given on political uses of video. In this project, students picked presidential candidates (Ford and Reagan), and used film clips from their campaigns as raw material for the video component of the essay. These clips included actual campaign speeches, as well as footage used in advertisements, such as a sequence showing happy workers in a clothing factory, and happy workers picking cotton. (It was not clear from viewing this material whether these were real workers as represented, or instead were happy actors.) In addition to the footage from the actual film clips, the students shot additional footage themselves. For example, they shot two "man on the street" interviews. One was a businessman giving his opinion on why Reagan would be a good choice. The other was a New York City cab driver similarly avowing that he was convinced of Reagan's superiority over Jimmy Carter. These shots were planned and created by the students—the scripts, directing, audio, shooting, retakes, and editing. The businessman and cab driver were talked into participating by the students.

In creating the essays, a number of decisions had to be made by the students. Demographics of the intended audience were considered. The decision was made to appeal to a broad range of socioeconomic levels: business people, cab drivers, factory and farm workers, and the cultures they represent. This was because they did not want "their" candidate to be branded as insensitive to low income and to minority groups (the cab driver was black). Decisions were made about the type of emphasis to construct. This involves issues about record of achievement versus personal qualities, positive versus negative campaigning, and others. An emotional tone had to be established.

Technical decisions mainly concerned the use of media (camera angles, based on what is available, sound, voice-over, annotation, graphics). Once the video footage was borrowed and shot and edited, further editing could be done when the script was written to present the final advertisement. The students implemented and evaluated and revised their decisions by creating objects consisting of text and pictures and other types of information, and writing a script in HANDY to put it all together, maintaining the particular type of thematic integration they chose.

The theme of the Ford advertisement was one of happiness and loyalty to Americanisms. As a single example, at one point in the Ford essay the script was written to play a video segment showing a Fourth of July celebration with fireworks displayed on a dark sky. In addition the script showed a computer-generated American flag the students had created to fit the video, and had superimposed on the video. At the same time, the audiocassette player played an excerpt from Beethoven's First Symphony.

In these political campaign advertisement video essays, the computer did not know what the students had done with it. The computer enabled a form of analysis, learning, feelings, and self-expression that cannot be expressed ahead of time in a way that could be computerized and predicted as a learning goal of a teaching system. In fact, in a certain sense the 10th graders who created the essays did not know what they had done. They had intended to create effective campaign advertisements for their candidates. However, a group of eighth graders (apparently young liberals) who happened to view the finished products thought the advertisements were intended as satires on Ford and Reagan.

A related video essay project was based on a videodisc containing civil rights news clip footage from the 1960s. The video was excerpted from several of the *Visual Encyclopedia* videotapes. Students (in eighth grade) used shots of speeches (e.g., Martin Luther King Jr., George Wallace, and Julian Bond), as well as police and crowd scenes (e.g., federal troops sent to Little Rock and to Detroit). Their essay consisted of an opening scene showing King's "I have a dream" speech at the Lincoln Memorial, and then a menu shown on the screen that allowed the viewer to select how he or she wanted to explore the ideas about civil rights contained in the essay. A viewer could browse through the material, for example, or could pursue a topic such as how King's enemies used speeches to marshall negative feelings Whites already had about Blacks.

When a viewer selected a scene, he or she was shown the still frame that began the scene. The voice synthesizer announced the name of the speaker, the event, the location, and the date. For example, "George Wallace, Sworn in as Governor, Atlanta, Georgia, 1963." The speech contained one of Wallace's most famous lines: "segregation now, segregation tomorrow, and segregation forever." The video then began. At any point during the video, the kids had programmed the script so that the viewer could stop the video, replay parts of it, request the identifying information again, and could also return to a menu to select some other part of the essay or quit. When the viewer chose to quit, a brief segment was shown of Ralph Abernathy conducting King's funeral services, and then the essay froze on King's tombstone with the inscription, "Free at last, free at last, thank God Almighty I'm free at last." The script then superimposed on this shot the title of the video essay, "What King did and what They did."

In creating this video essay, the students viewed footage of an era that had not previously existed for them. They became familiar with unfamiliar names: Wallace, Faubus, Abernathy, Ghandi, Bond, Brown, Carmichael, Selma, Montgomery, Resurrection City, and others. The names are not names in a textbook. They became names associated with speeches and soldiers on horseback riding through the streets of American cities. After a series of discussions, the students constructed an organizing principle for selecting and rejecting footage, and for presenting the essay itself. The students, all of whom were Black, discovered various aspects about "civil rights" and American history of a specific period that contained an experiential quality. A social studies teacher could argue with the way the students presented the materials, or the choice of speeches, or the lack of explicit chronology. A teacher could argue that there was no "assignment" the students were doing. However, a teacher could not easily argue that what the students did could have been predicted in a Teachers Guide or computer program.

In the video essay projects, the students actively used a computer and a specialized environment to produce a type of essay that could not feasibly be produced without computer support. The computers were an integral part of one aspect of the expression, but not a focal point in the overall experience.

In this interactive video type of essay, the computer does not know what the student will create, or think, or learn. The most significant aspect of what the student does is not related to concepts about computers. The civil rights essay was a moving multimedia interactive presentation that was a relevation to students for whom the 1960s did not previously exist. The Ford campaign was for some of the students a persuasive advertisement, based on a shrewd analysis of what it takes to convince people to vote for a certain perceived type of person.

Student Participation in the Video

Another form of self-expression we are exploring involves the students themselves as performers in the video. One example is a project in which a group of fifth-grade children created a "disk jockey" program, where a viewer could request a song. They drew a picture of a disk jockey, including mustache, Mohawk hair cut, and sweater with "WPLJ," their favorite radio station's call letters (New York City). They also created a menu that had a list of tour songs, "Private Dancer," "West End Girls," "Working on the Highway," and "I Call Her Darlin', But She Calls Me Collect." They wrote a HANDY script for a scenario in which the disk jockey bounced onstage, and the menu appeared, and the disk jockey said, using the voice synthesizer, "Pick a song."

The children had created their own videotape. On the tape they were singing and dancing to each of the songs. They had made costumes, picked the songs, done the choreography, and handled the production details. Then they viewed the tape through HANDY, in order to assign the segments they wanted to show for the different song choices their viewers would make.

Once the viewer of their disk jockey program made a song choice, the disk jockey would bounce offstage. The script would locate the beginning of the song on the videotape, and an object would open up on the screen, showing the singing and dancing. The script was written so that, at any point in time, the viewer could interrupt the song and dance, by pressing a certain key, and then return to the main menu.

This project involved a considerable amount of group interaction and planning, from picking the songs, to scheduling time when all four children could get together after school to shoot the video. Again, the point is that rather than learning only arithmetic, or computer programming, or a style of problem solving that could be predicted and could be described in terms that also were programmatic, the focus was on using a computer environment to create in this case a rock video, where the most important elements involved in the creation were in terms of social interaction, aesthetics, music, humor, popular culture, and production.

Two more examples are mentioned here, which were more ambitious in scope. The first was a television game show. The second was a soap opera. The television game show project was done with a group of children, Grades 3 through 5. The project began simply as an effort to teach a version of HANDY to the children, in order to determine where there were problems in HANDY that had to be corrected before the language could be used on a wider scale.

This project evolved into an elaborate satire of a popular television program, "Family Feud." On the "Family Feud" program on television, two families vie against each other by trying to guess how people on a previously conducted survey answered certain questions of general interest. Each family consists of five or so members, standing together behind a raised table, facing the other family across the stage. The five or so most frequent answers to the selected questions are on a large electronic board, but covered up. If a family member guesses one of the answers on the board, the answer is uncovered. A rectangular cover is retracted into the board. If the guess made is not one of the answers on the board, an "X" appears and a buzzer is sounded. Key elements in the television program are the fawning attitude of the moderator, and the exaggerated way in which members of the two families overreact to the moderator, to the questions, the answers, and to everything else. The children called their project "Family *Fools.*"

In this project, we used the computer screen to make an "answer board" like the one on the television show. Using HANDY, the children created the objects for the answers to questions, and objects with decorative patterns to cover the answers until they would be guessed. A script was written to check for an answer to be typed in, and, if there was a match (incorrect spellings and other types of approximate answers were accepted as correct), the relevant answer was uncovered. If not, then one, two, or three "X's" was or were displayed on the screen, and a buzzer noise was sounded by the computer. The computer part of the project, thus, constituted the technology used in the actual television game show production.

Questions to be used were generated by the children. For example: "What's the best excuse when you forgot your homework and have no excuse?" Four or five answers for each question were generated ("My dog ate it," "My dog ate my brother," "It was stolen by the school bully," and so on). The answers were rated. The generation of the questions and answers and ratings was done after extended discussions on a range of topics of relevance to the lives of grade-school children, as well as society at large. Children in one family generated questions, answers, and ratings to be used for the other family.

The game show itself included the children, the sycophantic moderator, and the computer. The children divided themselves into two different families. I was given the role of the moderator. Two video cameras were used to tape the production. One was focused on the action—the moderator, and the two families. The other camera was focused on the computer screen. The two video sources were selectively mixed, sometimes showing only the family or the moderator, sometimes only the game board (the computer screen), and sometimes some combination. The show was taped before a live and motley audience consisting of children waiting for their turn on camera, researchers, and passers by who wandered in because of the noise.

The "Family Fools" project, although started as a computer activity, and based in large part on a computer program, was considerably different in content and feeling than a computeristic activity. The computer was a catalyst and tool for a set of creative efforts that were experientially familiar to the children, that were expressed creatively, and that reached into diverse content areas.

The final example to be sketched is a soap opera project done with eighth-graders from Dalton School in New York City. The name of the soap opera is "Dalton Crest." The kids wrote a screenplay for the story that involved a complex set of personal relationships among six people. A murder occurs. Each child acted in the story.

A range of factors had to be dealt with in writing the screenplay. Each child invented the character he or she wanted to play, and was then responsible for writing the scenes in which he or she was the focal character, or collaborating on a scene that was equally focused. The screenplay was written so that each character had a plausible motive for the murder, but so that one character in subtle ways was implicated. Each character had a well-delineated personality and set of idiosyncracies. It was necessary to maintain the integrity of the characters in the story throughout their interactions with all others. Considerable group discussion was necessary to do this because this is a difficult task to begin with, and since the totality of the story was written by six different people.

The story was intended for viewing by third graders. This meant that the complexity of the mystery interwoven around the interrelationships among a set of definitely unusual, soap opera-like eccentrics, had to be accessible to and interesting to children who were 8 or 9 years old. A program of investigation was initiated to find out what a third grader is.

At a more general level, the soap opera was intended to function as a means for studying problem-solving activities of kids of different ages. The solution path a viewer of the soap opera took was recorded by the HANDY script controlling the presentation. This profile data could then be used as experimental data to compare third graders to eighth graders. The actual statistical value of such data would be meaningless by journal standards. However, studying such data, discussing it, and making hypotheses about it would provide a setting for reflecting directly on the notion of problem solving as an activity. It is unusual for kids to do this in school, due in part to the importance attributed to getting the facts, holding them until test time at least, and then returning them to the teacher on pieces of paper.

The videotaping of the soap opera was an involved process. Lighting, audio, camera angles, locations, costumes, rehearsal, retakes, editing, scheduling, directing, and so on, took considerable time, and was all done during the regular school day. The story was written so it could be taped entirely on school premises, due to time constraints. The directing and camera work were done by me. The videotape version was converted to videodisc for integration with HANDY.

A viewer of the soap opera encountered the following situation when he or she interacted with it on the computer. A short initial video segment was shown, with superimposed computer-generated text, to introduce the characters in the story and to establish that a murder had occurred. Then it was up to the viewer to solve the mystery by requesting more information. The additional information was presented in terms of video segments. For example, all six protagonists were shown as part of a party scene including extras as well. The viewer would then touch the person he or she wanted to know more about. Background information, using both video and text was then given about that character, followed by a menu listing scenes in which the character appeared. The viewer could touch the menu to invoke the scene desired. At any point in time, the user could return to the party scene in order to pick another character to explore or re-explore. The viewer could also, at any time, offer a solution to the mystery. This was done by touching a certain point on the screen. Then the viewer touched the hypothesized culprit on the screen, and a "window" would open up for the viewer to type a reason for selecting the character selected. If the viewer was correct, notification was given, and the murder scene was shown. If they did not select the murderer, they were returned to the main party scene showing all the main characters.

The system was scripted to keep a record of how the viewer traversed through "Dalton Crest." The script also saved the explanations given for the solutions proposed.

This project was conceived as a means of exploring ways the computer could be used unpredictably, in partnership, and whereby boundaries of classroom content area divisions would be unimportant, and where a sense of ownership of what had been done was strong. What the students did was hard work, thought provoking, creative, and contributed a sense of satisfaction to them. What they did was a project rather than an assignment; they worked together rather than divisively; they were the creators rather than students; they were reflective rather than receptive; and they had an experiential relationship to their work rather than just a school relationship. The computer played a part in enabling the kids to think about a range of issues, and then to be able to creatively explore those issues in a highly motivational, personally meaningful and publicly entertaining way.

This does not mean the kids learned nothing about school topics. Areas such as sociology, personality theory, creative writing, computer literacy, and video technology were integrally involved. If we had done a soap opera set in 19th-century Russia, one could add economics, history, and so on, to the list of content areas that would be relevant. One could obviously use this *Making-a-Scene* approach for didactic purposes.

The reason for sketching these representative projects in some detail is to try to give a tangible indication of how this genre of computers in education differs from "computers in education." The projects are described in order to contrast this new genre and its possibilities with other modes of using computers in education. They are intended as suggestions for further explorations, not as a new curriculum to replace the old. Upon consideration of these descriptions, or observations of or participation in these and other related projects, it is obvious that something quite different is going on, when compared to what one would normally observe in schools or research laboratories. The computer is decentered enabling technology for experiences whose significance transcends computeristic ideas. The children work together. What they work on is relevant to their own feelings and thoughts. Their work consists of creating something. The computer could not know what they were doing.

CONCLUSION

These projects had a special impact on the participants. They were fresh air. In some cases, the children only gradually realized that they really were not functioning in ways based on their normal school patterns. The impact of the projects stems to a large degree from the noncomputer components. In significant ways, these projects are not about computers at all. In significant ways, these projects could have been done without computers—just as they could be and were mainly done without books and assignments. The role of the computer was not central. This is the point of this genre of computer uses in education. The computer was a means for bringing together what the students were doing, and of presenting what they were doing in a manner that could be interacted with, enjoyed, and discussed by others. The computer was a means for enabling a focus on how to express the ideas being developed with each project. The computer was analogous to a text editor in the sense that text editors provide a tool for expressing and organizing thoughts. It was, however, different from a text editor as acting and feeling are different from writing words about acting and feeling.

The *Making-a-Scene* projects are intended to exemplify a *genre* of using computers in education. The style of the projects is the point. The content examples such as civil rights, soap operas, and silly game shows are not the main point. One may disagree with the content, and want content that is more identifiable as "academic," and still explore teaching that content and making it more meaningful by making a scene.

Can the *Making-a-Scene* type of project make any difference in the way students think and feel? The projects described here were all exploratory in nature, and evolved while being done. Further exploration is necessary to be at a point where actual recommendations might be made, or models of computer use be given. Can computers have any effect at all, other than simply teaching a mediocre level of content knowledge in some specific domain? Writers who have considered the good and the evil of computers in society, and for children more specifically, including Papert (1980), Weizenbaum (1976), Turkle (1984), Dreyfus and Dreyfus (1986), most contributers in Sloan (1985), as well as Woody Allen and comic denizens of late night television, assume that computers do have effects as a result of direct interaction with them over a period of time. Little if any empirical evidence is given of the type usually considered necessary to establish a cause and effect relationship. This has not been empirically tested in a fair manner to a satisfactory extent, and perhaps cannot be, given the limitations of the testing paradigms used, which are usually based on experimental psychology. The relationship is assumed, and the arguments start there, in terms of whether the results are good or bad.

This type of question as applied to the *Making-a-Scene* genre of computer activities is shifted somewhat. The focus is not directly on whether or not the computer makes a difference. It is on whether or not the nexus within which the computer is decentered, and which involves aesthetics, social interaction, humor, and so on, makes a difference. In this environment, it is easier to believe that a difference could be made. One can watch the children as they work on these projects, and compare what is going on in this environment to what goes on when students are taking tutorials or computer drills, or doing computer programming. In making a scene, the students are involved with more of their personalities. They more directly own what they are doing, both in terms of the cognitive and the affective elements. It has in general been shown that the deeper the processing of information, and the wider the range of types of processing, and the greater the motivation and sense of ownership, the greater the impact. The working assumption, then, is that computers in education, a la *Making-a-Scene*, can have a significant impact on children. This type of computer use is not an affront, either explicitly or implicitly, to one's sense of dignity.

The concern about dignity is not that computers may ultimately be as smart as, or no different than, the brain of a child. Whether or not computers are theoretically limited in comparison to human intelligence is not of direct interest here, despite its importance in other circles. If computers can never "know" or "feel," then their predictability is particularly depressing when viewed in the context of their being a model of human thinking and feeling. If computers in their own deterministic way can theoretically match or surpass humans, if there is a "geometry in our restlessness" (paraphrased from Pynchon, 1973), then the software and hardware that define them will be unlike current implementations. The problem is that computers as they *now* exist in education either are not conducive to, or else limit, dignity. The *Making-a-Scene* genre of computers and children is a means of dealing with this problem.

In a meaningful way, the computer does not know and can not know what the child will learn. Computers so far cannot create soap operas that elaborate complex interpersonal relationships and act them out with conviction, and can't experience strong feelings when confronted graphically with the realities of the racism of the 1960s. Artificially intelligent computers, as they now exist, represent a "cognition" that if evidenced in a human would probably be classified clinically as schizoid, retarded, lacking affect.

Computers as they now exist in education (and elsewhere) are limited. The type of computer and child interaction using the *Making-a-Scene* environment is an additional way to study the impact of computers on education. It is basically an unexplored environment at this point in time. There are significant questions to ask, and there are significant impracticalities. However, a computer that does not know what the child learns is a way of avoiding some of the concerns about inimical effects of computers on the dignity of being different than computers. Most positively, it is a way of considering a wider range of potential enhancements of education by computers. The use of the computer is creative; the creativity is not predictable; and the child in his or her interaction cannot be replaced with a tiny gadget.

REFERENCES

Allen, W. (1965). *Album number four*. New York: Capitol Recording Company.
Visual encyclopedia of the 20th century. (1986). CEL Educational Resources, 515 Madison Avenue, NY 10022.
Dreyfus, H. L., & Dreyfus, S. E. (1986). *Mind over machine*. New York: The Free Press.
Papert, S. (1980). *Mindstorms*. New York: Basic.
Pynchon, T. (1973). *Gravity's rainbow*. New York: Viking.
Sloan, D. (Ed.). (1985). *The computer in education: A critical perspective*. New York: Teachers College Press.
Turkle, S. (1984). *The second self*. New York: Simon & Schuster.
Weizenbaum, J. (1976). *Computer power and human reason*. San Francisco: Freeman.

7

Cognitive Flexibility and Hypertext: Theory and Technology for the Nonlinear and Multidimensional Traversal of Complex Subject Matter

Rand J. Spiro
Jihn-Chang Jehng
University of Illinois at Urbana–Champaign

Traditional methods of instruction rely on linear media (e.g., textbooks and lectures). Linearity of media is not a problem when the subject matter being taught is well structured and fairly simple. However, as content increases in complexity and ill-structuredness, increasingly greater amounts of important information are lost with linear approaches and the unidimenionality of organization that typically accompanies them. The advent of random access computer technologies makes practicable new forms of nonlinear and multidimensional learning and instruction that are better suited to conveying complex content. For example, it becomes a straightforward matter to *revisit* the same content material in a variety of different contexts, with each visit bringing out additional aspects of that content's complexity that are missed in the single pass of linear coverage. We use the expression *random access instruction* to refer to a cluster of fundamental issues brought into play by nonlinear learning with random access media. This chapter discusses a unified theoretical approach to those fundamental issues, an approach that provides a foundation of principles to guide random access instruction.

The research discussed in this chapter illustrates aspects of a general theoretical orientation to knowledge acquisition and application in complex content domains, *Cognitive Flexibility Theory* (Spiro, Coulson, Feltovich, & Anderson, 1988; Spiro, Vispoel, Schmitz, Samarapungavan, & Boerger, 1987). We argue for the suitedness of this theory to the special needs of random access instruction. The generality of the theory is attested to by the fact that it has been applied in roughly the same way to such diverse areas as literary comprehension and interpretation, biomedical cognition, history, and military strategy (Feltovich, Spiro, & Coulson, 1989; Spiro, Feltovich, Coulson, & Anderson, 1989; Spiro et al., 1987; Spiro et al., 1988; Spiro, Feltovich, Coulson, Jacobson, Jehng, & Ravlin, in preparation).

Although this chapter is primarily concerned with the application of theoretical issues of advanced learning on complex topics to a particular instructional approach, there is also a focus on one illustrative context for that discussion: a computer program in the area of *literary comprehension* and the understanding of complex patterns of individual behavior. Again, however, the chapter has a general theoretical point, it is not limited to the one area chosen to illustrate the theoretical concerns.

Because the meaning of literary works transcends the mere chronicling of the events they contain and also tends not to be reducible to any single interpretation, representation of *patterns* of thematic deployment often form the most useful scaffolding for their comprehension (rather than a single event-oriented schema). A literary work usually contains many themes and symbolic structures. A given theme is likely to be used in diverse ways, be relevant at irregular intervals throughout the work, and form intricate patterns of combination with the other themes. We argue that mastery of complexities such as these, which are found in all rich content domains, is greatly facilitated by the kind of guided nonlinear and multidimensional explorations typified by the instructional program (based on Cognitive Flexibility Theory) discussed in this chapter. (Furthermore, we have accumulated considerable evidence that more advanced understandings of this kind very frequently *not* to be successfully attained in typical instructional settings—see, e.g., Feltovich et al., 1989; and Spiro et al., 1988; Spiro et al., 1989.)

The project that is the primary focus of this chapter uses a random access (i.e., interactive, programable) videodisc of the complexly structured classic film *Citizen Kane* (Welles & Stein, 1984). A large number of short segments drawn from several scenes of the film have been closely analyzed for their patterns of instantiation of the film's thematic and symbolic structure. This analysis forms the basis for a very large number of computer-generated re-editings of the segments as a function of their patterns of thematic relatedness. In one use of the program, after students/subjects see the full scenes in their natural sequence, they are then exposed to variously rearranged traversals of the scenes in different contextual arrangements. Commentary is appended explicating the thematic and symbolic contrasts illustrated by each traversal (i.e., each thematically based re-editing of the scenes).

This use of programable video to construct multiple "texts" is intended to prepare learners (better than instruction with a standard linear schema for the film would) to go beyond the ability to merely *reproduce* the instruction they received, and instead to be able to independently apply the instructed knowledge to new situations that differ in their characteristics from those of initial learning. That is, the goal is *transfer*. An example of a transfer goal that the program is intended to facilitate is an improved ability to comprehend scenes from the film that have *not* yet been seen. Or the knowledge acquired from instruction should serve more effectively as background knowledge to support the comprehension of critical texts written about the film. It is also hoped that more *general* transfer might occur: by having the need for complex analysis of literary works clearly demonstrated to students, they will be more likely to avoid typical tendencies toward oversimplification in other literary works; and by fostering skill in the processes of complex text-based interpretation, the students should be better able to carry out the more complex analyses of new works. More generally still, this instructional program could be combined with similar ones developed in other domains to form a staging ground to alert students to *generic* hazards of oversimplification and to prepare them to deal with complexity across domains. (Note that an aspect of the instructional approach that is considered crucial for transfer but that receives less attention here is the *active involvement* of the learner. The role of student participation and exploration becomes clearer in the detailed example presented later in the chapter.)

OVERVIEW

The chapter begins by posing a set of problems for cognitively based theories of learning and instruction. These problems revolve around concern for *advanced knowledge acquisition* (i.e., post-introductory learning) in a content area. At advanced stages of knowledge acquisition content becomes more *complex* and the relationships across the cases that knowledge has to be applied to become more *irregular*. We call domains that have these features of content complexity and irregularity of application contexts *ill-structured domains*. At the same time that greater ill-structuredness must be dealt with by advanced learners, the *goals* of learning shift: (a) from the attainment of superficial familiarity with concepts and facts to the mastery of important aspects of conceptual complexity, and (b) from knowledge reproduction to knowledge use (transfer, application). (See Feltovich et al., 1989; Spiro et al., 1988; Spiro et al., 1989, for detailed discussions of advanced knowledge acquisition.)

After presenting a brief discussion of problems in dealing with advanced knowledge acquisition in ill-structured domains, we present a remedy: the Cognitive Flexibility Theory of learning, knowledge representation, and knowledge transfer. By *cognitive flexibility* we mean the ability to spontaneously restructure one's knowledge, in many ways, in adaptive response to radically changing situational demands (both within and across knowledge application situations). This is a function of both the way knowledge is *represented* (e.g., along *multiple* rather than single conceptual dimensions) and the processes that operate on those mental representations (e.g., processes of schema *assembly* rather than intact schema retrieval). We then discuss the instructional approach systematically derived from that theory and implemented in computer learning environments, the Cognitive Flexibility Hypertext approach to random access instruction. Key features of the approach are illustrated by a functioning hypertext prototype that teaches aspects of the complex multithematic structure of the film *Citizen Kane* using random access videodisc. The generality of the approach is underscored by a brief presentation of highlights of Cognitive Flexibility Hypertext prototypes in other domains (e.g., cardiovascular medicine and military strategy).[1]

We are especially concerned with how the knowledge representations that are built by using programs like KANE support the application of old knowledge in new situations. We stress the process of situation-dependent *schema assembly* as against the views of schema theories that depend on the mere retrieval of precompiled generic knowledge structures that are monolithically superimposed on the concrete case at hand. The latter approach is simply too unwieldy to support transfer when there is a lot of complexity in the individual case of application and when cases vary considerably, one to the next. If you may have to use knowledge in many ways, in a diverse set of circumstances, you cannot rely on a small number of rigidly prepackaged schemas (see Schank, 1982, as well).

A Note on Hypertext. The term *hypertext* refers to computer-based texts that are read in a nonlinear fashion and that are organized on multiple dimensions (see Marchionini, 1988, for a review). The same material (which can be any kind of randomly accessible medium, e.g., text, video, audio) is capable of being explored in different ways, with the different exploration paths producing what are essentially *multiple texts* for the same topic. We discuss hypertext later—in particular how the features of our approach avoid problems commonly found in other hypertext systems, such as the problem of pre-stored links and the problem of getting lost in a labyrinth of connections between ideas. For now, however, it is worth pointing out that the outline of the chapter just presented also corresponds to a systematic response to widespread problems in the development of hypertext learning systems. In particular, work on hypertext has tended to be *atheoretical,* driven by the power of the technology rather than by a clear sense of how to respond to two key issues: (a) the *stages* of learning and *purposes* of learning for which this unfamiliar kind of instructional environment may be best suited—not all

---

[1]The three hypertext systems are fully functioning prototypes. However, because they are currently used only for research, they contain a limited number of cases and commentaries. They are not fully developed curricula, although preparing them for that function would simply be a matter of adding more cases and commentaries—nothing in the computer programs themselves would change.

kinds of learning require so complex and potentially confusing an approach; and (b) the cognitive psychology of nonlinear learning—hypertext systems would be easier to use and would support greater educational attainment if they were systematically designed in accordance with a theory of how the information will be processed, mentally represented, and later used (see Spiro et al., 1988). This chapter can be thought of as being sequenced to correspond to these questions about hypertext (as well as forming a natural sequence for the presentation of problems of advanced learning and their solutions—as described in the overview).[2]

Our answer to the questions that we said should be posed for any hypertext systems are that they are best suited for *advanced* learning, for *transfer/application* learning goals requiring cognitive flexibility, in *complex and ill-structured domains*—rather than *introductory* learning, for *memory* tests, in *simpler domains*. (Incidentally, we were able to avoid the endemic atheoretical approaches to hypertext development only because of a fortunate coincidence of sorts: Our work on the cognitive psychology of learning for transfer in ill-structured domains happened to *precede* our interest in computer- supported instruction; Spiro, 1980; Spiro & Myers, 1984; Spiro et al., 1987.)

ADVANCED KNOWLEDGE ACQUISITION AND THE PROBLEMS OF ILL-STRUCTUREDNESS, COGNITIVE FLEXIBILITY, AND KNOWLEDGE TRANSFER

Two important things happen as you move beyond the initial introduction to a content area to more advanced stages of knowledge acquisition in that area: First, the conceptual content tends to become more complex and the basis of its application more ill-structured; and second, the goals of learning and the criteria by which learning is assessed shift (or *should* shift): (a) from superficial or introductory level familiarity with concepts to the mastery of *important* aspects of complexity (despite their difficulty); and (b) from accu-

---

[2]One further note may be helpful. The terms *hypertext, hypermedia,* and *HyperCard* are often confused. Hypertext has already been discussed. HyperCard is merely one kind of programming environment for hypertext development; it was not used for the Kane program. Hypermedia refers to nonlinear computer learning systems in any medium (including multiple media). In that sense, it is a more general term than hypertext. However, because only one of the nonlinear learning programs that have been based on Cognitive Flexibility Theory employs multiple media (the *Citizen Kane* program), we feel uncomfortable referring to the set of systems as hypermedia. Yet the set should have a common name, given that a common theoretical basis is shared. So we refer to all of the systems as hypertexts. This designation is consistent with the more general usage of the term *text* in post-structuralist literary theory to refer to any object of rich interpretation, including pictures. So, the instructional program using *Citizen Kane* is a nonlinear 'text' that relies heavily on film segments, as well as written text.

rate reproductive memory and imitative rule-following for instructed material to the ability to apply what was taught in new and greatly varying contexts—knowledge transfer.[3]

What do you have to do to attain a deep understanding of a complex concept, to "get it right"?[4] What has to be done to be ready to apply conceptual knowledge in a domain where the phenomena occur in irregular patterns? How can one be prepared to use knowledge in the great variety of ways that may be required in a rich domain? Unfortunately, the indications are that what should be done in all of these cases is very often just the *opposite* of what tends to be done in conventional instruction practices (Spiro et al., 1987). Learning and instruction for mastery of complexity and application in a complex and ill-structured domain *cannot* be compartmentalized, linear, uniperspectival, neatly hierarchical, simply analogical, or rigidly prepackaged (Spiro et al., 1987; Spiro et al., 1988). Yet it much too often is, and the result is the development of widespread and serious misconceptions and difficulties in knowledge application (Feltovich et al., 1989; Spiro et al., 1988; Spiro et al., 1989). This is because complex and ill-structured knowledge domains are characterized by such features as nonuniformity of explanation across the range of phenomena to be covered, nonlinearity of explanation, nonadditivity following decomposition, context-dependency, irregularity of overlap patterns across cases (reducing the effectiveness of prototypes and simple analogies), absence of wide scope defining features for category application, and so on (see Spiro et al., 1987; Spiro et al., 1988, for discussions of domain ill-structuredness).

We have shown in a number of studies that the learning of complex content material in ill-structured domains requires *multiple representations*—multiple explanations, multiple analogies, multiple dimensions of analysis (see, e.g.,

---

[3]An example of a transfer measure for *Citizen Kane* is comprehension of critical commentary on the film. It has been amply demonstrated that text comprehension requires the mobilization of an appropriate background knowledge scaffolding. This requisite background knowledge changes across the many texts written about the film. Ability to assemble comprehension-supporting background knowledge across a *wide variety* of texts (compared to comprehension scores of control subjects) would indicate the acquisition of one kind of flexible transfer ability.

[4]A note on terminology is helpful before continuing. In this chapter we use the term *concept* very broadly. We sometimes call schemas *concepts*, and we frequently refer to the complex themes of *Citizen Kane* as concepts. Sometimes abstract perspectives are called *concepts*. No theoretical significance should be attached to this usage. It is merely a convenient way to make a very gross distinction between abstract, conceptual knowledge and information about concrete cases. Similarly for our use of the term *case*. We refer to the short scenes from *Citizen Kane* as mini-cases (or sometimes, in more general theoretical discussions, as cases). Sometimes we call examples or events *cases*. We are simply lumping together as cases anything that is an actual happening or a description of an actual happening, whether it is a scene from a film, a medical case, or an historical event. This is part of the same fundamental distinction we draw between conceptual knowledge and cases (things that actually happen).

Spiro et al., 1987; also see White & Frederiksen, 1987). Mental representations need to be open rather than rigid and closed; nonlinear instructional sequences need to be followed to avoid missing key points; assumptions of regularity and homogeneity have to be replaced by acknowledgment of irregularity and heterogeneity. Learning that has these characteristics of openness and plurality produces *cognitive flexibility:* the ability to adaptively re-assemble diverse elements of knowledge to fit the particular needs of a given understanding or problem-solving situation. In an ill-structured domain, one cannot fit the wide variety of real-world cases of a given type that will be encountered to the same "plaster-cast" knowledge structure (although a common failing of advanced learners is that they will try very hard to do this).

Standard technologies (e.g., books, lectures, etc.) are not well suited to these requirements for the development of cognitive flexibility. But the problem goes beyond the limitations of traditional instructional technologies: *Theories* of cognition and instruction too often focus either on introductory learning or advanced learning in well-structured domains. They therefore have features that are antithetical to those required to deal with the complexities that need to be mastered at advanced stages of knowledge acquisition, as described previously. (See Spiro & Myers, 1984; Spiro et al., 1987, for discussions of limitations of earlier versions of schema/frame/script theories. Cognitive Flexibility Theory is a response to those limitations.)

Actually, although there has been considerable research attention devoted to differences between experts and novices, the intermediate stage of advanced knowledge acquisition that bridges between novicehood and expertise remains little studied. This neglect has had serious consequences given the indications from our research that characteristics of early learning are *inimical* to advanced knowledge acquisition—many of the strategies of learning and instruction that are most successful in introductory learning (e.g., the use of analogy) form impediments to the eventual development of more sophisticated understandings (Feltovich et al., 1989; Spiro et al., 1988; Spiro et al., 1989). So, new theories are needed, as well as new technologies appropriate to those theories. In the next section we first discuss Cognitive Flexibility Theory and then the technological instructional orientation derived from that theory, the Cognitive Flexibility Hypertext approach.

LEARNING AND INSTRUCTION FOR COGNITIVE FLEXIBILITY: CRISS-CROSSING CONCEPTUAL LANDSCAPES

The central metaphor of Cognitive Flexibility Theory is the "criss-crossed landscape." The metaphor derives from Wittgenstein (1953) who, in his preface to the *Philosophical Investigations,* despaired that all of his attempts to weld his complex ideas into a conventionally unified exposition, to force his ideas in any *single direction*, crippled those ideas. Rather than reducing the complexity of his ideas for purposes of expositional elegance and (spurious) theoretical parsimony, he opted instead to write a different kind of book. He would treat the philosophical topics that were his subject as forming a complex landscape, and he would sketch those topics as sites within the landscape. He would then arrange these sketches of local regions of the landscape to form a kind of album. The sequences in the "album" would represent different traversals of the (conceptual) landscape. So in order to insure that the complex landscape would not be oversimplified, he would endeavor to "criss-cross" it in many directions; that is, the same sketches of specific issues (or cases) would reappear in different contexts, analyzed from different perspectives.

Although Wittgenstein did not explicitly make the following claim, it seems likely he would agree (and in any case *we* argue) that because the complexity of a single region (issue, example, case) in a landscape would not be fully graspable in any single context, its full multifacetedness would be brought out by rearranging the sequence of sketch presentations in the album so that the region would be revisited from a variety of vantage points, each perspective highlighting aspects of the region in a somewhat different way than the other perspectives. A synoptic view of the complexity of the conceptual landscape would cumulatively emerge over a number of traversals—the richness of the subject matter would not be crippled if the content was examined in many different ways.

Cognitive Flexibility Theory generalizes Wittgenstein's metaphor of the criss-crossed landscape to apply to *any* complex and ill-structured knowledge domain. Furthermore, the metaphor is extended beyond Wittgenstein's concern for exposition (i.e., a style of writing). We use the metaphor to form the basis of a general theory of learning, instruction, and knowledge representation. One *learns* by criss-crossing conceptual landscapes; *instruction* involves the provision of learning materials that channel multidimensional landscape explorations under the active initiative of the learner (as well as providing expert *guidance* and commentary to help the learner to derive maximum benefit from his or her explorations); and *knowledge representations* reflect the criss-crossing that occurred during learning.

By criss-crossing topical/conceptual landscapes, highly interconnected, web-like knowledge structures are built that permit greater flexibility in the ways that knowledge can potentially be assembled for use in comprehension or problem solving. The likelihood that a highly adaptive schema can be assembled to fit the particular requirements for understanding or acting in the situation at hand is increased. In other words, the range of differing situations that the knowledge could be transferred to is increased. In ill-structured knowledge domains, with their great heterogeneity across potential instances of knowledge application, this flexibility is essential. Because one cannot have a prepackaged knowledge structure for every situation that might be encountered, the emphasis must shift from *intact schema retrieval* to flexibility of *situation-specific schema assembly* (see Spiro et al., 1987; Spiro et al., 1988). By criss-crossing a conceptual landscape in many directions, knowledge that will have to be *used in many ways* is *taught in many ways*.

Random Access Instruction as the Ideal Medium for Criss-Crossing Ill-Structured Domains: New Kinds of Learning and Instruction for Cognitive Flexibility Made Possible by Computers

Clearly, Cognitive Flexibility Theory, with its emphasis on repeated presentations of the same material in rearranged instructional sequences and from different conceptual perspectives, is most efficiently implemented in delivery systems with random access capabilities (e.g., programable videodisc, as in the program discussed in this chapter). The "random access instruction" implementation of Cognitive Flexibility Theory acts as an *antidote* to the various forms of failure in advanced knowledge acquisition frequently associated with traditional learning and instruction (Coulson, Feltovich, & Spiro, 1989; Feltovich et al., 1989; Spiro et al., 1988). If typical approaches have overlinearized, one can construct nonlinear presentations. If material has been presented from just one point of view, one can re-present it from different points of view. Cases that have been slotted in a rigid hierarchical structure can be repeatedly re-presented to attain heterarchical or montage-like structural representations. If partially overlapping exemplars have been indiscriminately lumped under one category in a way that causes important differences among them to be missed, one can demonstrate the diversity amongst the similarity. Or, if exemplars that partially overlap in important ways have been separated into different conceptual categories, the similarity amongst the diversity can be demonstrated. If aspects of knowledge have been overly compartmentalized, their insularity can be overcome by joint presentation. If decomposed elements are not additively assemblable, they can be reassembled with a more complex combinatory logic. If an old example/case is employed too monolithically as a precedent for a new one, you can decompose examples and then recombine aspects of different examples to achieve the most accurate (the most closely fitting) set of *multiple* precedents for understanding in a new situation.

We call the computer-based instructional programs derived from Cognitive Flexibility Theory and built to carry out such operations as those just listed *Cognitive Flexibility Hypertexts*.

A Note on What Kind of Hypertext We Are Talking About. The *Citizen Kane* program and the other Cognitive Flexibility Hypertexts have a specialized function—they are concerned with *structural* characteristics of the cases they try to provide help in understanding. Rather than trying to provide a diverse and entertaining experience, they are trying to simulate experience, insofar as structural aspects of experience are relevant to the knowledge representations that must be developed to support cognitive processing of subsequently encountered cases. The presented material is only that which is needed to form a fairly full representation of a case's internal structure. We are not saying that other material, such as information about an author (or the director of *Citizen Kane*) would not be helpful as well. It is simply our intention to deal with one important and difficult aspect of the hypertext problem: Having the hypertext convey complex knowledge structural characteristics.

A Note on the Use of the Terms "Random" and "Flexible." Two potential misunderstandings should be mentioned. First, the designation *random* is not intended to denote an absence of systematic structure underlying the instructional approach. Far from it: There is an abundance of structure in Cognitive Flexibility Hypertexts, albeit a highly multidimensional and web-like structuration. The randomness concerns the computer system's ability to utilize the underlying structure in a great variety of ways and without inconvenient delays (as when you need to fast-forward videotape to get to a distant segment). The same information is easily accessed in various combinations with other, perhaps distant information in a large number of different contexts.

Second, by promoting cognitive flexibility we are not advocating an "anything goes" mentality. To say, for example, that a text may support multiple alternative interpretations is not to say that interpretations may be offered without warrant. Learners must always be encouraged to find evidence for their claims: A strength of our systems is that their structure and operation make the search for evidence more manageable.

Beyond Access: A Note on the Need for Grounding of Hypertext Development in a Theory of Learning and Instruction. We refer to the systems that we have built as *hypertexts* because of their nonlinear and multidimensional nature. (See Marchionini, 1988, for a review of hypertext work.) However, we wish to emphasize again (see the earlier "Note on Hypertext") our belief that the debate on the hypertext notion has been too narrowly concerned with issues such as data access and too little concerned with the atheoretical character of much of the hypertext work (Spiro et al., 1988). We believe that it is vitally important that hypertext development not be divorced from underlying theories of cognition and instruction. We must know more about how people think and learn in the radically novel form required by hypertexts. We offer Cognitive Flexibility Theory and its extension to random access instruction as a grounding for hypertext approaches. Furthermore, we do not believe the additional cognitive load placed on learners by nonlinear instruction is always desirable. In more well-structured and simple knowledge domains, and, perhaps, in some introductory learning, the disadvantages of hypertext approaches may outweigh their advantages, and traditional approaches are likely to be more efficient and effective. We contend that hypertexts should be used primarily in those situations where traditional approaches would interfere with the goals of knowledge acquisition, namely, for advanced learners striving to master complexity and prepare for transfer in ill- structured knowledge domains.

A COGNITIVE FLEXIBILITY HYPERTEXT FOR MULTITHEMATIC EXPLORATIONS OF *CITIZEN KANE:* AN EXAMPLE OF RANDOM ACCESS INSTRUCTION

The Cognitive Flexibility Hypertext, "Exploring Thematic Structure in Citizen Kane"[5] (referred to by the shorthand designation KANE, which can also be read to stand for *Knowledge Acquisition by Nonlinear Exploration*), is a random access instruction approach to advanced understanding of a film that has a complex and subtle structure. Segments of the film, combined with text, are systematically re-presented at different times, in different content combinations, in different sequences. The result of these arrangements is *multiple texts* about the film, for different learning purposes, produced by *automatic computer re-editing*. The program has been designed for use by advanced high school students and college students. The intent of the program is to go beyond traditional instructional approaches that tend to be overly linear, one-dimensional in their abstractions, and, in general, reductive of the complexity found in literary works. In addition to the goal of fostering advanced understandings of this specific film, the more general intention is to demonstrate to students the complex nature of literary comprehension and to help students to begin to build a more adequate repertoire of cognitive skills for the processing of complexity and for the application/transfer of complex knowledge to new situations. The work on KANE is part of a larger research program whose goal, currently being explored in several domains, is to discover general principles of effective advanced learning and instruction for complex subject matter.[6] (In addition to their intended use in advanced knowledge acquisition, the hypertext programs can also function as helpful research tools for expert specialists, and of course, in experimental studies of nonlinear cognition and instruction).

---

[5]The program was conceived by the first author, who also conducted the content analysis of the film. The second author wrote the program code from the specifications provided to him. Michael Jacobson helped with some of the user-interface design.

At this time, the KANE program does not try to teach all aspects of the film. Rather, our more restricted current focus is a case-based understanding of the internal "semantic" structure of the film, particularly as it bears on the Kane character (i.e., his motivations, values, beliefs, and so on). (Obviously, if we wanted to be more ambitious and teach the entire film, rather than just the complex makeup of its main character, the film's convoluted narrative style and many technical innovations would be ideally suited to the random access approach.) Also, at this time the program uses a preestablished underlying structure, albeit a highly complex, pluralistic, and flexible one. Upcoming versions will incorporate more options for users to generate their own structural schemes in addition to those provided for them. However, the current version does allow users considerable leeway in the secondary structures that they may *add* to the provided underlying structure; and freedom of student-initiated exploration of the landscape as it is complexly mapped by the provided structure is a key feature of the program (as its title indicates). As is illustrated later, the provided underlying structure retains the potential for quite considerable openness in the interpretation of the work (Barthes, 1967).

"Exploring Thematic Structure in Citizen Kane":
A Brief Description of the Operation of the Program

The following is a brief description of the program intended to provide just enough familiarity with its operation to form a context for the discussion of the theoretical implications of the program's features that comes after this context-setting section. It is important to remember that the main intent of this chapter is to present our theoretical perspective and the systematic approach to computer-supported instruction that follows from the theory; discussion of the KANE program per se is not the purpose of this chapter. Accordingly, the reader interested in more information about KANE is directed to a more detailed, archival description of the program that will appear elsewhere.

Before going any further, however, an important disclaimer should be noted: Given the limitations of space, the accumulation of a critical mass of highly interconnected knowledge by a large number of "landscape criss-crosses" cannot be fully illustrated here. The examples that are discussed

---

[6]It is worth noting again that the Cognitive Flexibility Hypertext approach is a *general* one—the same principles lead to very similar hypertexts in radically different knowledge domains. The issue of *domain-independence* is relevant here. We believe that there are considerable differences across domains, but the *principles of domain exploration* are the same (just as New England and Southwestern landscapes differ, whereas general principles of how to explore a landscape can be applied to both). For example, in any landscape or complex knowledge domain, *multiple* traversals will be important.

can give only the faintest hint of the experiences provided by more extended exposure.

Preliminaries. It should be kept in mind that KANE is an *advanced knowledge acquisition* environment, not a tool for introductory learning. Thus, in the initial phase of working with the program, it is expected that students (college or advanced high school) will have already watched the film in its natural sequence at least once and preferably two or more times to become very familiar with it, and that they will have been thoroughly introduced to the major themes—before you can "play" with content, examining it in a variety of new and interesting ways, the content to be played with must be well learned.

Thematic Organization: Multiple Wide-Scope "Schemas of the Whole." For the main instructional part of the program, an extensive and detailed thematic analysis was carried out of Side 2 of the *Citizen Kane* videodisc, containing several scenes and lasting approximately 30 minutes. The analysis was based on 10 themes chosen for their prominence in the critical literature on the film. The themes have *wide scope:* Each theme has been put forward by some experts as being capable of providing a complete account of the Kane character's behavior, motivations, failings, and so on. In a sense, each of these complex and powerful themes has been thought of by some subset of expert analysts as providing *a complete schema for understanding Kane.* Examples of themes include: "Hollow Man" (Kane's inherent soullessness), "Wealth Corrupts," and "Outsized Ambition." Additionally, two of the themes involve Kane's relationships to important symbolic characters in the film, Leland and Thatcher. The course of Kane's development can be conceptualized as a dynamic movement toward and away from a complex of features crystallized in those characters (roughly: populism, friendship, and principled behavior for Leland, and wealth and emotional detachment for Thatcher).

As is seen later, the use of several comprehensive themes makes it more likely that an appropriate one (or subset combination) will be available to be adaptively fit to the particular needs of situations encountered in the future. Furthermore, the variability of usage of each theme is stressed in instruction (see the discussion of variability in concept application). So, *knowledge transfer is facilitated by having a large number of wide-scope interpretive schemas available and by enabling learners to use each of those schemas in a flexible manner.* The use of multiple organizing perspectives/schemas in the instructional program is an illustration of one of the most important recommendations of Cognitive Flexibility Theory: *Use multiple representations* for advanced knowledge acquisition in ill-structured domains.

The choice of themes does not involve an especially delicate selection process. In an ill-structured domain, more schemas are better than less; so each time you add another credible schema you are adding to the scope of coverage. (Again, each of the themes could be treated as a full schema. The themes are also called *concepts* at times. See footnote 4 for a discussion of the terminology used in this chapter.) Therefore, there is no need to adjudicate between alternative wide-scope schemas offered by different experts, discarding some because they are not as "good" as others. In an ill-structured domain any widely supported candidate schema is likely to be useful on many occasions and less relevant on others—they are all "correct," but only to a *limited extent.* The more of them you have, the more likely you will be to have an available subset that is especially useful for the needs of processing some new case (keeping in mind that in ill-structured domains there is considerable variability across cases and each case is individually complex). By the time you get up to 10 or so wide-scope schemas, a lot of territory has been covered (certainly *much* more than with just one schema). So, given the need for an *expansive* theme selection policy (the theory requires that as many credible perspectives as possible be incorporated up to limits of cognitive tracking capacity, to support future knowledge transfer), there is little pressure to choose between competing themes for inclusion in the instructional program. In any case, any theme list will be insufficient by itself given the necessity of knowledge assembly in the context of new cases in ill-structured domains (i.e., new knowledge structures will typically have to be built for a new case by *combining* themes).

It should also be noted that it is all right for the themes to overlap somewhat (it would be difficult to find any set of themes that are mutually independent, yet still have wide scope of application). However, the themes in KANE only partially overlap: Each makes some novel contribution not made by the others. (Obviously, it would be undesirable to use a set made up of very similar themes, themes that are not much more than paraphrases of each other.)

Case Organization: Division into Mini-Case Scenes. The second side of the videodisc was divided into 25 natural units. As is seen later, the precise subdivision chosen is not particularly significant so long as it is a defensibly reasonable one, because any of a number of possible subdivisions produce roughly equivalent effects—the important thing is that the chosen segments provide a rich staging ground for instruction. These scenes function as mini cases: Self-contained units that are short enough to permit rapid study (they mainly range from 30 to 90 seconds), but rich enough to allow for the complex interplay of multiple themes. Each of these scene "units" is coded with a vector that specifies which of the eight themes and two symbolic perspectives has a relevant role in a given scene; this information is the basis for the computer program's theme-based search (see later).

An example of a mini-case scene, which is referred to in later sections of this chapter, is the following segment of the film (that takes less than 1 minute to view):

In this scene, Kane has just recently taken over the newspaper "The New York Enquirer." The first edition of the newspaper since he took control of it will come out in the morning. Kane, his associates, and the newspaper staff have worked all night remaking the paper. Dawn is breaking. Kane's two exhausted associates are remarking on what a long day it has been. "A wasted day," says Kane. He complains that all they did was alter the surface of the paper. He wants to do something that is not superficial. He wants to make the Enquirer "as important to New York as the gas in this light." He then blows out the flame on the light, and the scene ends.

This is a very short scene, but it can teach many important lessons (and the number of lessons it can teach increases when the scene is contrasted with other scenes to draw additional lessons beyond those of the scene in isolation). Some of the lessons taught in the context of this 45-second scene are illustrated by the following optional theme commentaries drawn from the program (with theme and subtheme information included in brackets):

It's been a long day and night, but there is a weary sense of accomplishment in the group. Kane, however considers it a "wasted day." He has completely remade "The Enquirer," from top to bottom, but that is not enough for him. The changes are too superficial. He wants his newspaper to become of central importance to New York. He wants the people of the city to depend on the "Enquirer" as much as they depend on the gas for their lights. [An illustration of the Outsized Ambition theme, and its Grandeur/Sweep and Egomania subthemes.]

By getting the people of New York to consider his newspaper to be as vital to them "as the gas in this lamp," he wants them to depend on him (through his newspaper, which Kane always treated as an extension of himself). [An illustration of the Power theme ("Control Others by their Dependence on You" subtheme).]

His reference to the gas in his lamp as typifying something that is essential to the city is ironic. Soon the gas lamp will be obsolete (as will Kane). This is one of the many instances of conspicuous misjudgment on Kane's part (as when he guarantees in 1938 that there will be no war in Europe). He underestimates the forces of change and consequently is a frequent misreader of the future (whether it is about gas as a source of power or newspapers as the dominant media for influencing people). He is constantly shown to be fallible, a trait that undermines his egomaniacally pitched ambition. [An illustration of the Fallibility/Morality subtheme of the Outsized Ambition theme.]

Everyone has worked all day and all night, but Kane is the only one who is still going. This is typical of the energy and enthusiasm of his early years. (His youthful energy contrasts starkly with the deathlike torpor and stagnancy of Kane when he is older.) [A negative example of the Hollow Man theme illustrating the Lifelessness subtheme. His energy and vitality in this scene are opposed to his later lifelessness and lack of inner spark.]

A lot of the complexity of the domain has begun to be illustrated from just one mini-case lasting less than 1 minute. As we see later, there are several purposes served by this design strategy of structuring in small segments (e.g., acceleration of experience acquisition, making complexity tractable for the learner, facilitation of subsequent restructuring of knowledge, and others).

An important note that will help to avoid confusion in the exposition throughout the remainder of the chapter is that instances from the film are treated as *"cases" from Kane's life*. So, when our theoretical discussions refer generally to the role of cases, that means larger scenes from the film, while mini-cases correspond to very short scenes from the film. Again, *scenes* and *mini-cases* are used as interchangeable terms in this chapter.

Contextual Support, Thematic Commentary and Guidance. After a scene has been viewed the frame is frozen and several options are presented. Because the scenes are studied out of sequence, the user always has an option to request "stage-setters," information about the context in which the scene is occurring, what has just happened before the scene, and so on. Thus, the "out-of-the-blue" effect of nonsequential presentations is lessened. (It should be remembered, however, that the film has already been viewed in its natural sequence prior to this advanced stage of learning.) Also, of course, it is possible to use the program to watch clusters of scenes sequentially; that is, the student can study cases with a larger "grain size" than the mini-cases. This is recommended only for later stages of using the program, in order to avoid the confusion likely to result from starting right in with a complex multithematic analysis of too large an amount of case information. (See the later section on "experience consolidation" for a discussion of the cognitive advantages of introducing complexity in "bite-size chunks.")

Each scene is presented with a text overlay in a corner of the screen listing the themes the scene contains. The themes that were targeted in the menu selection (see the section immediately following) are presented at the top of the list in a different color than the themes present in that unit but not targeted for search by the student. The student can choose to see text commentary on the particular nature of any theme's instantiation in that scene. Two important kinds of information included in the commentaries concern *access/tailoring* (why the particulars of that scene constitute grounds for saying that the given theme is illustrated there—how the generic theme is tailored to apply to that particular context) and *across-scene relations* (how a particular instantiation of a theme relates to instantiations elsewhere in the film).

Finally, the student can choose to see the scene over again, exit back to the menu, or continue with the next scene in the stack. Also, the student can examine a "road-map" of his or her prior explorations.

In summary, instruction on complex subject matter must be made as tractable for the student as possible. We have found in our research that ignoring complexity leads to unacceptable learning outcomes (Coulson et al., 1989; Feltovich et al., 1989; Spiro et al., 1989). Essential content complexity and application irregularities must be faced, even if they are difficult to learn and teach. However, every effort must be made to help the student to *manage* that important complexity.

Theme-Based Exploration: Re-Editing the Film as Function of Thematic Content. Students operating in the program's *self-directed* mode (there is also a *sequential* and an *experimentor-controlled* mode of operation) are presented with a menu of themes and instructions for combining themes. They can choose to examine the occurrences of a single theme (which may be specified as to whether it is a positive or negative instance of a theme, if desired—for example, some event related to poverty would be a negative instance of the wealth theme). Or they can choose to search for scenes that illustrate *combinations of several themes* (conjunctively or disjunctively). The menu selection leads to a search for minicases/scenes whose vectors have the targeted thematic properties. For example, the student may choose to look for scenes that illustrate both the Wealth Corrupts and Hollow Man themes. Those scenes that fit the request are then put in a stack of scenes that the student can view.

In other words, in a very short amount of time, a *re-edited version* of the film that highlights *just* the theme(s) that the student wants to explore is ready to be presented. Because of the large number of scenes and themes, there are literally thousands of potential re-editings, each of which has some instructional significance (some, obviously, having more significance than others). This plentitude of re-editings relates to one of the important lessons of ill- structured domains: Because of domain irregularities and novelty resulting from the exponential explosion of the multiple factors in a complex concept, you always gain from additional experience—for example, a physician can never have "enough" experience.

Non-Preprogrammed Special Initiatives: User-Construction of Interpretive Essays. Adding to the flexibility of the program is a miniature author-aiding system of sorts in which "special initiatives" to teach structures in the film that are not included in the theme menu can be developed (either by the student or by an experimenter or teacher). For example, if the instructor wanted to construct a visual essay about Oedipal themes in the film, he or she would enter a listing of the scenes that are pertinent to Oedipal interpretations. The film would then be rapidly re-edited to show the relevant scenes upon a request to study the Oedipal interpretation. Or the symbolic significance of snow could be easily demonstrated by using the special initiative option to direct a re-editing to show the several scenes from different parts of the film that utilize snow symbolically. These special initiatives can be saved and incorporated into lessons under the instructor's control.

Enabling KANE (Pardon the Pun): The Virtues of HANDY

KANE was programmed using the experimental HANDY authoring language, developed by Don Nix. It would have been difficult if not impossible to incorporate all the features of KANE without HANDY. And those features that could have been incorporated with other authoring aids would not have been so convenient to incorporate. HANDY is a *very* useful tool for multimedia instructional development.

CRITICAL FEATURES IN THE APPLICATION OF COGNITIVE FLEXIBILITY THEORY TO RANDOM ACCESS INSTRUCTION: THEORETICAL RATIONALE FOR DESIGN DECISIONS IN THE KANE HYPERTEXT

In the last section, we offered a moderately uninterpreted description of the operation of KANE. With that description as background, we now highlight a number of fundamental *design decisions* that were made in that instructional program (and in each of the other Cognitive Flexibility Hypertexts), calling special attention to the theoretical motivation for these decisions in light of the goals of advanced knowledge acquisition, as the achievement of these goals is constrained by the presence of complexity and ill-structuredness in a knowledge domain.

Cognitive Flexibility Hypertexts, including KANE, are the result of a large number of design decisions. Each of these decisions is motivated by Cognitive Flexibility Theory, and most of them have more than one justification. To illustrate the web of support underlying the design decisions, we discuss in our limited space just *one* of them in fairly elaborate detail: the decision to use the *mini-case* (in KANE, a short scene) as the fundamental unit of organization for the search and presentation-display processes in the hypertexts.

We then more briefly highlight several other important design features of Cognitive Flexibility Hypertexts, with particular reference to their instantiation in KANE. The discussion again focuses on those features of learning and instruction that are affected by characteristics of complexity and ill-structuredness, as those characteristics relate to the attainment of the goals of advanced knowledge acquisition (mastery of complexity and knowledge transferability/applicability).[7] In other words, wherever possible, the rhetorical form for these discussions follows the basic frame that was originally used to move from Cognitive Flexibility Theory to the instructional implementation of the theory's implications for application:

> Because ill-structured domains have property X, the structural and processing requirements for attaining transfer are therefore Y. So, to get a learner to have the skills and knowledge to be able to achieve transfer, instructional systems ought to have design feature Z.

A *sample instantiation* of this frame would be:

> Because concepts in ill-structured domains have the property of substantial variability across their case applications, the structural and processing requirements for attaining transfer are therefore to understand the nature and scope of that variability, as well as the way that concepts get tailored to cases and cases signal the need for accessing concepts. So, to get a learner to have the skills and knowledge to be able to achieve transfer, an instructional system ought to have the following design feature (among others to address this need): The system should allow the student to sequentially study just those parts of cases that contain examples of uses of the concept; that is, teach conceptual variability by demonstrating it in one place (accompanied by appropriate commentary on the nature of the conceptual variability).

The Mini-Case as the Fundamental Unit of Instruction: Structuring in Small Segments for Tractably Accelerated Acquisition of Case Experience and the Development of Flexibly Assemblable Knowledge

The mini-case (a segment drawn from a larger case) is the starting point for all instruction in Cognitive Flexibility Hypertexts. The rationale for this design decision is discussed in detail in this section.

---

[7]It should be noted that KANE also allows well-structured aspects to be taught (e.g., besides showing how themes differ across instantiations) the program teaches what distinguishes each theme (i.e., what theme instantiations have in common). However, given limitations of space, we emphasize the more novel treatment of complexity and ill-structuredness.

Case-Based Exploration: The Central Importance of Actual Occurrences in Ill-Structured Domains. In an ill-structured domain, across-case variability is, by definition, too great to allow abstract conceptual knowledge to have a dominant role. By the definition of ill-structuredness, any abstraction or generalization will inadequately account for what happens across the range of cases that the knowledge will have to be applied to. Thus, in any ill-structured domain a more case-centered approach is needed.

Cases Cause Problems, Too: The Rationale for the Mini-Case. However, even the individual case is too complex and unwieldy a unit. Each case means too many things to be useful when treated as a monolithic unit. For example, isolated parts of a case may have instructional value but go unnoticed because they appear to lack significance within the frame of reference of the case as a whole. More seriously, intact cases used in instruction are frequently the cause of a problem in subsequent knowledge application: the tendency to map a new case completely to a single well-learned prototype, when part of the old case is *misleadingly related* to the new one—in ill-structured domains multiple representations are the rule, and that includes understanding a new case by reference to multiple prototypes. When cases are taught monolithically, their representations are harder to pull apart in the way that is necessary for transfer-enabling flexible reorganization of knowledge. Thus, in an ill-structured domain, an *intermediate* course must be followed: Just as one must not rely too much on abstract knowledge when dealing with a new case, one also can not rely too much on intact case-based reasoning, when the latter is taken to mean reasoning to a new case from a single precedent case.

Accordingly, as we have already mentioned, Cognitive Flexibility Hypertexts use segments drawn from cases—*mini-cases*—as the focus of instructional organization. KANE uses very short pieces of larger scenes as the mini-cases. Each mini-case receives interpretations across all of the multiple thematic dimensions that are relevant to it. (It is important to note that the *entire* case is always reconstructible in the hypertexts, and at some point during instruction the student should combine the mini-cases that belong to a larger case, so that they can learn how mini-cases configure to make up an intact case. The programs make it very easy to do this.)

It is worth calling special attention to a serious potential misinterpretation of what we mean by a mini-case. Mini-cases are not cases decomposed into their constituent features—they are not "abstract slices" of a case (e.g., the parts of a medical case that relate to vascular impedance). Such an approach would be antithetical to Cognitive Flexibility Theory because it would convey the mistaken notion, which is eagerly accepted by students, that the features of cases are independent, that one can study the aspects separately and then additively reassemble the whole case from those separately considered conceptual parts. Rather, mini-cases are chronological segments of a case (e.g., the first 3 hours of a battle, or frames 254–416 in a film). Thus, they retain some of the complex multiplicity found in the case as a whole. In a sense, they are *microcosms*, cases in miniature rather than separate case "compartments."

Advantages of Mini-Cases. There are several advantages to using mini-cases as the primary instructional organizing unit. We discuss them in turn in order to show how design decisions in our hypertexts are bolstered by converging theoretical considerations:

1. *Experience-consolidation and the mini-case: Accelerated acquisition of experience by compacting and elaborating cases.* In an ill-structured domain you need to see lots of cases—the more case experience you have, the better your performance will be (especially independent transfer performance). For example, that's why experience is so valued in the professions (such as medicine); professional domains are notoriously complex and ill-structured, and professional training can not possibly provide sufficient experience in the limited amount of time available. Even with "problem-based" curricula, only a small number of cases actually get covered (which is very helpful for teaching the processes of intact case analysis, but less helpful for providing the multidimensionally analyzed, criss-crossed knowledge structures that need to be derived from case experience).

By breaking full cases into several mini-cases, and then conducting a rich analysis of each mini-case (i.e., compacting and elaborating case experience), and by focusing mainly on knowledge structural characteristics of each case, many more case experiences are provided, in an instructionally reasonable amount of time. *The process of acquiring experience is consolidated.* Again, better performance in ill-structured domains requires more cases and more case-processing experience.

It might be argued that the advantage of covering much larger numbers of cases by using mini-cases is lessened by the quality of the coverage. In fact, the learning made possible by our richly analyzed mini-cases is quite potent. Consider all of the lessons taught in the context of just the one 45-second scene and few minutes of processing of commentary described earlier (the "gas in the lamp" scene). In that scene, it was clearly shown how four themes were simultaneously relevant, important lessons about the general nature of each of those themes were taught, illustrations of how the general themes had to be tailored to that particular scene (case of application) were presented, connections were drawn between that use of the themes and others in the film, and so on. All in less than 5 minutes, and all in the context of a *real* application of the conceptual/thematic knowledge that is being taught (not an artificial, *contrived* textbook example tailored to teaching the concepts but not representative of the types of cases that the concepts will eventually have to be used to understand—here, real scenes from the film). Now imagine what would happen if the in-depth understanding derived from that one mini-case presentation were to be *compounded* by similar rich lessons for 10 other mini-cases, with each one related to the others. And that would take approximately 1 hour. The effects of dozens of these experiences over several days is obviously quite potent.

Again, however, it is worth pointing out that we do *not* claim that learning with our mini-cases *substitutes* for actual case experience. Rather, we contend that *one* important thing that comes from case experience can be more effectively conveyed by covering compacted and elaborated mini-cases in the way that we do: namely, the criss-crossed, multidimensional representation of the structure of case-based knowledge. Furthermore, these structural characteristics are taught more efficiently in our systems than in real-world case experience for a number of different reasons: conceptual structure is highlighted for the case, rather than having to be inferred; optional expert guidance is available; one is not dependent on serendipitous occurrences of instructionally useful cases in fortuitous sequences; etc. To get a lot of useful case experience, you don't have to actually physically experience the case. Again, if the fullness of the case's structural characteristics is successfully extracted, the effects may be better than actually "being there", because of the larger number of cases that can be covered, because of sequencing for instructional impact, and so on.

Summarizing, an important function of Cognitive Flexibility Hypertexts is that they consolidate the *process* of experience acquisition. By using mini-cases, the student sees many more examples of rich case analysis (e.g., of how concepts interact in a single case), in a much shorter amount of time. Each mini-case scene in KANE is a case-based demonstration of the processes of complex thematic analysis. Furthermore, each scene provides a rich lesson in the complex thematic structure of the film. And it deals with the conceptual information in the way that it is needed in ill-structured domains: namely, *concepts are embedded in "practice"*—the treatment of concepts is tied to the cases they are being applied to (and remember, in an ill-structured domain concept application is far more variable across instances, and thus more difficult, than in well-structured domains).

2. *The mini-case and the problem of early introductions of complexity: Making complexity cognitively tractable for the learner.* The use of mini-cases not only allows more cases to be covered, it also has beneficial effects on the cognitive manageability of the complex case instruction required in ill-structured domains. We have referred to our research findings that indicate difficulties with the traditional instructional approach of incremental additions of complexity (i.e., "start simple and then get more complex"). The early simplifi-

cations create impediments to the mastery of complexity introduced later (Feltovich et al., 1989; Spiro et al., 1989). This would suggest that complexity needs to be introduced earlier. The problem, obviously, is that complexity brings with it learning difficulties—you do not want to overwhelm or confuse the learner. Hence, a great advantage of the mini-case: It allows the earlier introduction of manageable *complexity* by presenting it in *"bite-size" chunks*.

In other words, Cognitive Flexibility Theory leads to a *reconceptualization of instructional incrementalism*. Instead of going from simple to complex treatments (with the attendant problem of creating barriers to advanced learning for the specific topics initially oversimplified, and the more general problem of instilling in students the mistaken belief that knowledge is organized more simply than it actually needs to be), instruction starts with complex treatments but situates them in cognitively manageable mini-cases. The extra cognitive difficulty of having to process multiple thematic representations of the same case is lessened by only having to understand and apply the multiple representations to a *small* case. So the student learns from the outset that the cases they will have to apply their knowledge to are complex (in that they require that multiple aspects of their knowledge representations be simultaneously and interactively superimposed) and they receive an easily graspable set of lessons about how some specific conceptual themes get instantiated in a particular context. A complex lesson in the application of conceptual knowledge is made much easier if the site for the application is as easy to grasp as, say, a 45-second scene from a film.

So, instead of making early instruction on a topic manageable for learners by oversimplifying the content (which will be counterproductive for more advanced knowledge acquisition), hypertexts like KANE present the conceptual complexity necessary for applying the knowledge to actual cases; but they do it in bite-size chunks that will help the students to avoid being overwhelmed.

3. *Avoidance of maladaptive over-reliance on prototype cases.* One thing that makes a domain ill-structured is that the processing of some new case is unlikely to benefit from a direct mapping (of structure or content) to any single prior case serving as a prototype. The individual case is complex, and there is considerable variability across cases. This is not to say that there is nothing to be learned from earlier cases. Far from it. Cognitive Flexibility Theory is case-centered (rather than knowledge-centered), and cases are not just important to learn from: They also have a crucial role as precedents in the processing of new cases. But there is likely to be more than one antecedent case that will be useful for processing a new case. The Cuban Missile Crisis, as it was developing, was partly like the Appeasement of Munich, but partly unlike it, partly like Korea and partly unlike it, and so on (despite the fact that the policy arguments on President Kennedy's crisis team tended to

revolve around which of the similar antecedents should be *the* precedent used in forming strategy for the United States' response). By using mini-cases, the monolithic integrity of the intact case is undermined, with the result that the tendency to over rely on an exact mapping to just one precedent case is considerably lessened. Correspondingly, the need of mapping to *multiple* precedent/prototype sets, drawing on those *parts* of prior cases that are relevant is made clear, and the ability to appropriately assemble pieces of several precedent cases is enhanced.

4. *Principled fragmentation for adaptive flexibility: The importance of mobile, recombinable knowledge elements.* A key feature of ill-structured domains is that a single prepackaged schema or prototype case will typically be inadequate as background knowledge to support the processing of a new case. Thus, intact schema retrieval (or prototype retrieval) as a knowledge-based processing mechanism must be replaced by situation-specific schema- and precedent-case assembly. In a complex and ill-structured domain, small bits of information (either about prior cases or about abstract concepts) recombine in a large number of ways in the new cases that prior knowledge must be applied to. The use of mini-cases allows for easier situation-dependent knowledge assembly, because the cognitive processes of knowledge compilation are much easier to execute if they are operating on, say six mini-cases rather than six full cases.

More importantly, however, availability of a large number of mini-cases permits a greater range of potential precedent-case assemblies for use in understanding new situations. Paradoxically, decomposition into very small discrete units enables a wider range of nondiscrete representations (similar to the paradoxical effect of breaking things into many very small units to approach a continuum in integral calculus). By using very small units that are then recombined with several others, it is much more likely that you will be able to assemble a precedent set to fit the many kinds of new situations that will be encountered in an ill-structured domain (a process facilitated by the mental record of and experience with recombination derived from past "crisscrossings"). A domain must be substantially *de*constructed in order to have a wide range of possible *re*constructions. Think of the way the use of small dots in comic strips allows more flexibility for developing different kinds of shadings than do bigger dots. In an ill-structured domain, cognitive flexibility to adapt to case variability requires a rich variety of potential shadings of the knowledge that is to be assembled. By structuring with small case segments you will be able to better match knowledge representations to the complexity of the world.

5. *Retaining openness of interpretation.* Meaning in ill-structured domains is multivalent. The goal must always be to resist the premature "closing down" of the interpretive process as soon as one account is identified. This is

especially true in literary domains where the typical literary work will support many interpretations. Structuring over small segments (i.e., using mini-cases) helps to retain openness and plurality. Analyses based on large units will tend to stress elements found across the whole unit, and thereby miss elements that have more local occurrence; this will be true to a greater extent for domains that have complex cases (as in literary domains). Similarly, the larger the unit of analysis, the more that interpretation will tend to *narrow* to some "common denominator" that fits all the constituents, again missing the more irregularly occurring local complexities. Because cases tend not to be homogeneous in an ill-structured domain, representing at the mini-case level helps to avoid these reductive biases and thus offers greater opportunities for representational fidelity to a heterogeneous reality.

Barthes has made similar arguments. In his analyses of literary works (e.g., 1967), he made the short segment, which he called a *lexia* (ranging in length from parts of a sentence to several sentences) the organizing unit for his analyses. He argued persuasively that this would result in an "open" and "plural" text, whereas if the text were structured over larger segments, it would be more likely to become closed to alternative interpretations. This is because many of the bases for opening up interpretation would be found only in parts of the text, but would be lost when the "grain size" is the text as a whole. As a result, the text would tend to have a more singular interpretation, uniformly applied throughout (again, because much of the basis for realizing that the text has to be seen in multiple ways would have been narrowed away).

The avoidance of closed and narrow representations by structuring in small case segments is particularly important for adaptive flexibility in schema assembly, which requires rich diversity in the way cases are represented. If narrowing occurs in case representations, then you will have fewer "shadings" available to you to optimize the fit of prior knowledge to new cases.

6. *Power and efficiency of the program.* Besides the cognitive and instructional advantages already discussed, the use of the mini-case also has several "logistical" benefits for the development and operation of the computer hypertext program. For one thing, by having a larger numbers of mini-cases, each coded with a 10-slot vector with three possible values in each slot, the number of case contrasts and traversal routes for "landscaping criss-crossing" that can *automatically* be generated by the program (without pre-programming of instructional sequences or pre-storing links across mini-cases) grows *exponentially*.

A time-saving advantage in hypertext development is that fewer cases have to be produced when each case results in several mini-case units. As we have already seen, quite a bit of instructional mileage can be gotten out of even a few cases if they are segmented into many complexly analyzed mini-cases. Of course, the efficiency of the program is further increased by the fact that Cognitive Flexibility Theory *requires* that each mini-case be used more than once (i.e., the same landscape site, or scene in this case, is revisited on different traversals of the landscape).

Also, by using mini-cases it is much easier to effect a connection between a small part of one case and a small part of another case to which the former case is instructively related. It is more difficult to accomplish this when monolithic case blocks are used as organizing units.

7. *Mini-cases help to avoid two common problems of hypertext: a confusing labyrinth of connections and the need to pre-store links.* These technical issues in hypertext methodology are addressed at the end of this chapter.

We have devoted considerable space to the motivation for just one design choice in Cognitive Flexibility Hypertexts (including KANE), and the advantages that accrue to that choice: the principled decision to use mini-cases (short scenes in KANE) as the primary organizing unit of instruction. In the sections that follow we talk about other design decisions; although these are also considered to be crucial, we do not illustrate their rationale and benefits as exhaustively.

Multiple Knowledge Representations and Theme Selection to Maximize Transfer

In an ill-structured domain no single schema will provide sufficiently complete coverage, which will account for sufficient variability in the way things happen in the domain. With the more limited view that results from a single representational system, the learner is not prepared to apply his or her knowledge to those new situations that are less relevant to that representation—and in an ill-structured domain there will be many such situations by definition. Or, in the less extreme situation where multiple schemata are provided, it usually happens (either through instructional influences or because of learner biases) that one or two of the schemata assume precedence over the others. Although this is not as serious a problem as that when only one schema is provided, it is nevertheless the case that in an ill-structured domain any reduction in the operative perspectives for analyzing the wide variety of cases encountered will be disadvantageous. To make up for the inadequacies of any single representational perspective, additional perspectives must be added. With a sufficient number of perspectives, a fuller, more "three-dimensional" view of the domain is achieved. By providing 10 co-equal, frequently applicable themes in KANE, we are making it clear to the student that any one theme permits only a limited view of the landscape. The student learns that the abstract conceptual world for the ill-structured domain is complex and not easily simplified.

So, advanced cognition in complex and ill-structured domains requires *multiple knowledge representations.* As we have already indicated, each of the 10 themes used in the Kane program is more than a mere descriptive attribute—each is a schema in itself. Each could be argued to provide the best full account of the Kane character. Rather than trying to show which is best, the program illustrates how they are all correct, and how their *joint* consideration produces the most adequate account. You cannot impose one interpretive scheme on the film; any scene mixes and blends several interpretive schemes. This lesson is amply taught in KANE, as each mini-case (scene) is viewed from several thematic and symbolic perspectives. By helping the student to fully cover each case/scene by pluralistically representing it, transfer is fostered in several ways: (a) the student learns how to fully interpret cases, facilitating the full interpretation of new cases encountered later; (b) the multiple coding of cases provides a larger number of access routes for their later retrieval from memory as background knowledge precedents for understanding new cases; (c) the interaction of conceptual perspectives is taught by their simultaneous consideration within a single mini-case context; and (d) having 10 wide-scope themes will "cover the landscape"—it gives you more flexibility in tailoring for schema assembly. Also, having 10 themes helps students to avoid the reductive bias of a "uniformity of explanation" (Coulson et al., 1989; Feltovich et al., 1989): with many equal themes none can dominate the others, and therefore all of these (now more minor) perspectives can be readily available to make their contribution as benefits to some new case.

Re-Reading and Rearrangement: Repetition Without Replication

The Kane program, like the other Cognitive Flexibility Hypertexts, relies heavily on the repetition of case information. However, this use of repetition is completely opposed to the *typical* purpose and consequences of repeating information in learning and instruction. Conventional uses of repetition in instruction are intended to strengthen the learning of some aspect of knowledge, with successive presentations each intended to *mean the same thing each time.* In contrast, our use of repetition is *non- replicative.* The aim is to illustrate the *complexity* of case information. Following the metaphor of the criss-cross landscape, the same content is presented in different contexts. This helps to keep interpretation from rigidifying toward an overly narrow subset of the lessons that the content should be teaching (and that the learner must be prepared to utilize in transfer situations). That is, the repeated presentations aim to point out for students how the same case information can take on importantly different shades of meaning at different times and how each case has many facets, some of which will tend not to be noticed in any single context of occurrence. In complex and ill-structured domains, each unit of content is multifaceted. Each presentation of that content in a different context highlights another aspect of that multifactedness, as well as illustrating context dependencies. There is a limit to the number of lessons that can be learned in any single presentation of content material, in any single context of presentation. Furthermore, by presenting the same case information at different times, in the context of various other cases, and with different conceptual elements stressed, a web of case and context interrelationships of the kind necessary for flexible knowledge assembly and transfer in ill-structured domains is established.

Relationship to Poststructuralism in Literary Theory and Philosophy. A similar role for re-reading in order to avoid reducing complexity was a central feature of Barthes' (1967) analysis of Balzac's short novel, "Sarassine," in *S/Z*. In fact, our general approach has many affinities to poststructuralist literary theories (like that of Barthes in the late 1960s), which also stress such factors as multiple codes, the importance of knowledge fragments, and the nonunifiability of rich cases by any *single* unifying logic. Not coincidentally, Wittgenstein's later work, which strongly influenced our thinking, also has been adopted by many poststructuralists. (Interestingly, Wittgenstein had originally intended to have an elaborate set of cross-references placed below each sketch in the *Philosophical Investigations* to enable criss-crossing the landscape of sketches in various directions with frequent re-readings in new contexts.)

Theme-Based Exploration: Teaching Conceptual Complexity and Variability in Conceptual Application

One of the main features built into KANE is the ability to have the program search for occurrences of any chosen theme and then re-edit the film to show just those scenes found in the search (along with accompanying commentary, stage-setting information, etc.). Theme-based explorations of the film are intended to teach both the complexity of the themes and the nature of their variability of instantiation in actual scene contexts. An important feature of abstract concepts in ill- structured domains is their irregularity of application (see also Barsalou, 1987). That is, each concept is used in a lot of different ways. Also, the same concept will apply to a variety of kinds of cases. These features have the consequence of making it hard to: (a) go from cases to concepts (problems of knowing which concepts are relevant from the case information), and (b) go from concepts to cases (problems of tailoring the way a concept is used to a particular context of its application). (Once again, in this chapter we use the term *concept* very broadly to make a gross distinction between abstract knowledge and case information. With this loose criterion, a complex theme in KANE can be referred to as a concept.)

Theme-Based Search and Variability of Instantiation. In general, the concepts of an ill-structured domain cannot be transmitted to learners the way they are in well-structured domains, namely by some direct process of providing general principles or definitions (perhaps with one or two examples as illustrations of the general principles). Instead, knowledge of concepts comes from having their uses (instantiations) *demonstrated*, rather than the concept being specified in the abstract. In an ill-structured domain the meaning of concepts is implicit, at least partly, in the pattern of its *uses* of the concept (Wittgenstein, 1953). The theme-search feature of KANE (and a similar feature in the other Cognitive Flexibility Hypertexts) does what must be done in an ill-structured domain: It allows the nature of concepts to be *shown* (by a guided presentation of their actual occurrences), not *told*. The nature of the variability of theme-instantiation in KANE is conveyed in part by sequentially viewing an entire series of scenes that are instances of the theme. For example, the user can ask to view a series of brief scenes that all illustrate the Hollow Man theme. Thus, the program *shows* the variability in conceptual use—you *see* a set of different cases that are said to be instances of the concept. (Of course, you also see what is in *common* across the uses—but this is much easier to teach.)

Commentary and Expert Guidance: Tailoring, Integrating, and Preparing for Access. The thematic commentary that accompanies scenes also helps to convey conceptual complexity. Commentaries provide several kinds of assistance. First, they explain how the scene instantiates the theme; that is, they *tailor* the theme to the case. Second, they discuss features of the scene that lead one to consider it to be an instance of the theme, information that helps students learn the difficult process of accessing concepts from case information. Third, the commentaries help with two kinds of integration functions: They relate the theme to other themes in the same scene (building *theme connections* and reminding learners about the importance of the *simultaneous* use of multiple perspectives); and they relate the current instance of the theme to other instances of the theme elsewhere in the film.

Also helping in the management of conceptual complexity is the use of more differentiated subtheme designations that tell what *type* of instantiation of the theme is being observed. That is, each theme is analyzed into various "senses," and the instantiated sense is presented in the header for the commentary. For example, a subtheme of the Power theme is "Kane controls others by having them depend on him." The subtheme information also accompanies the viewing of a scene (i.e., whenever a theme is instantiated in the film, that theme's name is presented in colored print that overlays the film, accompanied in parentheses by a subtheme designation). Of course, the problems of ill-structuredness apply at the level of subthemes as well: Subthemes lack definiability in the same way that concepts do and, like ill-structured concepts, must have their uses shown or demonstrated.

A Note on "Situated Cognition" and the Relative Importance of Conceptual Knowledge. A popular call has been raised recently for "situated learning" (e.g., Collins, Brown, & Newman, 1989). The emphasis that has been placed on situations at the expense of conceptual knowledge has led some people (although not Collins et al.) to suspect that abstract conceptual knowledge is relatively unimportant, that all that matters are the situations or cases in which learning occurs. The emphasis in Cognitive Flexibility Theory is clear: Concepts and cases are *both* essential. However, conceptual knowledge must be taught in the context of actual cases of its application (not "in the abstract"), and the ill-structured nature of the *use* of conceptual knowledge must be acknowledged and directly addressed in theories of learning, knowledge representation, and instruction. The approach of Cognitive Flexibility Hypertexts is intended to effect an *integration* of conceptual and situational learning, in which each is appropriately thought about *in terms of the other*.

Theme-Combination-Based Exploration: Avoiding Compartmentalization and Assembling Higher Order Knowledge Structures

An important feature of Cognitive Flexibility Hypertexts is their ability to search for mini-cases that are instances of some *combination* of abstract concepts. For example, the KANE program has a menu option that allows for traversals of the film (i.e., re-edited scene juxtapositions) to be selected that highlight combinations of themes.

Non-Insular Treatment of Themes. A common problem in traditional instruction is *compartmentalization:* Conceptual areas that are highly related are presented in separate chapters, lessons, classes, and so on. As a result, the knowledge ends up being represented as if it were in separate compartments. When knowledge from across compartments later has to be combined for use in some situation, the representational basis for the conceptual combination is weak. In ill-structured domains, conceptual combination is the rule rather than the exception. Thus, by allowing the film to be explored as a function of theme-combinations, students learn about the patterns of interaction of conceptual themes, their context dependencies (i.e., the way theme meanings are altered by the context of other themes that they occur with), and so on. These lessons (as well as KANE's approach to teaching *several* themes in the context of each mini-case scene) help to vitiate the force of the compartmentalization bias and to provide knowledge and skill for processing conceptual information in a noncompartmentalized way.

Thus, not only is there a multiplicity of themes, but they function as something more than a list of independent items. As befits an ill-structured domain, the themes are not treated as insular, separable "compartments"; rather, the themes are shown to interpenetrate, to have complex patterns of mutual dependence on each other.

Schema Building. Another use of the theme-combination feature is in generating hypotheses about complex structural models of the film, and then enabling explorations to test and refine those models. These hypotheses can be triggered by such things as chance observation of patterns in the haphazard exploration of theme co-occurrences (i.e., noticing two themes going together in a few different scenes). Or they can be explicitly suggested by the film itself (as in the example presented in the second paragraph following). Or, by exploring small combinations of themes, larger explanatory structures are suggested (also illustrated here). These hypothesized larger structures can then be explored using theme-combination search to validate the hypotheses. This kind of activity provides practice in situation-sensitive schema assembly (e.g., preparing to write an essay, as in the example in the second paragraph following), as well as helping to build "mini-schemas"—complex theme combinations that have partial applicability.

An example of a mini-schema would be the combination of the Wealth Corrupts and the Outsized Ambition themes, as in "Kane's tendency as he got older to buy things instead of earning accomplishments [Wealth Corrupts theme] interfered with the attainment of his earlier ambitions [Ambition theme]." One could then test this mini-schema or examine its variability across instantiations in the same way that variability for a single theme is learned, namely, by juxtaposing a set of scenes that constitute instances of the theme combination.

A lengthy example of using KANE to build a higher order schema (a complex model) is the following sequence of steps using the program to answer an essay question: *Why did Kane fail to achieve the ambitions which seemed within his grasp during his more youthful years?*

A start toward assembling knowledge to answer this question might come from the mini-case scene that immediately follows the one presented in detail earlier in the chapter (the "gas in the lamp" scene). After Kane says that he wants his newspaper (which he equates with himself) to be "as important to New York as the gas in this light", his friend Leland asks him *how* he is going to achieve that goal. Kane goes on to say that he will do it by putting a "Declaration of Principles" on the front page of the paper. He will be honest with the citizens of New York, he will look after the interests of the disenfranchised, and so on. His associate Bernstein pointedly responds by telling Kane "You don't want to make any *promises* you're not going to be able to keep." Kane says that he will keep these promises. That is, he will achieve his ambition for the newspaper (and thus himself) by *principled behavior.* This suggests a possible relationship between the Ambition theme and the Principled Behavior theme. Another part of the puzzle might suggest itself if the student recalls another mini-case scene: at a difficult moment Kane states with some gravity that he could have been a great man if he had not been very rich. Summarizing thus far, we have three themes that might figure in an answer to the question about Kane's failed ambitions: the themes of Principled Behavior, Wealth Corrupts, and, of course, Ambition. The hypothetical model for responding to the essay question at this point might have the form "Kane's ambition was thwarted by his wealth interfering with the path he had chosen to attain his ambitions, principled behavior."

This suggests a re-editing of the film to look at the joint occurrences of these three themes. After the program executes the search, among the scenes encountered will be one mini-case that is especially provocative. The newspaper has become a huge success, and Kane and the staff are celebrating at an extravagant (and mildly decadent) party. Kane is about to embark on a vacation trip to Europe, and Bernstein stops the party to ask Kane if he intends to buy a lot of statues while abroad. Kane says yes, and then Bernstein keeps saying, with emphasis as indicated, *"Promise* me, Mr. Kane. *Promise* me." There is no apparent reason for Bernstein to go on and go about Kane promising him that he will buy those statues (at least when viewing the film sequentially). However, in the context of having recently encountered the scene in which Bernstein pointedly suggested to Kane that he not make any *promises* he was not going to be able to keep, a clear link is established to the principled behavior that was mentioned in that scene as what was going to make the newspaper and Kane great. Once that allusion to the earlier scene is established, it becomes especially significant that Kane responds to Bernstein: "Yes, I promise you. *But you don't expect me to keep any of those promises, do you?"* Clearly, the whole unusual interchange about promising (as well as Bernstein's earlier unusual emphasis on Kane not making promises he could not keep) is intended to signal a connection between the two scenes (or at least supports such a connection, if it was not intended), a connection that is portentous for the theme of Kane's failed ambition. What might have seemed to be a trivial (although odd) statement about making promises now takes on an enriched meaning by its juxtaposition with a more serious scene that also had an odd emphasis on promising (tied to Kane's promise of principled behavior as a way to make him and his newspaper great). Furthermore, the point about Kane not keeping any of his promises is made in a context in which Kane has begun to clearly show that he is allowing his wealth to corrupt him (i.e., in several scenes, obvious connections have been drawn which tie unprincipled behavior by Kane to the corrupting influences of his wealth, as revealed by having the computer do a two-theme search. For example, he repeatedly indicates that he thinks he can act in an unprincipled manner towards friends and then buy them off.

Indeed, after the "promise me" scene at the party, Kane does begin to slide downhill, his lofty ambitions fading further and further from possibility with the passage of time.

Thus, the KANE program provides a substantial start toward a cohesive interpretation of Kane's failed ambitions in terms of his renunciation of principled behavior because of the corruption of his wealth. Especially striking is the way the program helps to make connections that would otherwise be very difficult to make. Of course, this is only one of many possible responses to the essay question. What is important is that the KANE program helps students to respond to situational demands in a manner that is *original*, *complex* and *warranted* (i.e., the program helps the student to assemble justification for a budding complex interpretation). After a short time working with the KANE program, very intricate weavings of themes, of the kind just illustrated, become very straightforward.

Sequencing to Produce Cognitive Structures With Woven Interconnectedness

A topic that we do not treat in detail in this chapter and that is not yet fully implemented in the Cognitive Flexibility Hypertext systems is *sequence and arrangement*. Following Wittgenstein (1953), we consider the *strength* of representations in ill-structured domains to depend not on a single thread running throughout—that is too reductive of the domain's complexity—but rather on the overlapping of many strands. This criterion increases the possible hinges for schema or precedent assembly, the number of access/retrieval routes in memory, and so on. So, it is not just important that a domain's landscape be criss-crossed—how it is criss-crossed is an important consideration. Of course, it should be criss-crossed in such a way that useful instructional contrasts are highlighted. Furthermore, sequential arrangements should be such as to promote knowledge representations characterized by highly woven interconnectedness along several conceptual dimensions, rather than highly compartmentalized structures with connectedness of many elements determined by some single organizational system.

One important sequencing principle that we will incorporate into our systems is that of *"intermediateness"*: Mini-cases should be sequenced for presentation in such a manner that two representational extremes will be avoided. First, a case should not be the next one presented if it would too closely parallel the thematic interactions in several recently presented cases;

this would help students to *avoid overgeneralizations,* a major hazard in ill-structured domains. Second, at the other extreme, a case should not be so dissimilar from those that were recently presented that it would give the learner the mistaken notion that there is no role for conceptual abstractions that extend across cases; this would help students to *avoid the perception that each case is unique.* Rather than either of these extremes, cases should be selected because their strength of relation to preceding cases is *intermediate,* partially overlapping and partially nonoverlapping (see Spiro et al., 1987). This would promote an appreciation of the importance of both knowledge-based and case-based analysis, without either assuming precedence over the other.

The KANE program allows for both experimenter-controlled and student-controlled sequencing. The program keeps track of student-selected traversals. The relative efficacy of different sequencing patterns in the nonlinear presentation of materials, or of different patterns of spontaneous student exploration, is a central concern of our theory, and one that is deserving of considerable empirical investigation generally.

Other Features

There are many other features of the KANE program and Cognitive Flexibility Hypertexts that cannot be discussed in this chapter because of reasons of space (e.g., options related to user-*customization;* user- and teacher-*construction of interpretive essays*—for example, one has been built for the famous reference to Rosebud in KANE; and *active-learner participation).* We have focused in this chapter on those features that cast the most direct light on the most important theoretical underpinnings of the instructional approach.

To take just one example of a potent feature that can not be discussed in depth, consider the "special initiative" option, which allows for the easy development and use of mini-case sequences that illustrate new themes not covered in the provided set. Obviously, this option makes the computer program more flexible. However, it also has some cognitive significance. For example, this option increases the program's power to deal with thematic combinations. Because the "special initiative" option presents specially programmed sequences that are accompanied by their thematic overlays, one can be thinking analytically about the various themes represented in a scene at the same time that a symbolic feature, the topic of the special initiative, is affectively *"coloring"* that thematic analysis. For example, if snow is supposed to symbolically evoke feelings of contentment and security associated with childhood, that mood can be experienced in the background while one is consciously thinking about the role of the Wealth Corrupts theme in the same scene (just as, when you are angry, you can be thinking about something unrelated to your anger, but be doing it angri*ly*—the emotion effortlessly *overlays* the other cognition). *Thoughts* about one topic can be colored by the *feelings* evoked by another topic, thus expanding the scope of possible literary understanding and mental representation (Spiro, Crismore, & Turner, 1982).

Generality of the Approach Demonstrated by Parallels to KANE in Cognitive Flexibility Hypertexts for Random Access Instruction in Other Domains

We have stressed the point that the approach taken in the KANE program is based on principles of random access instruction derived from Cognitive Flexibility Theory (Spiro et al., 1987; Spiro et al., 1988). It is very important to make clear that that theory has the same implications for random access instruction in other, very different domains. That is, the systematic, theory-based approach in Cognitive Flexibility Hypertexts is domain-independent—essentially the same hypertext approach may be employed across ill-structured domains. There are currently two other functioning hypertext prototypes besides KANE, one in cardiovascular medicine and one in military strategy. All three of these Cognitive Flexibility Hypertexts have the same primary features discussed in this chapter (as well as many others we did not have time to present here). All of them: are organized around mini-cases (e.g., parts of battles in the military strategy program); impose multiple conceptual perspectives on each mini-case; allow for concept-based search across cases (highlighting conceptual variability of application and instances of conceptual combinations); provide commentary on the relationship between conceptual and case elements (i.e., they teach the concepts in the context of cases and show how the concepts have to be tailored to the individual case); and so on. (The Cardioworld Explorer hypertext is discussed in Spiro et al., 1988. A detailed treatment of all of the hypertexts will be found in Spiro et al., in preparation, a paper about hypertext generally and about our approach specifically.)

However, by claiming domain-independence for our hypertext approach we are not saying that we dispute the widely reported findings of domain-dependence in cognitive science. In fact, there *are* extensive differences in the nature of knowledge and in the way the knowledge must be used between the domains of literary interpretation, biomedical cognition, and military strategy. However, as we mentioned before, it is not the same thing to say that two landscapes are radically different as it is to say that there are important principles of landscape exploration that are general across domains (e.g., multiple representations; repeated presentations in different contexts; etc.)—it is principles of the latter kind that form the basis for the commonality of Cognitive Flexibility Hypertexts across domains. When the specific content of a domain is used to instantiate the general frame that underlies

Cognitive Flexibility Hypertexts, domain-specific features emerge. Again, the fact that the same primary features were successfully incorporated into hypertexts for three highly dissimilar domains attests to the generality of this theory-based instructional approach.

BENEFITS OF THE COGNITIVE FLEXIBILITY APPROACH TO RANDOM ACCESS INSTRUCTION: DEVELOPING KNOWLEDGE REPRESENTATIONS AND COGNITIVE PROCESSES APPROPRIATE TO ADVANCED LEARNING IN COMPLEX AND ILL-STRUCTURED DOMAINS

The application of Cognitive Flexibility Theory to advanced instruction using computer hypertexts, as illustrated in this chapter by the KANE program, results in several major benefits. These can be briefly summarized as follows here.

Toward a New Incrementalism: Tractability of Learning and Instruction Without Inhibiting the Acquisition of Complexity by Early Oversimplification

The attention to covering necessary complexity is not achieved at the expense of overwhelming and confusing the learner. By using *bite-size chunks of complexity* in the early stages of advanced instruction (mini-cases), followed by the use of more complete cases later, instruction that addresses complexity may be introduced from the outset because it is staged in the context of a limited and manageable (but nevertheless moderately rich and ecologically representative) example—that is, the use of mini-cases reduces the *cognitive demands* on the learner without the hazards of oversimplified "concepts-first" approaches. (A number of other features of our approach also help learners to manage the complexity that is presented, including the various options available to the learner to get theme commentary and guidance, stage-setting information, scene re-viewings, verbal overlays of active themes during film viewing, and so on.)

Advanced Learning in Instructionally Reasonable Amounts of Time: Accelerated Acquisition of Case Experience

Another problem associated with the need to cover complexity and to cover a large number of cases (a prerequisite of advanced performance in ill-structured domains) is the amount of time required. It would be desirable to achieve these goals in the time available for instruction (i.e., a course, or a program of study). The process of acquisition of complex case experience is accelerated in our approach by the use of elaborated mini-cases and by making use of the same, increasingly *familiar* mini-case in different contexts (thus eliminating the need to spend time learning as many new cases). Thus case experience can accumulate far more rapidly with this approach than it does in either: (a) case-based curricula that spend much more time on each case (again, you need to see *lots* of cases in ill-structured domains because of the many different forms cases assume), or (b) the natural exposure to case experience (which is haphazard, and thus not tailored to instructional needs, or guided as to properties of conceptual structure).

Teaching Concepts-in-Practice: Avoidance of Over-Reliance on Knowledge-Based or Case-Based Representational Extremes

The way that advanced topics are usually taught in instructionally reasonable amounts of time is by stressing abstract conceptual knowledge at the expense of exposure to cases. The hope is that the abstractions will have wide scope of application to new cases. In an ill-structured domain, this is a vain hope. For one thing, in an ill-structured domain, concepts vary too much in the way they apply to cases. Cognitive Flexibility Hypertexts like KANE directly address conceptual variability across cases of conceptual application. And these hypertexts *situate* the teaching of concepts in the context of actual cases, demonstrating how concepts are tailored to cases. Thus, our programs neither neglect cases to teach concepts, nor concepts to teach cases—*both* are taught in the context of each other. Learning is situated, but abstract knowledge is not ignored. Our approach teaches concepts and cases *simultaneously*, not separately: *concepts-in-practice.*

Avoidance of Counter-Productive Compartmentalization

A serious problem in the preparation for knowledge transfer by traditional instruction is the presentation of information in highly *compartmentalized* forms. Different conceptual topics are treated in different parts of texts and at different times. When cases are presented, they are usually dealt with in isolation and very seldom related to other cases. But in an ill-structured domain, knowledge can rarely be used intact—parts of topics/schemas/concepts must be combined to form schema-assemblies, and cases must be combined with other cases to form precedent sets. These processes are inhibited by the compartmentalization of knowledge representation that results from compartmentalization in instruction. In our approach, compartmentalization is avoided in a number of different ways. *Several themes are simultaneously considered* when each mini-case is being processed. Search for examples of any possible *theme combination* is facilitated. Commentary on one theme will contain *allusions* (cross-references) to other themes.

Similarly, the likelihood of compartmentalization by cases is minimized. An intact case is less likely to be rigidly treated as a monolithic entity after having been broken into several mini-case segments. Also, the multiple conceptual codings of each mini-case causes it to fall into several conceptual categories. And the ubiquity of case juxtapositions when using the KANE program, as well as the allusions to other cases in the theme commentaries and the thematic overlap across cases, are all designed to build interconnections among cases, not separation.

Teaching Situation-Adaptive Knowledge Compilation: From Intact Schema Retrieval to Schema Assembly

Schema and precedent assembly, as opposed to intact schema retrieval, is, again, a crucial tenet of Cognitive Flexibility Theory. You cannot have a prepackaged schema for every situation you will encounter in an ill-structured domain. A new case will be kind of like an aspect of one prior case, kind of like an aspect of another prior case, and so on. Similarly for the relevance of parts of different concepts, appropriately assembled to fit the new case. So you need to *build schemas* to fit new situations. This requires *flexibility* in knowledge representations. For flexibility you need many movable/recombinable knowledge elements (meaningful *fragments* of knowledge—"partial theories") within a *web-like* structure. This is accomplished in Cognitive Flexibility Hypertexts by such features as the use of minicases/scenes (for later *precedent assembly)* and by having a fairly large number of wide-scope themes/schemas/perspectives for *conceptual schema assembly.* The larger the available set precedent cases and conceptual perspectives, the greater the likelihood that you will have an optimal combination for dealing with the odd new case. The more *pieces* you have to work with that each make some nonoverlapping contribution compared to the others, the greater the *adaptive flexibility* you will have to *respond to complex and changing case realities.* As we said earlier in the chapter, an ill-structured domain must be substantially *de*constructed (while retaining complex interactions of the parts) in order to have a wide range of possible *re*constructions. And facilitating the adaptive assembly of these pieces of cases and fragmentary "theories" is the earlier record of and experience with *criss-crossing* them during instruction (e.g., assembly routes are suggested—you can get between more places in the landscape in more different ways by having a rich network of interconnecting routes).

So, for schema assembly you need: (a) lots of little pieces of reality (mini-cases) and of conceptual knowledge (multiple themes/concepts/partial theories), and (b) a way of assembling them, of putting them together to fit a new case. These needs are supported by features of the approach such as theme combinations, repetition in new contexts, the more rapid accumulation of experience due to the use of compacted and elaborated mini-cases, and single theme search. Consider single theme search: It demonstrates that even routes with the same theme-name can be differentiated, which allows you to even better tailor your knowledge to highly diverse and complex new cases: You can pick just the right flavor of thematic connection—your palette for painting case reality has a much richer and more subtle range of colors. All of the other features similarly contribute to promoting schema assembly ability.

ADDRESSING SOME PROBLEMS IN HYPERTEXT METHODOLOGY

The work on KANE and the other Cognitive Flexibility Hypertexts contribute many new ideas to the growing literature on hypertext methodology. Two especially important ones are addressed here. First, the use of hypertext is made less daunting for the student. Second, it uses a procedure that automatically generates connections, rather than having to have all links stored in advance. These are discussed in turn. (Of course, we consider the most important contribution to be the *theoretical* one that is the subject of this chapter.)

How to Avoid the Problem of "Getting Lost in Hyperspace"

A common problem with hypertexts is that the user soon gets lost in a labyrinth of connections, and loses track of the sense of his or her exploration, as well as his or her physical place in the hypertext (collectively referred to as "getting lost in hyperspace"). The use of a case-centered instructional scheme with mini-cases as instructional and programming foci solves this problem. You can never get lost because you are never more than one connection from the focus of instruction. In a sense, each mini-case, begins a complete and independent unit of instruction. All departures for commentary, guidance, context setting, and so on, take you right back to the case at hand. Each mini-case starts a new lesson (constitutes a new experience).

Latent Rather than Programmed Links: Multithematic Coding of Cases

In conventional approaches to hypertext development (e.g., those using HyperCard), it is usually the case that any connections between knowledge nodes (between "note-cards") that will be available for the user to explore have to be anticipated and explicitly built into the program. This is a limitation of most hypertext programs that does not apply to Cognitive Flexibility Hypertexts. By coding each mini-case with a vector of relevant themes, the KANE program *automatically generates* instructive case sequencings (and many times more of them than would be possible if all links had to be pre-stored— the number of mini-case juxtapositions is so large a number because very many mini-cases are used, and there are many values in the search vector for each of them). So the program can be used for much longer without duplication of instruction and with many more lessons being taught.

We have seen how connections are automatically identified by the program for presentation to the user. But the mere juxtaposition of cases (even with appended commentary) does not guarantee that important connections between them that are not *explicitly* drawn out will be represented in the mind of the user. How, then, do the connections that are *implicit* in the program get formed in the mind (e.g., connections across mini-cases)? The same way they are in *actual* experience. After all, the computer program merely presents experiences (albeit, stripped down to their structurally-relevant features). However, the experiences in Cognitive Flexibility Hypertexts are different from actual experiences in several important ways that make it easier to induce interconnected knowledge representations from exposure to cases: (a) the cases are immediately juxtaposed (hours or days do not pass between nonroutine cases); (b) the cases are thematically related (whereas there is no guarantee of instructive relatedness across naturally occurring adjacent cases); (c) the cases are stripped down to structurally significant features, making it easier to extract dimensions of structural relatedness; (d) the cases are accompanied by expert commentary and guidance; and, finally (e) because the cases are short, they are each easier to remember and more of them can be presented in a short amount of time, facilitating the recognition of relationships across cases.

CONCLUSION

The overall effect of the features of random access instruction that are derived from Cognitive Flexibility Theory and embodied in "Exploring Thematic Structure in Citizen Kane" is a program that allows the Kane character to be viewed from a very large number of valid perspectives. The result of overlaying more and more points of view on the same content material (while at the same time reducing initial demands on the learner resulting from this extra complexity by working with easily digestible mini-cases) is a kind of "stereographic" representation—the multidimensional fullness of the content is increasingly approximated with each additional perspective that is presented. Furthermore, the theme combination feature of the program permits an incremental buildup of a picture of the *interrelations* among the thematic perspectives. Instead of just having a set of independent conceptual perspectives that have to be additively assembled, the complex pattern of their intertwinement in the actual cases (scenes) can emerge. By re-presenting the same information in different contexts and from difference perspéctives, the complexity of that information is made more resistant to oversimplification. As a result, knowledge representation is made more multidimensional—and knowledge that will have to be used in many different ways has to be represented in many different ways, with the potential to form various combinations with other aspects of knowledge as required by new contexts of knowledge use.

The result of instruction of this sort is deeper understanding of complexity and nuance, understanding that provides learners with a basis for going beyond what was explicitly taught. In ill-structured domains, there is considerable variability in the way knowledge has to be used across the set of potential knowledge application situations. Correspondingly, there is a greater burden on learners to be able to *independently* apply their knowledge, rather than relying on prepackaged "prescriptions" for knowledge application provided by teachers and textbooks. Therefore it is essential that learners be presented with a cognitively tractable picture of the landscape of varieties of knowledge use. And learners must be guided in the development of cognitive skills for effectively traversing those landscapes to independently and adaptively assemble knowledge to fit the new situations that that knowledge must be applied to. These are the aims of the hypertext instructional systems that implement Cognitive Flexibility Theory. In Cognitive Flexibility Hypertexts (like "Exploring Thematic Structure in Citizen Kane"), these aims are achieved in an instructional environment that reconciles agendas whose seeming incompatibility would be expected to impose extreme obstacles: Instructional material is presented in a manner that does not sacrifice complexity, yet takes an instructionally reasonable amount of time to cover, and does not overwhelm the learner.

A final point: The instructional approach described in this chapter *is* difficult. But sometimes advanced knowledge acquisition has to be hard. There are data that indicate that difficult instruction tends to be neglected, at great cost to learning outcomes (Feltovich et al., 1989; Spiro et al., 1988). The trick is to make advanced learning as easy as possible *without sacrificing the integrity of the material to be learned.* That is what Cognitive Flexibility Hypertexts attempt to do.

ACKNOWLEDGMENTS

The research reported in this chapter was supported by grants from the Army Research Institute (MDA903–86–K–0286) and the Office of Educational Research and Improvement (OEG 0087–C1001). The International Business Machines Corporation is thanked for providing equipment for the KANE project. An earlier version of this chapter was presented at the Annual Meeting of the American Educational Research Association in 1987. Although much of this chapter was written in 1986 and based on work conducted earlier, later revisions of the chapter have incorporated theoretical advances during the intervening years that the senior author made in collaboration with Paul Feltovich and Richard Coulson in their studies of biomedical cognition (see the co-authored papers in the reference list). The senior author is immeasurably indebted to these close collaborators. Don Nix has been a major help to the KANE project from the start. By making available his ingenious programming language, HANDY, he made it possible for us to build a program with the features that we wanted. Also, he offered many useful suggestions on the substance of the project. Judith Orasanu of the Army Research Institute has on many occasions made very insightful comments on the course of the entire program of research of which KANE is a part. Michael Jacobson provided helpful comments on an earlier draft of the chapter. Finally, Rita Gaskill's expert assistance on manuscript preparation is much appreciated.

REFERENCES

Barsalou, L. W. (1987). Instability of graded structure: Implications for the nature of concepts. In U. Neisser (Ed.), *Concepts and conceptual development: Ecological and intellectual factors in categorization* (pp. 101–140). Cambridge: Cambridge University Press.

Barthes, R. (1967). *S/Z*. New York: Hill, Wang.

Collins, A., Brown, J. S., & Newman, S. E. (1989). Cognitive apprenticeship: Teaching the crafts of reading, writing, and mathematics. In L. B. Resnick (Ed.), *Knowing, learning, and instruction: Essays in honor of Robert Glaser* (pp. 453–494). Hillsdale, NJ: Lawrence Erlbaum Associates.

Coulson, R. L., Feltovich, P. J., & Spiro, R. J. (1989). Foundations of a misunderstanding of the ultrastructural basis of myocardial failure: A reciprocating network of oversimplifications. *Journal of Medicine and Philosophy, 14,* 109–146.

Feltovich, P. J., Spiro, R. J., & Coulson, R. L. (1989). The nature of conceptual understanding in biomedicine: The deep structure of complex ideas and the development of misconceptions. In D. Evans & V. Patel (Eds.), *The cognitive sciences in medicine* (pp. 113–172). Cambridge, MA: MIT Press.

Marchionini, G. (Ed.). (1988). Special issue on hypermedia [special issue]. *Educational Technology, 29*(11).

Schank, R. C. (1982). *Dynamic memory*. Cambridge: Cambridge University Press.

Spiro, R. J. (1980). Prior knowledge and the processing of stories: Integration, selection, and variation. *Poetics: International Review for the Theory of Literature, 9,* 313–328.

Spiro, R. J., Coulson, R. L., Feltovich, P. J., & Anderson, D. K. (1988). Cognitive flexibility theory: Advanced knowledge acquisition in ill-structured domains. In V. Patel (Ed.), *Tenth annual conference of the Cognitive Science Society* (pp. 375–383). Hillsdale, NJ: Lawrence Erlbaum Associates.

Spiro, R. J., Crismore, A., & Turner, T. J. (1982). On the role of pervasive experiential coloration in memory. *Text, 2,* 253–262.

Spiro, R. J., Feltovich, P. J., Coulson, R. L., & Anderson, D. K. (1989). Multiple analogies for complex concepts: Antidotes for analogy-induced misconception in advanced knowledge acquisition. In S. Vosniadou & A. Ortony (Eds.), *Similarity and analogical reasoning* (pp. 498–531). Cambridge: Cambridge University Press.

Spiro, R. J., Feltovich, P. J., Coulson, R. L., Jacobson, M., Jehng, J-C., & Raulin, S. (in preparation). *A theory of hypertext: Nonlinear learning for the development of cognitive flexibility in ill-structured domains.*

Spiro, R. J., & Myers, A. (1984). Individual differences and underlying cognitive processes in reading. In P. D. Pearson (Ed.), *Handbook of research in reading* (pp. 471–501). New York: Longman.

Spiro, R. J., Vispoel, W., Schmitz, J., Samarapungavan, A., & Boerger, A. (1987). Knowledge acquisition for application: Cognitive flexibility and transfer in complex content domains. In B. C. Britton & S. Glynn (Eds.), *Executive control processes in reading* (pp. 177–199). Hillsdale, NJ: Lawrence Erlbaum Associates.

Welles, O. (Producer/Director), & Stein, R. (Videodisc Designer and Producer). (1984). *Citizen Kane* (Videodisc No. Catalog No. CC101). Los Angeles, CA: The Criterion Collection.

White, B. Y., & Fredericksen, J. R. (1987, November). *Casual model progressions as a foundation for intelligent learning environments* (BBN Rep. No. 6686). Cambridge, MA: Bolt Beranek & Newman.

Wittgenstein, L. (1953). *Philosophical investigations*. New York: Macmillan.

Author Index

Subject Index